CONTENTS

PREFACE

This book is written in the belief that studying is one of the most interesting and satisfying things we can do – and that learning how to study well is among the most challenging. The book is for students of arts and humanities subjects (though not primarily for those who are studying fine or performance arts). Whether you are just thinking about taking up study, are returning to study later in life or are a more experienced student, we aim to help you improve your study skills.

Like its 'parent', *The Good Study Guide*, the book offers practical help with key study processes such as reading books and articles, making useful notes, writing essays, and preparing for exams. We include other methods of studying too – learning from lectures and tutorials, from the audio-visual media, from visits to museums and galleries and through project work; and we discuss use of the computer for word-processing, multi-media study and exploring the Internet. There is also a chapter about the *nature* of study in the arts and humanities, in which we consider some of the processes of textual analysis, interpretation and evaluation involved. Discussions are all based on practical exercises: on analysis of real students' work, and on your own 'reading' and understanding of an article, paintings and a poem reproduced in the book. Since none of us improves our study skills just by being given good advice, we aim to help you explore and develop ways of studying that suit *you*, in the light of your particular purposes and circumstances.

Most of those who worked with us on the book are students (or, like us, staff) at The Open University. So the book draws mainly on the experiences of adult part-time students working independently from home. But we hope it will be useful to students everywhere. It is not meant to be read from cover to cover. Rather, it is organized so that, as you approach a particular study task, you can dip into the relevant section of the book and take what you need. It is a reference book that you can return to over many years, as you continue your studies and meet new challenges. It is based on the authors' experience of teaching, of researching into study processes and discussing them with students. Andrew Northedge originally wrote *The Good Study Guide* with students of the social sciences in mind. With his help, Ellie Chambers has here adapted it for arts and humanities students. (Although we are joint authors, for convenience we use the singular, 'I', throughout the book.)

Many other people have contributed to its writing and production. As part of our preparation, we asked some students to volunteer their work. We are very grateful to them, and to their tutors. Grateful thanks also to Blanche Gaskell and Vina Quinn-Searle who, as student-assessors, gave us their comments on draft chapters. Members of the OU Arts Faculty's A103 course team offered helpful advice or assistance, especially its Chair,

Cicely Havely, and also Colin Cunningham, Julie Dickens, Lorna Hardwick, Liz Manning, Derek Matravers, Jim Moore, Nora Tomlinson, Linda Walsh, Nigel Warburton and Roberta Wood. So too did colleagues in the School of Health and Social Welfare, host to the access course *Living Arts*: Martin Robb (Chair), Margaret Allott and Stella Waraker, with secretarial support from Val O'Connor. Other colleagues in the University who gave us their time and ideas include: Tim Benton and Hilary Robertson, Arts Faculty; Ann Brechin and Tony Walton, School of Health and Social Welfare; Nicola Durbridge, Magnus John, Jan Rae, Mary Thorpe and Olwyn Wilson, Institute of Educational Technology; Giles Clark, Book Trade Department; Tony Coulson, Library; Simon Rae, Academic Computing Service. I am grateful to Trevor Herbert of the Arts Faculty for supplying the guidelines for 'active listening' on page 190. Thank you to Clive Baldwin, the editor, and Sîan Lewis, who designed the book. Thanks also to our friend Gill Parsons, of North Hertfordshire College, for her help with Chapter 6.

Special thanks are due to Nora Tomlinson, who read every word and made many insightful, detailed suggestions for improvements; to Margaret Allott for her efficient organization of the project and friendly support; and to Clive Baldwin for his skill and patience as editor of the book. Its shortcomings are, of course, our own. Finally, we are grateful for permission to use Joyce Ellis's article as a basis for study exercises.

Ellie Chambers
Andrew Northedge

April 1997

CHAPTER ONE

GETTING STARTED

1 STUDYING ARTS AND HUMANITIES SUBJECTS

Why have you chosen to study the arts and humanities? Because you really enjoy reading novels, looking at paintings or listening to music, and you want to know more about these things? Or is it that you are fascinated by a particular time and place – Classical Greece, Renaissance Italy, Victorian or modern Britain? Perhaps what you love doing is tossing ideas around, arguing about things and really getting to the bottom of them. Whether you decide to study literature or history, art, the mass media, music, philosophy, religions, drama, languages, law – or some combination of these subjects – you will certainly learn a lot about human cultures and societies, past and present. You will learn about what people did and made and believed; the ways they lived, wrote and thought. You may also learn quite a lot about yourself: about what you really think, and why. And you will learn how to present your thoughts with confidence, in discussion with other people and in writing.

You may even find new 'worlds' opening up. Do you regularly tune in to the debates going on in newspapers, radio and TV? Are you the type who always has your nose stuck in a book, or who goes to the theatre, art galleries and museums? If you think these things are not for you, you may surprise yourself. They are all much more satisfying when you understand them at a deeper level and can share your ideas and pleasure with others.

If you are interested in any of these things then this book is for you. It will help you understand what studying arts and humanities subjects is all about. In particular, it deals with the *study skills* you need and helps you practise them. For example, it will give you advice and help in:

- finding the time to study, and organizing yourself so that you get the most out of your course
- reading texts and getting to grips with the ideas in them
- getting the most out of other ways of studying; for instance, from lectures and group discussions, watching TV or video and listening to cassettes, using a computer
- making useful notes
- planning and writing essays
- getting exams into perspective, and tackling them constructively.

In short, this book is meant to help you learn successfully and enjoy your studies.

2 HOW TO USE THE BOOK

This is not the kind of book you sit down to read from cover to cover. It is a book to dip into, taking what you need when you need it. That is because you can't just read about the skills of studying and understand what is involved once and for all. You learn these sorts of skills gradually: through trial and error, through repeated practice, and by stopping to reflect on your experiences. The way you understand and approach challenging study activities, such as note-making or essay-writing, will change as your abilities as a student develop.

But the subject of study skills is not for beginners only. A pianist does not stop practising and seeking help because she has 'finished' learning to play. Whatever stage you reach in a particular skill there is always something to be gained from going back over your techniques and trying to refine them. And you do not necessarily need very *different* advice when you are more expert at something. There are basic truths about performance that you need to return to from time to time and understand again at a new level. So you will need to return several times to the sections of the book that are relevant to *your* particular concerns. They will take on new meanings as you come back to them over a period of years. For this reason it is not easy to grade the various parts of the book as 'beginners' material, 'intermediate', or 'advanced level'. You will find some ideas relevant straight away because of the particular study tasks you are engaged in. But you may find them just as helpful in a year or two.

This book, then, is written for students at all levels: from absolute beginners to those who are relatively experienced. This first chapter starts with the assumption that you have not studied for a long time, but the following chapters include both introductory level discussion and more advanced ideas. You will need to select what is useful to you.

To help you find your way around the book there is quite a detailed contents list at the front and an index at the back. The text has also been organized with the main points picked out in boxes – the idea being that you can skim through, just reading the boxes, if that is all you need. There are two sorts of box.

> ### KEY POINTS
> ● These boxes contain very brief summaries of the main points made in the text.

> ### Discussion boxes
> Discussion boxes contain short discussions of specific topics, which you can read without going into the main body of the text.

However, if you are looking for a fuller discussion you can settle down to read the text. In many places this includes closely worked examples to show exactly what is meant. To get the most out of these examples you will sometimes need to stop reading and carry out an activity.

ACTIVITY

This is the first 'activity'. Make sure you are properly organized for studying this book.

- Where are you reading it? Will you be able to concentrate without being disturbed too much?
- Have you got enough space to work in?
- Do you have a pen and paper handy in case you need to do some writing?

If not, get yourself sorted out.

Often an 'activity' asks you not only to *think* about what you are doing (as this first activity does), but also to *write down* your ideas on paper. This is a basic study technique. You do not learn by just soaking things up like a sponge. You need to work with a pen in your hand so that you can write thoughts down as they come to you. Once you have your ideas on paper, you can get to work on them; refine them, extend them, make connections between them and other ideas. When you do this you are studying *actively*, and learning.

The various boxes and activities in the text allow you to read different parts of the book at different levels of detail, depending on what you need. But each chapter does contain a fair amount of detail, and this is another reason why you shouldn't try to take everything in at one go. In any case, you need to mix *reading about* studying with *practising* it. If you sat down to read through a manual on all the skills of perception and muscle control used in skating before you'd had a go at doing it, you would probably be so confused or intimidated you would never even put your skates on. You would have far too many abstract things to think about. Similarly, there is a real danger that if you wade too quickly into a lot of detailed discussion of study principles you will freeze up when you try to do the real thing. As with skating, the best way to start studying is to pitch in, have a go and not worry too much if you fall over. Then pick up any advice you need as you go along. Use this book as a resource when you are not making progress and you feel ready for some fresh ideas.

You have probably been given good advice about how to study before now – to be organized, keep to time, plan before you write, present your work neatly, and so on. That sounds straightforward enough. The difficulty is connecting *advice* about how to study with studying as *you experience* it.

General advice may not help much in your particular circumstances. To develop study techniques you can actually *use*, you will often have to work things out for yourself. This book aims to present thought-provoking activities which connect with your own experience: questions and tasks that stimulate you to reflect on your situation, and on your strengths and weaknesses as a student. The aim is to bring to the fore what you already know about yourself and the way you learn, so that you can work out study solutions that suit *you*.

The ideal way to use the book is as part of a course, in company with a teacher and other students. You can then study sections of it a bit at a time, as the course demands. The book was specifically written for use with the Open University's undergraduate courses in Arts and Humanities and with the introductory course *Living Arts*, but it works perfectly well on its own. If you are using the book by itself, you will need a plan of attack. I suggest that you work either by the skimming and dipping method outlined earlier, or by taking about ten to twenty pages at a time and then leaving the book for a while.

KEY POINTS

- If you are starting to study for the first time in many years, you will probably find that this book goes into a lot more detail than you need at first.
- Don't be put off. Take a little at a time. Skim through and find the bits that are relevant to what you are currently working on. The contents list at the front of the book, the index at the back and the boxes in the text will help you find what you need.

3 WHY READ ABOUT STUDY SKILLS?

Why should you need a book about studying anyway? Isn't it all fairly obvious? You read the texts, or you listen to the lectures, and then you write your essays. What could be more straightforward than that?

But perhaps it isn't so simple…

Jan put her pen down with a sigh and looked up at the clock again. It was now 8.17. She had started three-quarters of an hour ago and couldn't believe she was still only on page two.

'Have to be up early tomorrow – can't afford to be too late tonight. Perhaps I'll make a cup of coffee and really concentrate until 9.30 when Don gets back. Oh, and then Phil's coming over for a drink. I've got that other really long piece to read by Thursday too. And Wednesday night's out because of squash.'

She looked at her note pad. The title of the article was written neatly across the top. The rest was blank. They'd said you should make notes as you read.

> 'Right. "Sum up the main points of the article". But what *are* the main points...? I can't even work out what it's saying half the time. It's really irritating the way they just assume you know things you've never even heard of. And I might get on faster if I didn't have to keep stopping to look up every second word. Who on earth is this written for? Not me, that's for sure. I really liked the look of this article – I thought it was going to be interesting... I'd better just tidy up the table a bit I think.'

There was a wail from upstairs. One of the children...

She made another cup of coffee and flopped into the chair again.

> 'Only half an hour left now. Must concentrate. I'll go back to the top of the page – on second thoughts, I may as well start all over again and really try to get some notes down this time since I can't remember a word of it. Will I ever be able to remember anything I read? I wonder why Charlie keeps waking up like that. I hope there's nothing wrong with him... Oh I'm so tired. This is so *boring*. Every sentence is a battle. It's too late to get anywhere with it now. I'll just put my feet up for a bit, watch the news...'

Meanwhile, in another room a few streets away.

Nathan screwed up yet another sheet of paper and aimed it at the waste-paper basket. He stared blankly at his pad. What now? He had made half a dozen starts and hadn't once reached the end of the paragraph before crumpling the page up in disgust.

> 'How can I be stuck when I've hardly started? How long is this whole thing going to take? "Did eighteenth-century women migrate to towns mainly because of the attractions of the towns, or mainly to escape from life in the countryside?" How should I know? Even these historians don't seem to be able to make up their minds. What if I said it was a bit of both, probably. Or maybe I'll just take a few sentences from here and there and change the words around a bit – then at least they can't say I've got it *wrong*. But the tutor said write in your own words...'

As his mind wandered back to the tutorial he winced. Why hadn't he just kept quiet, as he'd meant to? He hadn't really understood what all those clever types were going on about – but the tutor seemed so keen for everyone to join in. By the time he'd wound himself up to say something the subject had moved on. He couldn't get a word in edgeways. But then the tutor had looked straight at him and he'd just blurted it out anyway. He'd actually been shaking and feeling hot as he spoke. Ridiculous at his age. They had pretended to 'use' what he'd said as they carried on the discussion, but he knew he had made a complete fool of himself. How could he face going back again?

'Anyway, I didn't get much out of it – no notes. In fact I can hardly remember a thing that was said. I'll give it a miss next week. Or would the tutor be offended if I didn't turn up? ...Oh well, must get back to this wretched essay. I just don't know where to start. Perhaps I'll rescue some of the bits I wrote before and try to sort of cobble them together. No. I can't bear to look at them again... *Why* am I doing this to myself?'

Is studying really as bad as that? Surely not. But sometimes things do look pretty bleak. Although Jan and Nathan are fictitious, their problems are real enough. And these kinds of difficulties are not only experienced by new or 'weak' students either. They are general problems that we all face when we study: of *struggling to understand*, of *managing time*, of *completing tasks*, and of *keeping our spirits up.*

ACTIVITY

Maybe you have experienced some of Jan's or Nathan's difficulties. What do you think they are doing wrong?

Write down what you see as Jan's main problems and some ideas about what she could do to improve things. Then do the same for Nathan.

I'd say one of Jan's main problems is finding enough *time* for study, between the demands of child-rearing, her social commitments and her leisure pursuits. And both she and Nathan are having problems *using* the time they do have effectively. Both are concerned about *what* they should be doing and *how long* it should be taking them. They are both 'stuck' and cannot see a way forward. Jan is repeatedly *distracted* – by a child's needs, her own thoughts, by making coffee and tidying up her table, and most of all by the frustration and 'boredom' she experiences as she reads the text. Nathan is held up by the revulsion he feels when he reads his own words, and by believing he is inadequate as a student. He is overawed by the tutor and the other students and sees himself as less clever than they are. Because of this he is approaching the essay in a very tentative way, which makes it difficult for him to get a good grasp of the subject and concentrate on expressing his thoughts. Instead, he is sitting almost hypnotized by the essay title, casting around in desperation for a way of getting though the task. Both of them are feeling fed-up and have lost the enthusiasm they had when they started their studies. They are in danger of giving up and wasting all their good intentions. They need some help! Exactly what they might do to improve things is what the rest of this book is about.

However, they may both be doing better than they realize. Studying often feels like a struggle – and it is in the process of struggling that important learning starts to happen. We have been spying on them at a particularly low moment. But, since they are fictitious, we can join them again when things are looking up.

Figure 1.1   Henry Pickering, *Lady Dixie*, c.1750–3, oil on canvas, 122 x 99 cm. Lady Dixie typifies the accomplished young woman of the period, dressed at enormous expense for public view. (City of Nottingham, Castle Museum)

Jan, Nathan and some fellow students have decided to make a trip to an art gallery. They are grouped round a picture (in fact the one above, of *Lady Dixie*). Jan is listening as Carol finishes speaking:

'…but surely the whole point is that she's *supposed* to be standing about like a clothes horse, dripping jewels.'

'Horse is about right,' she adds.

'Yes,' Nathan cut in, 'I bet she's there to show the world how wealthy and powerful her father is. He must have commissioned the portrait I suppose. And paid for it. I wonder if we could find out…'

'Get him – "commissioned the portrait" indeed,' said Jan with a grin.

'But it's true,' Anna said to her. 'There's absolutely nothing in the background…'

'Mmm, nothing else to look at besides that glorious frock,' agreed Carol wistfully. 'It takes up over half the picture space.'

'And look at the colours in it!' said Philip.

'I see what you mean,' Jan replied. 'But look at her eyes too. She seems to be staring straight at me – well, down on me really – the mouth, kind of quietly pleased with herself. Obviously a thoroughbred.'

'Isn't her left arm a bit out of proportion?' asked Hansa, suddenly.

'Elongated,' mused Nathan. 'Elegant, trailing fingers…'

'Useless you mean. Those aren't rubber gloves she's dangling – *her* hands have never been *near* the washing up,' said Jan, to general laughter.

Later, as they stood at the bus stop, Jan said to Nathan, 'Really nice people aren't they.'

'Yes, they are. Quite a mixture too. At first I was terrified. I thought they were all teachers or something, real culture vultures. Didn't dare open my mouth.'

'Mmm. I never thought I'd be walking round a gallery, talking about art. I didn't even think I'd make it through the first chapter of the book. I'd never have done it without Carol – in the end I rang her up and she helped sort me out.'

'And I *never* thought I'd be talking about commissioning portraits…all that jargon,' laughed Nathan. 'Now I keep coming out with it – "and on the one hand this, and on the other hand that". In fact the problem is how to *stop* myself, even at work.'

'Yes – well, you seem to pick it all up pretty easily.'

'Oh yeah? You should have seen me struggling with that first essay. Nearly drove myself mad – and the whole family. The writing's the hardest part even now. Still, I seem to be improving a bit. I don't like the look of that next piece of reading though, do you?'

'Oh, I don't know – it could be quite interesting. Look, here's my bus! See you next week Nathan. Bye.'

And so they disappear off into the sunset, and we see how wonderful studying can be after all.

Well, I just wanted to show that although studying is frustrating and tough sometimes, it is also very rewarding and satisfying – and even fun. Many students say it not only gives them greater knowledge and understanding of the subjects they study, but also *more confidence, broader interests,* and an extra *purpose in life*. They begin to achieve more at work and at home. This is another reason for reading about study skills and thinking seriously about *how* as well as what you are studying. If you develop a wide range of study techniques and strategies you will not only improve as a student, you will strengthen your capabilities in other walks of life.

4 GETTING YOURSELF ORGANIZED

When you begin, studying is difficult just because it has no 'shape' for you. Until you have developed some kind of *system* for organizing your study – for deciding *what* needs to be done and *when* – you spend a lot of time dithering about, starting one thing and then another and wondering whether you are getting anywhere. Jan clearly suffered from the lack of a purpose and plan, which left her with a major problem: how to *manage* her study time.

4.1 Managing time

In fact she had two kinds of problems with time: *finding enough* of it and *using* it effectively.

Finding time

Jan had *social* commitments (spending time with her partner, having a drink with a friend), *child-care* commitments, and *leisure* interests (squash, keeping up with the news). All of these things are important. But is there enough time in between for studying? Students always have to make very difficult decisions about their priorities. When you take up studying it usually means that something else in your life has to go, or take a back seat. And yet we know what 'all work and no play' does – even students have to have their pleasures. So one of the first skills you need to develop is creating a balance between the various demands on your time. Studying requires quite a *lot* of time and in fairly long *stretches*. You have to become an expert at *making* time for study. One way to set about this is to draw up a chart of your 'typical' week and see where there is room for manoeuvre.

Here is one student's chart. Anna is studying part-time and also has a part-time job (Monday–Thursday). She has a child who goes to playgroup in the afternoons and spends Saturday mornings with grandparents. She is trying to 'find' about fourteen hours for study each week.

	Monday	Tuesday	Wednesday	Thursday	Friday	Saturday	Sunday
am	Study – 1 hr	Study – 1 hr	See parents	Study – 1 hr	Housework/ shopping	Study – 3 hrs	Free
pm	Work	Work	Work	Work	Study – 2 hrs	Washing etc.	Free
evening	Evening class	Study – 2 hrs Aerobics	Study – 1 hr	Study – 2 hrs	Free	Free	Study – 1 hr

Figure 1.2 Planning your study time.

Draw up a chart of this kind for yourself. Work out the total study time you can reasonably expect to set aside in the week, and where in the week it falls. Try to identify when clashes are likely to occur and whether you may have to cut back on some other things.

You don't need to go into great detail. You are just trying to give some shape to your week.

Don't be surprised if you found this activity difficult. It is. Life is usually pretty messy. Looking over her plan, Anna said:

> Not every week's like this of course. It varies. Sometimes I see my parents on Thursdays and, in a crisis (like a big essay to write), they'll have Susie for longer on Saturday – or she'll go round and play with friends for a while. I don't always manage to do an hour or so in the mornings either, depending on how she is. If I'm pushed I'll make it up on a Friday. But I like to keep Saturday nights free for seeing friends and things, and I try to spend Sunday going out and about with Susie.

So, having made your plan it is not always easy to stick to it. But sticking to it is not necessarily the point. Even if you have to keep changing your plans it is still worth making them, because each change of plan forces you to think about *what* you are doing and *why*. Planning makes you think *strategically* instead of just drifting along.

Using time

Jan was not only having trouble finding enough time for study, but also making *effective* use of it. She had not worked out exactly what she wanted to achieve in the two-hour study session ahead of her. By flitting about from one thing to another, she ended up finishing the session early without having achieved very much at all. To avoid this you need to develop an idea of *how much time* you need for *particular types of task*. You will find that you can do some study tasks only when you are reasonably fresh and have a good stretch of time ahead of you: for example, reading a difficult passage or writing part of an essay. Other, less demanding tasks – such as organizing your notes or reading through a draft of an essay – you can squeeze into odd moments, or manage when you are more tired. People *vary a lot* in their patterns of working, so you have to *experiment* and *find out what works for you*. You need to *reflect* every now and then on whether you could divide up your study time in a different way to get better results. Don't just plod on hoping for the best. You need to *manage* yourself more actively than that.

4.2   Completing a task

So far I have perhaps been talking as if studying comes as bundles of neatly packaged, clear-cut tasks. In fact, as Jan found, a lot of the work you have to do as a student is very *weakly defined*. It is a crucial part of your job to *create* the shape and size of the tasks you need to do. You have to define tasks for yourself.

Defining tasks

First you need to have an *overall idea* of what you are hoping to achieve in a given week. But, within that, you also need to define a number of *smaller tasks* for yourself – 'reading the next ten pages of the chapter', for example – so that you can decide how much time to give to each task. That way you can really take charge of your studies and manage yourself. *Managing yourself* involves:

- getting yourself started;
- keeping yourself going; and
- deciding when to stop and move on to another task.

It is particularly important to be able to break down a big task, such as writing an essay, into a series of smaller ones. Then, unlike Nathan, you will be able to see the way ahead. *When you have a clearly defined task to do, it is easier to focus your attention on it and keep yourself working at it* – and so resist some of the distractions we are all tempted to give in to.

Why is it so easy to be distracted when you are studying?

It is the feeling of drifting around in a meaningless way, with no end in sight, that makes us so ready to clutch at any distractions we can find. When you don't really understand the text you are reading, or haven't defined what you are trying to achieve, you feel restless and uneasy. Distractions offer the chance to focus attention on familiar and meaningful parts of your life and escape from the uncertainties of studying. The urge to avoid uncertainty is very strong. That is why it is so important to define clear-cut tasks for yourself and create a pattern to your work. This gives it purpose and meaning.

If you find that you keep stopping as you work, try setting yourself a smaller and more tightly defined task – something that involves you in an *active* way. For example, if your mind keeps wandering as you read, get a highlighting pen and search for key words and phrases. That gives you a specific task to focus on.

Here are some other examples of specific study tasks you can define for yourself:

- read the next two sections of the text you are studying
- make notes on an article you have read recently
- sort out and file the notes you have made over the past couple of weeks
- watch a video-cassette
- browse in the library, looking for useful articles and books
- gather notes together and sketch out a plan for your next essay
- write a first draft of the main section of the essay
- contact other students
- prepare for the next tutorial (and then attend it)
- make your study plan for the coming week.

You will get a fuller picture of the range of tasks you can define for yourself as you work through the rest of the book.

Having given some shape to your studies by identifying a number of tasks to be done in the coming week, you then need to divide out the time you have for study between them (see Chapter 2, section 3.2). It is unlikely that you'll be able to stick exactly to your plans because studying is too unpredictable. But you can *set broad targets* to help you decide when it is time to stop doing one thing and start on the next. And you can keep reviewing your progress, and adapting your plans accordingly.

KEY POINTS

As you start out on your studies, think carefully about how to:

- *manage your time*, and in particular how to
  - *find* time, by planning out your week;
  - *use* time effectively, by doing work of different kinds at the most suitable times;
- *define study tasks* for yourself, and then
  - *allocate* time to them;
  - *monitor* your progress as you attempt to complete them.

Managing time and task

Time management and *task management* are closely bound up with each other. You need to balance one against the other. If you become too obsessed with *time* (as Jan was) then you tend to think in terms of the 'hours put in' rather than what you have achieved. You may start 'filling in' time with relatively unimportant tasks, just to while it away until you can finish your study session feeling virtuous. To avoid this, you need to start with the aim of *completing certain tasks* by the end of the session (even if you don't always succeed). On the other hand, if you focus too much on the task you may let it drag on for far too long. You need to keep switching your attention between both task management *and* time management so as to strike a reasonable balance.

4.3 Practical matters

Social arrangements

Other people don't always realize how hard you need to concentrate when you are studying. If you live with others, you may have to negotiate specific times when you can use a particular table, or a room, and be left in peace. Show them your study plans, and make some kind of deal with them about when you will *not* be available: 'You look after the kids while I write my essay, and I'll take them to the park tomorrow'. Unless you can arrange to be left undisturbed while you study you are in for a very frustrating time. Similarly, friends may not realize how much time you need to spend studying. You will have to make it clear to them that you can't go gadding about as often as they would like.

If you get into the habit of discussing your work and study plans with the people who are close to you, they are not so likely to feel that you are shutting them out and are more likely to give you support and encouragement.

Setting up a place to study

Many people feel it's important to have a place where they regularly sit down to do their studying – where they can quickly settle into a businesslike mood and easily get hold of everything they require. On the other hand, you may find time to study during breaks at work, or on the train, and you may choose to do your reading in a comfortable armchair. For some tasks though, such as writing essays, you really have to be able to work undisturbed. You need access to your files, enough space to spread out your books and papers, and you may also need room for a computer. Ideally you should have good lighting and heating too. You may not be able to arrange everything just as you would like, but you should try to get as close to it as you can.

Equipment

The equipment you need will depend on the course you are studying, but here are some basic suggestions: a supply of pens; A4 note-pads and envelopes; a box of index cards; cardboard folders; filing boxes and labels; a good dictionary; and shelf space. This doesn't have to be too expensive – there are shops in most towns that sell in bulk, and stock cheap cardboard filing boxes. Or you could always adapt boxes you get from the supermarket, and arrange your books on a plank supported by a couple of bricks. For some courses, though, you will require more expensive, electronic equipment: a TV, video-recorder, radio, audio-cassette player, and possibly a computer.

Where to keep things

If you study for any length of time you will soon begin to accumulate large amounts of printed material: handouts; your own notes; old essays; books; illustrations, plans and maps; photocopies of articles, and so on. You may also build up quite a collection of video and audio-cassettes, and computer discs. It is important to be systematic about how you store all this material, right from the start. This is where storage space, folders, boxes and labels come in. In the end you will find that it is not so much what you can remember that counts as *what you can lay hands on* when you need it.

Bookshops and libraries

As you start out on your studies, it is worth finding out where the best bookshops and libraries in your area are and what they have available on the subject you are studying. Some people find it a bit daunting to walk into a big library or bookshop and try to locate the particular section they need, especially if they are not sure what it is called. But assistants can usually provide a lot of help if you go ahead and ask them. You will also have to learn how to order books and articles through the library (and, increasingly, how to use CD-ROMs and on-line databases). That means thinking ahead, identifying the material you will need and ordering it up in good time. This is another aspect of *managing* your studies, and a further reason for *planning* your work in advance.

KEY POINTS

As you begin your studies you have to make some practical preparations:

- set up a *place* to study
- get the *equipment* you need
- *organize* and *store* things so that you can find them again easily
- explore *bookshops* and *libraries*
- negotiate your study times and arrangements with *family* and *friends*.

---

5   WHAT IS STUDYING ALL ABOUT?

5.1   What are 'study skills'?

There are many different aspects of learning how to study, but they all tend
to be gathered together under the general heading of 'study skills'. This is a
bit misleading because it suggests that they are all the same *kind* of thing. It
also suggests you can become skilled in them in the same way you become
skilled at, for example, controlling the clutch of a car. You take some
training, keep practising over and over again, and then 'hey presto', one day
you have acquired the skill and don't crunch the gears any more. But many
of the capabilities you need to develop as a student are not skills of that
kind. You need to understand the *processes* of study involved in your subject;
you need to learn certain *techniques* for accomplishing different tasks, to try
out different *strategies* for approaching your work, and to establish certain
routines or *habits* of working. And with study skills the day never dawns
when you are sure you'll never crunch the gears again – there is no such
objective 'proof' of your success.

You improve your study skills all the time, not by hours of repetitive practice
but by trying out new ways of doing things and reflecting on how well they
work, by being realistic about yourself, and by thinking strategically.
Becoming skilled at studying involves picking up *practical 'know-how'*,
taking charge of your studies, *keeping your spirits up*, and *managing
yourself* shrewdly. The ultimate aim is to become an *independent* learner.
We'll look at each of these in more detail.

Practical know-how

Practical know-how is something you pick up from day-to-day experience. A
good example is recognizing the importance of having a simple and effective
filing system for your notes and other course materials. To see the need for it
you only have to lose a vital sheet of paper (such as the marking scheme for
an essay, or your exam timetable). Getting hold of folders and boxes and
designing your own filing system is not a high-level technical skill. It does
not require hours of practice. It just takes experience, thought, and
willingness to experiment.

Other kinds of know-how include:

● where to get information
● who to go to for help and support
● what to do when you are stuck.

You can also pick up vitally important know-how about what demands the
course you are studying will make, and what your tutors expect of you (from
book lists, past exam papers, and former students). And when you are facing

a particular study task, know-how enables you to judge:

- what kind of task it is
- how well-equipped you are to tackle it
- how long it will take you.

You accumulate all this knowledge through *doing* and *reflecting* on what you have done.

Taking charge of your studies

To be successful you also need the determination to 'get to grips' with things. It is easy to let a course happen to you – simply getting by from day to day – rather than taking control and making sure you get good value for your time and money. As we have seen, you have to be ruthlessly *practical* when it comes to keeping people at bay and arranging a place where you can work with your study materials around you. You can't afford to be half-hearted about these things. And you have to be *realistic* – alert to the danger of kidding yourself by:

- 'filling in' time rather than really studying
- telling yourself you understand when you don't
- avoiding facing up to deadlines.

To succeed you need to recognize things as they are, be determined, and keep driving towards your goals.

Keeping your spirits up

There is nothing more damaging to your progress than sagging morale. We saw just how little Jan and Nathan achieved when filled with doubt about their own ability or despair about completing the task ahead. To stay on top of your studies you have to know *why you are studying* the course and what you hope to get out of it: there is no point in setting yourself wildly ambitious targets that you are almost certain to fall short of. You have to find ways of persuading yourself that you are *making progress*. That is not always easy. We all experience disappointments, confusion and self-doubt at times. The skill is in knowing how to come to terms with these lows. Instead of comparing yourself unfavourably with other students, indulge in some positive thinking:

- think about your *strengths* as a student, and try to build on them
- recognize the progress you have made and 'congratulate' yourself on it from time to time
- keep reminding yourself what you are getting out of your studies.

As far as you can, try not to think too much about the question of your own ability – put it to one side. Whatever we set out to do there is *always* someone who seems to be better or more talented or 'brilliant' at it, and there is no point at all in measuring yourself against these people if it is not productive. Even they have their weaknesses. Just accept yours, and instead put your energy into working out ways of developing your skills.

Finally, be ready to recognize your needs as a human being:

- set out to get as much fun as you can
- mix tasks you don't enjoy with those you do
- don't drive yourself too hard – take a good break from time to time
- encourage your friends to flatter you when you feel low.

Being an effective 'self-manager'

Managing yourself effectively involves taking a *systematic, analytical, strategic* and *reflective* approach to your studies.

Being systematic

Think back to the study plan on page 9. Drawing up this kind of chart is being *systematic* (that is, organizing what you do according to a plan or method). You are saying, 'Right – I need to find fourteen hours a week for study. Let's set the week out so I can see all seven days. I'll divide each day into three parts and mark in the time that's already committed. Then I can sketch out a plan for spreading the work across the remaining time.' Instead of muddling along, you take a rational, structured approach to things.

Being analytical

This means breaking something down into its component parts, so that you can see exactly what it is made up of. If you approach the task of writing an essay by first 'defining' a series of smaller tasks for yourself (for example, thinking about the essay title, reading an article on it and making notes, sketching out a plan for your essay, and so forth), then you are taking an *analytical approach*. Having broken down this task into its component parts, you can work out a way to get started. Then you can go on to tackle each part of the process, moving towards your goal in an orderly way. Taking an analytical approach to your studies means thinking carefully about exactly what you need to do and why.

Being strategic

When you try to use the time available to you effectively, by weighing up which study tasks to do when you are fresh and which of them you can squeeze into odd moments, you are taking a *strategic approach*. This involves not only giving attention to study goals themselves, but also to your priorities, your levels of energy and how well you can concentrate at different times. These are key resources for reaching your goals. Being strategic means:

- identifying your goals
- weighing up your priorities
- reviewing your resources, and
- working out a plan for making best use of your resources to achieve the goals you have given top priority.

Being reflective

When you have looked systematically and analytically at the tasks ahead of you, and have worked out a strategy for achieving them, the final stage is to reflect back on how successful you have been:

- Did your plans work out?
- Did you misjudge the task, or the time, involved?
- Have you learned anything that will help you get it right next time?

Taking a *reflective approach* means that you think back over your past plans and achievements in order to develop principles that will help you shape more successful plans in future. You can also pick up ideas for the future from talking to other people, and from reading books such as this.

This approach – of trying things out and learning from your experiences – gives you the *flexibility* to tackle a wide range of study tasks. That is important at a time when the technology of education and the way education is organized are changing rapidly. Flexibility allows you to learn and adapt continually so that your abilities as a student improve *throughout your life.*

Keeping a study diary

This is one way of helping yourself take a reflective approach to your studies. Writing a page each week about what you have achieved and how you feel about it will set you thinking about why you have approached study tasks in particular ways. It will also stimulate you to think of other ways of doing things. Looking back over a few weeks and months, you will see certain patterns in your work and you will be able to think strategically about whether you are achieving as much as you could.

You can try organizing your diary under such headings as 'Feelings about my studies', 'Main achievements this week', 'What went badly', 'Lessons learned', 'Major tasks ahead', 'Strategies for tackling major tasks'. Even if you only write the diary for short spells every now and then, it can get you into a reflective and strategic way of thinking which carries on long after you have stopped writing it. In some courses you will be asked to keep a study diary. But there's no need to wait to be asked.

Eventually, the sequence of *analysis, strategic planning* and *reflection* will become a habit, so that you are hardly aware you are doing it.

Becoming an independent learner

The older you get and the higher you reach in the education system, the more you have to take responsibility for your own studies. In school, teachers are prepared to take a lot of the responsibility for what we learn and how we learn it, and they put pressure on us to work hard. But as an adult you have to make your own choices. It is up to you to choose a subject you want to study and decide how much effort to put into studying it. You have to set your own targets and priorities, and work out your own strategies for achieving them.

You also take responsibility for your own ideas and points of view. At school, much of what we are given to study is presented as 'facts'. We gain marks for remembering the facts and setting them out again accurately. As an adult student you are expected to *question* what teachers say and what you read in books, and to *think for yourself*. That is because, at higher levels of study, people recognize that we cannot be so sure about the 'truth' of things. If anyone wants to say that something is true they have to show you *why* they think so, and convince you that they are right.

In other words, they have to *argue* for their point of view and present you with the *evidence* that supports their argument. You have to weigh up what they say and come to your own conclusions about the strengths and weaknesses of the ideas they present – not just remember and repeat them. And you have to learn how to present an argument of your own, along with the evidence that supports it. The whole emphasis changes from being a *receiver* of 'knowledge' to being an active *seeker* after understanding, and a *maker* of sense and meaning.

This does not happen all at once, especially if you are returning to study after a long break. Nevertheless, your target is to become an 'independent' student; to be able to find your way around a subject for yourself. You have to start setting your own agenda.

KEY POINTS

Study skills are not a set of 'tricks' you learn once and apply for ever. Becoming skilled as a student involves:

- accumulating practical *know-how* about the kinds of things you have to do as a student, and how to set about doing them
- being determined to *take charge* of your studies and meet challenges in a practical and realistic way

- knowing how to *keep your spirits up*: by positive thinking, playing to your strengths, tackling your weaknesses, and being forgiving to yourself
- becoming an *effective self-manager*, by taking a systematic, analytical, strategic and reflective approach to study tasks
- becoming an *independent learner*, by taking responsibility for your own studies and thinking for yourself.

The accumulated effect of all this is that you will acquire a range of *robust* and *flexible* skills, abilities, techniques and habits of mind that will enable *life-long* learning.

5.2 What is learning?

Obviously, the point of studying is to *learn*. But what does it mean to 'learn' something? As we have seen, it is not just a matter of memorizing information. At higher levels of study, learning is more about getting hold of *ideas* than information, and it involves *understanding* rather than remembering.

Understanding ideas versus memorizing facts

TV shows like *Mastermind* and *University Challenge* give the impression that being clever involves knowing a lot of facts. Clever people often do know lots of facts, but the reason they can respond to questions so quickly is to do with how well *organized* the facts are in their minds. They are not stored as separate items in these people's memory banks. Facts are connected together in meaningful ways by the *ideas* people have, by their *understanding* of the subject as a whole and of where the facts *fit in*. As a student you have to do a certain amount of memorizing, especially just before an exam, so that you have the information you need at your finger-tips. But a good exam result depends mainly on the work you put into *understanding ideas.*

I am using the term 'ideas' in a broad way here, to include:

concepts – general notions about groups of things and distinctions between them (for example, we have the concept 'music' and within that we distinguish between the concepts 'classical' music and 'pop' music, and so on; we have a general notion of what is meant by 'the past' and we distinguish between it and 'the present');

principles – underlying ideas on which we base a lot of our thinking, arguments and actions (for example, a moral principle such as 'do no harm to other people'; the study advice offered in this book is based on the principles of 'strategic planning' and 'self-reflection');

theories – connected 'systems' of ideas, that explain something (for example, there are a number of different theories of art, which aim to explain why people make things and why other people respond to them and enjoy them).

Learning ideas consists of three things.

- *Taking in* new ideas; and by that I mean *making sense* of new ideas, not simply seeing, hearing or memorizing them.
- *Thinking through* new ideas and fitting them together with the ideas you already have, so that they become part of your *general understanding* of the subject you are studying.
- *Using* newly formed ideas: using them as you *communicate* with others in speech and writing.

Taking in new ideas

When you look at an unread book on your shelf, you know there is a lot of 'stuff' in there that you want to get into your head. But this involves much more than simply passing your eyes over masses of words, symbols and pictures. It means *making sense* of what you read and see, so that you understand it. For example, say you came across the term 'concordant harmony' in music, and were told that it means 'combinations of notes that blend together in a pleasing way'. You could memorize the term and the definition quite easily. But that is not the same thing as *understanding* what it means. To 'take in' this idea you would have to listen to some music that is made up of concordant harmonies – and listen to examples of the opposite kind of music, which is made up of discords. Or perhaps you are studying an historic building and reading a description of the way the space is organized on the ground floor. This kind of description is very hard to take in unless you can 'see' it in your mind. To make sense of it you need to sketch out a floor plan as you read, working out where the main walls go, where the different rooms are and the entrances to them.

The study techniques that will help you take in a text, a lecture or a TV programme are those that put the emphasis on making sense of things. That is why this book talks a lot about making notes as you read, listen or view. Deciding what to note down helps you pay attention to the *meaning* of what you study. Chapters 2 and 3 are about ways of 'taking in' ideas of various kinds from different sources.

Thinking ideas through

It takes time before you can get new ideas properly into focus. You have to connect them up with the ideas you already have. And when new ideas conflict with the old, you have to work out where that leaves you. But 'thinking ideas through' is not something we normally sit down to do in its own right. It usually happens while we are busy doing other things. Various study activities help the process along – discussing things with other students, jotting down ideas for an essay or 'boiling down' your course notes for exam revision. These activities may seem like 'extras', tagged onto the mainstream activities of reading and essay-writing, but they are *not* marginal. Odd moments when you are jotting down bits and pieces for yourself are often times when you are working your ideas into shape. There isn't a chapter specially devoted to these thinking activities because they tend to be meshed in with the other more obvious ones, but throughout the book you will come across them.

Using ideas

You do not *really* understand an idea until you can put it to *use*. This is why people say, 'When you want to know if you have understood something, try "teaching" it to someone else'. It is when you are the one who is pushing the thinking along that you grasp the full force of an idea. So activities such as tutorial discussions and writing essays play a key part in helping you to understand new ideas and 'make them your own'. Speaking and writing are not just things you have to do to show what you have learned. Expressing your ideas is an important *part* of learning. Chapter 3 of the book deals with discussion, and Chapters 4 and 5 take a close look at writing.

'Taking in', 'thinking through' and 'using' ideas are all *active* processes. They do not happen to you while you nod off over a book. Each requires purposeful, thoughtful action on your part. However, making a distinction between these three aspects of learning is artificial, because they are not clear-cut 'stages' you go through one after the other. They are going on, in an overlapping way, all the time. Nevertheless, the distinction is useful. It emphasizes that learning goes on at many different points in your studies, not just when you are reading a book or listening to a lecture. It reminds you to give as much attention to 'thinking through' and 'using' new ideas as to 'taking them in'.

A learning 'spiral'

Rather than thinking of these three aspects of learning as stages, it helps to imagine them as part of a continuing cycle. When you study you are taking in, thinking through and using ideas all the time and, as you do that, your understanding advances – as in a spiral. But this spiralling process is not a smooth one. Learning tends to proceed in lurches, with the occasional leap. And you can rarely identify the 'moment' when you learn a new idea (although some people say they can remember having suddenly understood something, as if a light bulb had been switched on in their heads). Yet if you look back over ideas you grappled with months ago, they somehow seem obvious. You realize you must have 'learned' them but you can't pinpoint when. And often you can't imagine why you found them so difficult at first. That is because your learning has advanced; these ideas have become part of your understanding and are now 'your own'.

Having 'your own ideas', in this sense, is what was meant earlier by 'thinking for yourself' and 'reaching your own conclusions' at higher levels of study. You are not expected to be chock-full of 'original' ideas. It is *understanding* what you are studying that counts. When you show your understanding, in a discussion or an essay, what you say is bound to be original (in the proper sense of the word) – because it is *your* understanding, and no two people understand things in exactly the same way. That is what makes studying other people's ideas so fascinating.

This raises an interesting question. Can you be original (in the sense that you have understood something 'for yourself'), and be wrong about it? I would say 'yes'. But that's another story, for later on in Chapter 6.

Ideas and skills in arts and humanities subjects

In this chapter, I have emphasized the learning of ideas and have not talked about the learning of skills in arts and humanities subjects – for example, how to analyse a poem, a painting or a piece of music. This gives a false impression, because learning these skills goes hand in hand with learning ideas. For instance, we saw the way understanding the concept of 'concordant harmonies' involves listening to many different pieces of music – the actual *objects* of your study. To hear these harmonies you need to know how to listen carefully, and be able to pick out and analyse particular sequences of sound. These are some of the skills you learn as you study music.

In arts and humanities subjects you study many *different kinds* of objects – written, aural and visual. You study poems, novels and plays; musical performances and scores; paintings, sculpture, artefacts, buildings and their plans; philosophical treatises and writings; historical documents and records for particular periods and events. We'll call these objects of study *primary sources*.

In your studying, you also read a lot *about* these objects in text-books, scholarly articles and teaching texts; you watch TV programmes and films, and listen to radio talks about them. In such texts and programmes, scholars, critics and teachers analyse and interpret the meanings of the particular objects they choose to study. We'll call these academic accounts *secondary sources*.

In this book we are mainly concerned with how to study secondary sources. How to study the objects themselves is what your arts or humanities course teaches you, though we will look at some of the issues involved in Chapter 6.

KEY POINTS

- Learning at higher levels of study involves a lot more than 'memorizing' information. At the core is *understanding ideas*.

- To learn new ideas you have to *take them in, think them through* and *put them to use*.

- Learning does not proceed in a straight line. It is not a clear-cut, smooth process. It is better to think of it as a continuing cycle, a 'spiral' of gradually increasing understanding and skill.

In this chapter I have talked about how to plan for the start of a course of studies, and get yourself into the right frame of mind. We have looked at the nature of studying and learning in general. In the next chapter we get down to some real studying.

CHAPTER TWO

1 INTRODUCTION

Reading academic texts is a core activity in studying the arts and humanities. Exploring other people's ideas about a topic is one of studying's main attractions. It is also one of its main challenges. But why should it be so challenging? You can of course *read*, or you would not be following these sentences: reading in that everyday sense is not the issue. Think back to Jan in Chapter 1 – why was she having such trouble? Her difficulties were having too much to read and finding some parts of it hard to understand. And she was worried about whether she would be able remember it all afterwards. When you are *studying*, then, the challenges are:

- coping with a *lot* of reading
- reading *difficult* material and trying to understand it
- trying to *remember* what you have read.

The best way to find out about these challenges is for you to have a go at some reading. At the back of the book you will find an article called '"On the town": women in Augustan England' (see page 265). It is by Joyce Ellis, of the University of Nottingham, and is part of an article published in the December 1995 issue of the journal *History Today. You must read this article* because a lot of the discussion in this chapter and in the chapters on essay-writing assumes that you have. We will go into some detail, so I have added paragraph numbers for ease of reference. I have also cut out parts of the article. These cuts are indicated by three dots (…).

Photocopy the article

You will find it helpful to make *two* copies of the article on pages 265–8 before you begin work on it – one to use now and one with Chapters 4 and 5. Then you can have a copy of the article *and* this book in front of you at the same time. And you can write all over your copies. You will also need a photocopy of the short essays in Chapter 4, pages 106 and 107.

It may be convenient to do all this photocopying at the same time. You should be able to use a photocopier in your local library or a shop.

ACTIVITY

Read the article '"On the town": women in Augustan England' now. Then write down your thoughts about the following questions. Don't spend too long on your answers – a few quick reactions are all you need. But you will find it useful to have a written record, so don't skip the writing.

1   Did you enjoy reading the article?

2   How did you go about it? Did you experience any difficulties as you read?

3   How long did it take you?

4   Where and at what time of day did you do the reading?

5   In a sentence, what is the article about? (Don't look back – just work from memory.)

6   What two or three points have stuck in your mind? Do you think you will be able to remember what is in the article in a few weeks' time?

7   Did you mark parts of it as you read (underlining or using a highlighting pen), or make any notes?

Here are the answers a student, Carol, gave.

1   Yes I did enjoy it, mainly because I am very interested in the role of women through history. It gave practical reasons for women's attitudes. But parts of it were very hard to understand.

2   I read it through once – fairly slowly – going over the bits I found difficult twice or more. I had to read and re-read some sentences carefully because they were very long and they needed to be 'unravelled' to get the true sense of what the author was saying. You had to pay attention to the punctuation to make sense of it (for example, para.10, 'Moreover, whereas in earlier periods…coffee houses'; the whole of para.12). And I didn't understand some words – 'Augustan' in the title, 'demographer' in para.1; 'dysfunctional' in para. 3; para.10, 'an assize'. I found it quite long.

3   Over half an hour.

4   In the living room at home, sitting in an easy chair. 6.00 in the evening.

5   The expectations of women in the eighteenth century.

6   The strength of opinion at the time against women moving into towns.
    How isolated women could be by lack of transport and bad weather in the countryside. Needing a bone-setter!
    The references to literature, for example, Jane Austen.
    I think I'll remember the general information, yes. But probably not the names of the people who are quoted.

7   No.

How do Carol's answers compare with yours? To throw more light on these answers, and your own, we'll look at the questions more closely.

2 YOUR REACTIONS TO READING

The first two questions are to do with the impact the reading task made on you. Were your experiences and reactions similar to Carol's? Possibly not. We all react differently to what we read. It depends on what we are interested in, whether we already know something about the subject and are used to that kind of reading, and how much effort we are prepared to put in. As a student you have to try to 'manage' your approach to reading, so you need to think about how *you* react in different circumstances. In studying, as with other things, how you *feel* about what you are doing has a profound effect on how well you do it.

2.1   Feelings about what you read

We have seen that Carol enjoyed the article, mainly because she was already interested in women's history. But it wasn't an easy read. She had to spend quite a lot of time re-reading some sentences because it was hard to work out what the author was saying. It sounds as if she approached these sentences rather like puzzles, trying to 'unravel' their meaning by looking for clues in the way they are put together and punctuated. And some of the words and terms used in the article were new to her. That slowed her down too. She ended up feeling that it took quite a long time to read.

I must say I had mixed feelings as I started reading. The mention of 'demographic research' in the very first sentence put me off a bit. The title 'On the town' sounded a lot more fun than that. Also, while I thought I knew what 'demography' means, I stopped to look it up in the dictionary just to be sure. This first sentence seemed long and complex – I found it quite difficult to read. By the time I got to 'a remarkable predominance of women', I was forgetting the beginning of the sentence and had to go back to it, and I had to read the last part of it a couple of times too. It is written in a complicated way: 'Modern demographic research suggests…, producing…in contrast with…'. I felt the writing was holding me very much at arm's length.

The first sentence of paragraph 2 struck me as off-putting in a different way. It seems to be written as if we are all 'in the know', or should be. If in fact you don't know anything about this 'standard cliché', where does that leave you? Speaking for myself, on the outside feeling pretty stupid. However, I was reassured by the next sentence. 'Underhand stratagems' sounded much more interesting and I set off again in a happier frame of mind. I was a bit held up by the word 'hangings' and re-read that sentence a couple of times, but I was stopped dead in my tracks by the start of the one after, 'In contrast…'. In contrast to what? That took a bit of working out.

Generally, I thought the author expected me to have a wide vocabulary so that I could take in my stride words like 'vindicated' and expressions such as '…meccas of unbridled consumption and frivolity to which women were irresistibly drawn'. At this point I began to feel rather frustrated by my slow progress.

Then, I went on to find the last half of paragraph 3 and paragraph 4 even more difficult to grasp – full of abstract ideas, complex sentences and difficult terms: 'Such claims, however, reflected long-standing literary conventions and equally long-standing male anxieties rather than contemporary reality.' The last sentence of that paragraph was particularly complex: 'It is much more plausible to argue…rural setting.' I stopped to try to make sense of it – underlining the word 'dysfunctional' (perhaps its meaning would become clearer to me later?) – but after that I decided just to push on. As I read through paragraph 4 I underlined the phrases 'conventional expectations', 'contemporary norms' and 'an ideal' so that I could come back to them later. Then, I highlighted paragraph 5 in the margin, because Ellis is describing an historical change that had a big effect on these women's roles in the countryside.

Unknown words

Should you always stop and look up unfamiliar words in the dictionary?

It depends. Obviously it slows you down if you have to stop a lot. You have to decide whether a word seems important. Does it keep coming up? Is not knowing the exact meaning interfering with your understanding of the text enough to make it worth stopping to find out?

On reflection, I think I should not have stopped as often in these opening paragraphs of the article. It was not until paragraph 6 that I was reading fluently and really began to get *engaged* in what I was reading. Perhaps I could have guessed what 'demography' meant from the context, well enough to be going on with at least. Instead, I think I should have read the article right through once, marking words I was not sure about so that I could come back to them later on.

From paragraph 6 I began to enjoy myself. I found it all quite easy and engaging reading. I was struck by how the writing 'flowed', with one part of the discussion seeming to lead naturally to the next, carrying me along with it. And I began to realize that, generally, Ellis would make a point (for example about the difficulty of travelling around in the countryside), then spend quite a lot of time explaining and illustrating it. I particularly enjoyed some of these illustrations – reading the very words of people at the time. To think that carriages would turn over and women break their bones simply visiting neighbours! And imagine being house-bound for four months on end. Although 'antique' writing can be difficult, I found these quotations quite readable. And I found myself thinking about how very different life is for women who live in the countryside now.

It was also intriguing to read about the views of visitors to England: it had never occurred to me that women went window-shopping in the eighteenth century. I didn't bother trying to remember people's names. But I did try to underline the *main points* the author was making as I went along, so that they would stand out. That way, I could keep these points separate in my mind from all the illustrations of them. It was only mildly disappointing to discover that these probably weren't 'naughty town-women' after all.

So, looking back, my difficulties were mainly at the start, in paragraphs 1–4. After that I found the article so interesting that, in the end, I felt it was worth going back to the difficult bits and spending some time trying to get to grips with them. What about you? How did you get on with the opening paragraphs? Some of the sentences are dense, and complex in structure – they are not at all easy to read and understand. And, generally, how did you cope with the level of the vocabulary?

Coping with difficult reading

What do you do when you cannot make sense of the text?

Take the first sentence in the article. When you are faced with this kind of complex sentence it's a good idea to break it down – make several sentences of it. So you might have 'Modern demographic research suggests that…/This produced…/That contrasts with…'. Then you need to fill in the gaps. As you do that, make it simple. The new sentences might go:

'Modern demographic research suggests that many women migrated to the larger towns.'

'This produced towns with far more women than men living in them.'

'That contrasts with smaller towns, where either the sexes were more balanced or there were many more men.'

When you need to do this, you can try doing it in your head. But sometimes you will have to write things down to make sense of them, even though that slows you down more.

You can often put off looking up various words and terms by paraphrasing like this as you go along, aiming just to get the gist of things. Usually, it *is* better to read through to the end of a text and get a sense of what the whole thing is about before worrying too much about the difficult parts. I've dwelt on some opening sentences here because it is rather depressing if you can't make sense of things right at the start. But in fact I found this article a lot easier to read as I progressed.

Often when you come across something you don't understand you can *keep moving on*, and still get a lot out of a text (see also section 3.5 on page 47). The difficult parts may make more sense when you come back to them another time, or from a different angle. Don't let the tough parts get you down.

Notice that Carol and I approached the job of reading the article differently. She worked her way through slowly, re-reading parts of it and trying to work out everything as she went along. I started off by doing that, but then I became frustrated because I wasn't making enough progress and didn't feel engaged in my reading. I made the decision to speed up and come back to the difficult parts later. In other words, I *changed the way* I was reading in response to how I was *feeling* about it. Otherwise, I might just have given up.

However, both of us were successful, in that we got to the end of the article and found it interesting. There is no 'right' way to read. The important thing is to be flexible in your approach; you need to be able to judge how well you are progressing, and how you are feeling, and to adjust your approach accordingly.

KEY POINTS

- When you find parts of an academic text difficult, it is generally best to read through to the end and come back to the hard parts later.

- You can often get the gist of complicated sentences by re-structuring them for yourself and putting them into your own words as you go along.

- There is no 'right' way to read this kind of text. You have to experiment and discover what works best for *you*.

Adjust your approach according to how you are feeling as you read. If you feel frustrated because you are not making progress or don't find things interesting, then try speeding up.

2.2   Your attitude to the topics you read about

Perhaps it seems odd to have begun by asking whether you *enjoyed* reading the article. You are studying, and you were asked to read it, so you just get on with it – does it matter whether you enjoy it? But as an adult isn't it rather unusual to feel that you *have* to read something (unless it's for work of course)? If you don't enjoy your leisure reading you probably just stop and turn to something more interesting. Here, you are in the position of having *chosen* to study but then being *told* what to read 'whether you like it or not'. Yet if you really don't like the topic you will surely find it hard to concentrate for long. Worse, what you read tends to slip from your mind unless you find it at least a bit thought provoking. So, even before you get down to reading a particular text, your feelings about the *topic* you are studying will have an effect on you. It is generally much easier for us to study and learn about things we enjoy.

KEY POINT

● You cannot *learn* well unless you can become *interested* in the subject to some extent.

When you are setting out on a whole *course* of study there are bound to be aspects of it you are not very interested in. You may often be asked to read texts about subjects that simply don't appeal to you at first sight. So the question is, how can you learn when you are a reluctant, or hostile, reader?

The best thing to do is look for ways of overcoming your reluctance, by *making* the subject interesting for yourself. Almost anything can be interesting if only you can find the right way to look at it. For instance, as I was reading the Ellis article I began to think about the irritations I sometimes feel travelling around in the countryside. And two days of being snowed in last winter were enough for me, though nothing at all compared to what poor Lady Jane Coke had to put up with. I can quite see why she would have preferred to live in a town. In other words, I began making connections between what I was reading and my own life and experiences. Carol also found the 'practical reasons' given for these women's attitudes particularly appealing. In arts and humanities subjects we can often make this kind of connection with our experience. Or we become personally involved in what we are doing by responding to a poem or a piece of music emotionally and in our imaginations.

However, this is not always the case. In some branches of philosophy, for example, the interest lies more in exploring intellectual puzzles and learning how to place a complicated problem into a conceptual framework that allows you to get to work on it. The key to becoming involved is to understand the problems the text is trying to solve: to see why the subject was interesting to those who developed it, and what hangs on the conclusions you reach. You cannot simply 'force' yourself to learn what is on the page. You need to try to grasp the underlying questions the text is grappling with.

So let's try to see what the underlying questions are in the Ellis article.

ACTIVITY

Read through from the middle of paragraph 3 again (from 'What women sought in the towns, the satirists argued...') to the end of paragraph 5.

Then home in on the last sentence in paragraph 3 ('It is much more plausible to argue...'): try to re-structure this sentence and put it into your own words – as I did earlier with the first sentence in the article.

Now write down what you think Ellis's underlying questions are: what questions is she trying to answer in writing the article?

First, the final sentence in paragraph 3. When I tried to paraphrase this, what struck me was that Ellis begins by telling us what this 'more plausible argument' is *not*. So I put that part to one side and started with the rest of the sentence. This is what I came up with:

> It is likely that so many of these women were attracted to the town because they could no longer fulfil their 'proper' function in the countryside – not because they objected to the very idea of there being 'correct' behaviour and roles for women.

So, reading this sentence in the light of the surrounding text, what questions is the text addressing? I think the broad question is quite a simple one: 'Why did these women migrate to the larger towns?' But there is a more subtle and difficult question too: 'Was it because they wanted to escape from or reject women's conventional roles – or was it because these roles had become much more difficult to play in country settings than in towns?' In other words, was going to towns a way of rebelling against their conventional role or a way of getting a lot more fun out of it?

This is the crux of the matter I think. Once you recognize it, you can see what Ellis is trying to do in the article. You can see that she is presenting an *argument* about this question, not just a descriptive account of what life was like in country and town then. You can try to follow her argument as you read – picking out the *main points* she makes, as I tried to do – and see whether you find it convincing. This makes things much more interesting.

So, as you start out on a text you hope that the writer is going to pose one or two interesting questions that will give you something to think about and enable you to search for meaning as you read. But you may have to keep your wits about you to spot them (as we have just seen). Or you may be unlucky. The writer may fail altogether to put across what questions she or he is setting out to explore. In that case you'll have to try to set some questions for yourself.

Setting your own questions

Questions make reading interesting. Unless you are reading with a question or two in the back of your mind ('Why did higher ranking women no longer have a satisfying role to play in the countryside?', 'What effects did this have on them?') you cannot *engage* with the words on the page.

When you can't get involved in the text you are reading it tends to be because you cannot see what *question* is being addressed, or because you cannot see the *point* of the question being addressed – why it is an important question, what hangs on it. You may need to stop reading closely, and skim right through an article; or with a book, look at the preface or the conclusion, or skim a few other chapters – anything that helps you see what questions the text is addressing and why they matter.

Figure 2.1 C. Bowles, 'A Morning Ramble, or…The Milliner's Shop', 1782. The multitude of shops in eighteenth-century cities offered young women more than just commercial temptations as this cartoon shows. (*History Today* Archives)

You were asked to read 'On the town' out of the blue. But, normally, you would be studying this kind of text as part of a course, and reading it in that context. It will be linked to other coursework you are doing: other texts, seminar discussions, an assignment. This context usually gives you clues to the text's meanings and the questions it explores. But, even so, if it simply does not stimulate your interest then you have to shift your strategy and work out a way to *create* an interest for yourself.

Creating an interest

To develop an interest in a subject, you can try to:

- link what you are reading to questions you are already interested in
- work out why other people have found the topic interesting – what questions they were concerned about and why
- make connections between the subject and your own experience.

However, if you find you *cannot* develop an interest in a subject, then find a strategy for 'getting through' the reading as best you can. Search for information on a particular aspect of the topic for instance, or focus on material you will need for your next assignment. In other words, if you can't find an 'intrinsic' purpose for reading the text, then create one by actively seeking something out. Then just move on. You are not achieving anything if, like Jan (in Chapter 1), you spend hours messing about with something that is not engaging your thought processes.

> **KEY POINT**
> ● You are the person who has to *do* the learning and you are the one the learning is *for*. So *you* have to take charge of it, and find ways to construct a positive approach to what you are studying.

2.3 Academic language

At the other end of the scale from the subject matter, you may find yourself reacting to individual words in texts. It is easy to be put off by the terms used if they are new to you or are used in unfamiliar ways. And when unfamiliar words fairly pepper a text, you can begin to feel rather excluded from the 'in-crowd' of people who seem able to bandy them around so freely. It can be very frustrating if you are constantly struggling to squeeze meaning out of the text. Sometimes it is almost as if you are reading a different language.

Using specialist language

Indeed, specialists do develop their own language. We accept this quite readily in the case of technical or 'scientific' language. But it is true even in subjects we tend to think of as 'subjective' – as involving our feelings and personal responses – such as music, literature and art. Specialist language gives authors extra power to explore the objects they study in a systematic and detailed way. This language ranges from the precise, technical terms used when we analyse or take apart a piece of music to see how it works (*chord, melody, harmony,* for instance); to style and period labels (such as 'Augustan', 'the Renaissance'), and the language used in theories of literature or history. If everyone uses this language when they discuss a poem or write about a painting then we can be sure that we are all paying attention to the same things in it (this 'rhyme', that 'figure'). And because it is a language we *share*, it is easier for us to understand what each other means to say about these things. It helps us see whether we agree or disagree with someone else's interpretation of the poem or painting, and just what it is we disagree about. And it helps us explore the reasons for our disagreement.

Specialist language

Everyone finds unfamiliar, specialist language off-putting and frustrating at times.

However, academic specialists always develop their own 'language'. It gives them a way of analysing and talking about the objects they study, which everyone can share. This language is constantly evolving. Developing new ideas and fitting new words to them is part of the process of producing new knowledge. As you study a subject, and become more of a specialist yourself, you will gradually 'pick up' the appropriate language and find yourself using it.

Sometimes the specialist language can be overdone, so that texts are unnecessarily obscure to the newcomer. On the other hand, you cannot hope to enter a new subject area without having to learn its specialist language.

So don't let irritation with the language or confusion over the words used in a text hinder your progress. If it is a problem, try to work out ways of tackling it.

Dictionaries

One solution to difficult words is to have a good general dictionary, and keep it right beside you when you are studying. It is an *essential* resource when you are studying arts and humanities subjects. You might use *The Concise Oxford Dictionary*, for example. Or, if you can afford it, get the two-volume *Shorter Oxford English Dictionary*. People can become quite addicted to it. But don't expect too much from a general dictionary, nor treat it as infallible. Some specialist words will not appear in it, and words that do may not be defined in the same way as they are used in your subject. If you try using a dictionary definition at the start of an essay, for instance, it may lead you off in the wrong direction because the nuances of meaning are not right for your area of study. Often you will get a better insight into the meanings of key terms in your subject from text-books and the other secondary sources you study.

You can also buy specialist dictionaries and 'companions', though they are sometimes rather difficult and technical themselves. I have listed some of these at the end of the book (see page 269).

Another approach is to have a system for writing down the difficult terms you come across, so that you can add new clues to their meaning as you see them used in different places and contexts. For instance, you could set up a 'concept-card' system using a card-index box, starting a fresh card for each new word you think is important. Keep them filed alphabetically so that you can find them easily and add new bits of information as you go along. Why not start one and see whether it suits your style of studying? It is probably worth buying a small card-index box anyway. Then you can try out various ways of using it in organizing your studies (see section 5.2).

Quoting words

While we are on the subject of words, why does Ellis keep putting some words in quotation marks?

In most cases she is in fact quoting *other people's* words: when you do this you must *always* show that's what you are doing by putting quotation marks around them. Although she doesn't always say who she is quoting, it is usually clear from the context when she is making this kind of direct quotation. But some are not quotations. What is she signalling then?

ACTIVITY

Have another look at the first five paragraphs of the article and find the quotation marks. Which are cases of direct quotation from past writing?

Then see whether you can work out what she uses the *other* quotation marks for (I found four cases).

My answers are as follows.

'the long eighteenth century'	She is signalling that this is a label used by historians to refer to a particular historical period. (In fact, the period 1688–1820.) This suggests she is writing for people who already know enough not to need reminding of the precise dates.
'female territory'	Here Ellis uses a suggestive phrase to bring certain ideas into our minds (did these females hunt in packs, we wonder). By using this kind of scientific language she signals that she is sending up the satirists: it sounds as if *they* thought they were very acute observers, whereas the exaggerated language *she* uses in the rest of the sentence confirms for us that she thinks they were quite the opposite.
'correct' (behaviour) 'accomplishments'	In these cases Ellis signals '*I'm* not saying this – it was what was expected in society at that time'.

Strictly speaking, these are not uses of quotation marks at all, but of what are often called 'scare-quotes' – I suppose because we are frightened of missing the significance of the words used inside them, or should be. (Incidentally, the term 'scare-quotes' is not in either of the general dictionaries I just recommended!)

Another common reason for using scare-quotes is to alert the reader to the fact that the term being used is not accepted by everyone, but is contentious – the claim that a painting's style is 'primitive', for example, or that a poem reflects 'reality'. Here, we are being invited to think about what we really mean by 'primitive' and 'reality', and whether these are the terms that should be used.

2.4   Academic writing style

Sometimes we are not so bothered by the words used in a text, but are thoroughly put off by the whole *way* in which it is written. What we read in everyday life usually starts from a well-defined point of view. A newspaper editorial might try to persuade you to see an event in a particular light, or a magazine article offer a straightforward 'solution' to a problem. You can agree or disagree, take it or leave it. But academic writers are generally much less committed to reaching speedy conclusions. Instead of making a direct attack on a particular question or problem, you may find they start by raising broad, abstract issues (such as demography). As we have seen, it is not always easy to discover just what questions *are* being addressed. And you may feel that the author is taking you all round the houses instead of coming straight out with a view. The text may be littered with qualifications ('in some cases', 'in part', 'somewhat', 'to an extent'), and conditional phrases such as 'it might be said that…' or 'it could be argued…'. Eventually, the writer may offer a conclusion couched in very guarded language: 'It would therefore seem that…', or 'The evidence tends to suggest that…'. Why is this?

Elaborately cautious language

Academic texts tend to be written in very cautious language.

In fact this is necessary. The writers are trying to be as *exact* as they can in their analysis, so they are careful to say only what they think can be justified. In everyday life we often use language as a rather blunt instrument for getting things said and done. However, in academic writing, language is used more like a scalpel, cutting precisely between closely related arguments so that they can be prised apart and analysed in detail. An academic writer aims to say exactly what he or she means to say, even if it takes a lot of extra words.

For example, take the first paragraph of 'On the town'. Notice that demographic research '*suggests* that…' and 'All the evidence *indicates* that…*principally* by…'. Why doesn't Ellis just say straight out that the female population of the larger towns expanded dramatically and that was because women moved into towns from the countryside? She doesn't because demographic knowledge is not the kind of knowledge we can be that sure about. In the nature of things it is *uncertain*. Research methods and techniques change over time, producing new knowledge. We may even come across new sources of information, new evidence, from this period – previously undiscovered records of births and deaths, for instance. So what we think we know now is likely to be challenged by the findings of future researchers. Ellis deliberately reflects this uncertainty in the way she presents her case. (And this is only part of it. In fact I cut a section of more detailed argument about facts and figures from the original text.)

Take another example, this sentence in paragraph 7: 'The education given to men from the social elite was almost expressly designed for a rural setting.' *Almost* expressly? Ellis is acknowledging that there were other sides to these men's education. What exactly they were is not important here so she doesn't go into them, but she does not want to give us a false impression either. You may have noticed that she is always careful to balance the picture she presents of women's life in the countryside with that of men's. In the passage just before this, about Lady Jane Coke getting marooned, she adds 'Of course, to some extent, her husband was marooned too…'. She does not want to exaggerate the woman's predicament by simply paying no attention at all to the man's. Also, she wants to build up a strong case. So she doesn't leave herself open to the counter-argument that men might have suffered just as much in the countryside: she says they didn't.

This reminds us that Ellis is presenting an *argument* here, not telling a story, and that she wants her argument to be convincing. So you have to pay close attention to what she says, and think about it. In the end, you are not likely to be convinced if she exaggerates one side of the case or just ignores whatever doesn't happen to suit her argument. Comparing her account of the subject with those given by other academics would help you make this kind of judgement.

KEY POINT

● An academic text is not a narrative, however instructive. It is an *argument*, written to be convincing.

Besides striving to be precise and accurate, academic writers tend to use a cool, *passive* voice: 'It would, therefore, seem that…', rather than the *active* 'I think that…'. The passive voice emphasizes the thing being discussed, not the person who is doing the discussing. When Ellis concludes, 'The steady migration of women into towns was the logical consequence of conventional perceptions of femininity...' (rather than 'I think women moved into towns because...'), she is drawing your attention to her *argument* rather than to herself as the thinker of it. And we never discover what she personally feels about these 'conventional perceptions of femininity'. In this kind of writing it is not supposed to matter *who* is doing the enquiring or what state of mind they are in. Only what is directly relevant to Ellis's enquiry is included in her account of it. For instance, she doesn't tell us anything about *how* she researched what she writes about: her enquiry is not presented as an exciting voyage of discovery involving the perils of wobbly ladders in libraries, the frustration of following tracks that lead nowhere, and eventual triumph. Rather, her account consists of analysis, description and argument presented in a calm, detached and impersonal manner.

This is because Ellis is writing as an academic, aiming her words at an 'academic audience'. She is assuming that you are a cool, detached and very critical reader. She takes for granted that you will be interested in the strength of her arguments, not in her as a person. But it would be wrong to think that the 'detached' stance and 'distant' tone of much of this writing means that academics don't care about their subjects, or don't have strong views about anything – far from it. And I do not mean to say that all academic writing is done well either. Some of it is *too* 'remote' and some far too stodgy, in my opinion. The point is to understand that academic writing follows certain 'accepted rules', or conventions, and why. Then you are less likely to be irritated or put off by the way the texts you study are written, although it can take a bit of getting used to.

KEY POINTS

- Academic writers aim to present a convincing argument, so they try to write in a precise and 'balanced' way.
- In order to be precise, they use a specialist language: when you enter a new subject area you have to learn its specialist language.
- They tend to write in a detached, dispassionate way, often using the passive voice, in order to emphasize what it is they are writing *about*.

2.5 Points of view

Finally, you can feel very frustrated because you do not agree with the point of view of the writer. For example, you might wonder why Ellis doesn't explore or present any evidence for the argument that town life attracted women because they were 'trying to esape from or subvert accepted gender roles'. You might feel she dismisses it out of hand simply by ridiculing the satirists who believed it. Perhaps you don't see why that is necessarily a less plausible argument at all. So you may feel increasingly impatient as you work through her version of things – like having a conversation with a very talkative person who goes on and on without giving you the chance to speak. It can feel very oppressive if you disagree at a fundamental level and want to raise an objection. It may be hard to keep driving on through the text.

On the other hand a lot of ideas seem unappealing or implausible when you first come across them. If you were only to read what you already agreed with you wouldn't learn very much. Part of studying is learning to cope with not feeling too happy about what the author is saying – distancing yourself from your hostile feelings and reading on to see what arguments are put forward. Eventually, you may decide the author has a point, or not, but first you need to give yourself the chance to find out what he or she is saying.

A detached stance?

It is said that we think most clearly when our thinking is not distorted by passions. So, when you are reading academic texts you are supposed to 'detach' your thoughts from your feelings and beliefs, to put your emotions and convictions to one side, and judge arguments by their strength and their soundness.

However, as a reader you cannot be entirely detached or you wouldn't have a position from which to think about, criticize and judge what you read. So perhaps 'semi-detached' is a better way of putting it.

Of course, detachment – even semi-detachment – is an 'ideal' rather than something we can always achieve (as are precision, clarity and the rest). You are bound to have feelings, especially when you disagree with what you read. The thing is to use those feelings constructively. When you disagree with a text, write down your criticisms and your counter-arguments point by point instead of just fuming. You can learn a lot by reacting against what you read because it often helps you sort out your own ideas.

2.6 Feelings and motivation

The reason we are discussing your reactions to studying is because it is not a simple process, nor a painless one. Often it is enjoyable, and sometimes exciting and exhilarating. But it is quite easy to lose heart too, especially if you are studying independently as a distance student. By its very nature, studying can make you feel edgy and uncomfortable. You are constantly being presented with new ideas. Trying to understand them, think critically about them and come to your own conclusions can be confusing and quite disturbing. And always there are more texts to read and make sense of, essays to write. Doing all this takes effort and determination. It is immensely satisfying when you feel you have grasped something quite complicated or important, but you never know when that moment is going to arrive. In any case, you then have to move on to unfamiliar territory again.

How you feel as you are studying a text makes a big difference to how well you manage to get to grips with it, take what you need from it, and then move on to the next task. To study effectively you need to be able to 'manage' your feelings. This involves:

- recognizing how various study texts (and tasks) make you feel
- thinking about the effect these feelings are having on you
- working out what to do about your reactions.

You have been thinking about the first two of these here – first, by reading the Ellis article and writing down your reactions to it, and then by reading on to this point in the chapter. You will have to explore the third for yourself, as you go along – by trying out different patterns of study, varying your activities when you begin to feel weighed down, and talking things over with tutors and fellow students or friends. If you are to learn well, and keep on studying over a long period, it is vital to work out how to make your studies enjoyable and interesting most of the time.*

KEY POINTS

As a student it is very important to be able to *manage* your feelings about your work. You need to find ways to:

- build on your enthusiasms, and
- avoid sinking into despair when the going gets hard.

Specifically, you need to:

- be able to make the subject matter interesting to you
- accept specialist language and take it in your stride
- become accustomed to academic ways of writing
- learn how to read arguments you disagree with – making constructive use of your reactions by writing down your criticisms.

---

*Incidentally, if you enjoyed reading the Ellis article you could find out what she says about why poorer women were attracted to towns by looking for the complete article in a library (see page 265 for the full reference). At the end of the article Ellis includes a list of 'further reading'.

3 READING STRATEGICALLY

We will now turn to the way you *set about* the reading task – the *strategy* you adopted when reading the Ellis article. Perhaps you think you didn't have anything as grand as a strategy. But that doesn't mean you didn't, just that you took it for granted and didn't think about it. After many years of reading it would be surprising if you didn't have some quite well-established ways of going about it. For example, some people skip to the end of a piece first, see roughly how long it will take to read and decide when to get started. Others skim quickly through to see what it is about, and whether they want or need to read it carefully. Some of us like to do our reading in a special place: a particularly comfy armchair or, in summer, out of doors. When you start out on any piece of reading you make lots of small decisions – about how, when and where to do it – that affect the way you read. You need to think about these habits of yours, and consider whether they are suited to a serious course of study.

3.1   Place and time

Where and when did you read the Ellis article? Were you lying in bed, sitting at a desk, on the train, or what? Was it first thing in the morning, late at night or, like Carol, early in the evening? It is worth pausing to think about how well this place and time worked for you.

ACTIVITY

Were you able to maintain a period of steady concentration, or would it have been better to do the reading when you were feeling less tired or were in a quieter place?

Did you have necessary materials to hand – pen, paper, dictionary? Do you need a surface to write on as you read?

Do you like to keep moving to different places to read, or is it better for you to establish a regular spot?

Stop and have a think about these things.

The decisions you make about these questions may make a significant difference to how effectively you read.

3.2   Reading speed

How long did it take you to read the article? The issue of 'reading speed' is a persistent worry for most people. There always seems to be much more to read than you have time for, so there's a tremendous pressure to read more quickly. In fact it is surprising how much you can pick up by pushing through a few pages at speed.

Scanning first sentences

If you just want to get a quick impression of what a piece is about it can be helpful to read quickly through the first sentence of each paragraph, picking out a key phrase in each one.

Doing this for the first four paragraphs of the Ellis article, I came up with:

'female population of towns expanded'

'women's enthusiasm for urban life'

'not only women preferred urban life'

'higher-ranking women's lives confined in the countryside'

I would say this list gives me a fair picture of what the article is dealing with. It tells me what topics it is about. But it doesn't save me the job of reading the article properly. I couldn't find out from this why and in what ways women's lives were confined in the countryside, or what was so attractive about the town. It is just a rough guide to some of the contents.

The list will:

- help me decide whether I want to go on and read the article properly
- put me in the right frame of mind to understand the article
- remind me afterwards what the article dealt with (in other words, this is one way of making notes).

Skimming

There will be many times in your studies when you need to move even faster than this, scanning very quickly through a lot of pages to get the gist of the topics and issues dealt with, or to find specific information. However, it is important to be clear that *this is not reading*. It is skimming. Skimming can tell you *about* a text, but it won't enable you to *learn* what is in the text.

Reading

In order to learn from a text you need to follow the argument at the heart of it. And to do that you need to *slow right down*, taking it bit by bit and making notes as you go. Some people claim there are ways of 'speed-reading' that enable you to grasp the contents of a text in a fraction of the time it takes most of us. Even if that were possible, it would be to mistake your purposes in reading the text.

The point of reading

The underlying purpose of reading is to *develop your understanding* of the subject – by encountering new ideas, arguments, explanations and information, and through the process of thinking about them.

If you try to 'bypass' this thinking process, you are not really learning as you read. Learning is to do with changing your ideas, combining them together in new ways, and taking in new ideas. Reading a text is one way you bring about these changes.

The point of reading is not to have a lot of words pass in front of your eyes. Nor is it just to add a few new items to a long 'list' of information in your mind. It is to *engage* your existing ideas and make you *rethink* them. And it is to give you new ideas to think about.

You need time to develop your thoughts as you study. But, even so, you can't afford to work at whatever speed just comes 'naturally'. When you are trying to keep abreast of a course of study you often have to push yourself to do a lot more reading than you normally would. What you need is a *range* of study strategies, so that you can work at different speeds according to what it is you are trying to achieve. At one end of the scale is the lightning skim through a whole book and, at the other, painstaking study of a difficult paragraph. You need to become accustomed to working at different points on this scale depending on the circumstances. How slowly you need to go will depend on:

● how much you already know about the subject you are studying

● how difficult the text is

● how thoroughly you need to understand it.

So how long did you spend on the Ellis article – and how long 'should' you have spent?

You might have spent twenty minutes on it and picked up all you needed. On the other hand, if you found parts difficult or it made you stop and think a lot, it could easily have taken more than half an hour. If you were taking notes it might have taken an hour, and if in the process you read it more than once it could have been an hour and a half.

Because of my own special interest in the article (for the purposes of this book) I spent several hours on it. The longer I worked on it the more interesting I found it and the more clearly I grasped the issues it deals with. You would have no reason to spend nearly so long, but it shows that there is no 'right' amount of time to spend. It depends entirely on what you are trying to achieve.

Time investment

By becoming a student you are choosing to invest your own time in developing your intellectual powers and your knowledge.

Sometimes you will get a good return by investing in a very detailed reading of a small section of a text which is central to your current interests or needs. At other times you will get a good return by dipping into several texts and skim-reading in order to broaden your ideas.

Basically, *you* have to decide what your current needs are and *distribute your time* in a way that will give you a good overall return.

This is easier said than done, of course. But a key test is to ask yourself 'Is this making me think?', 'Am I getting a better grasp of the subject?' If the answers are 'no', the time you are investing is being wasted and you need to turn to a different activity.

As a rule-of-thumb you might think in terms of the following 'study rates'.

1   Easy text/fairly familiar material: 100 plus words per minute.
2   Moderately hard text that you want to follow reasonably closely: 70 words per minute.
3   Dense or difficult text/unfamiliar subject-matter that you want to understand in depth: 40 words per minute.

I call these *study rates* because they include the time needed for you to think and work things out as you read, and for a fair amount of re-reading. (If they were simply 'reading speeds' they would be very slow, unless English is not your first language.) These rates would give you study times for the Ellis article (about 1500 words) of around 15, 25 and 40 minutes, respectively. You can apply these rates to any secondary source material you are setting out to study. By skimming through to assess the length and difficulty of the piece – and bearing in mind your familiarity with the subject-matter – you can decide which of the study rates 1–3 to apply to it. Then you can work out roughly how many minutes or hours you will need to spend studying it.

If you adopt this strategy it will help you to *assess in advance* the time you need to spend on reading tasks. This will help you *distribute* and *use* your study time more effectively. You may not be able to make your assessment very accurately, but some fairly reasonable idea is better than none.

Remember that we have been talking about secondary, 'academic' texts. When you read primary texts (poems, historical documents, philosophical writing) you do not read them for the same purposes, nor in the same ways (see Chapter 6).

KEY POINTS

You need to adjust the speed at which you read an academic text according to:

- the kind of text it is ('easy', 'moderately hard', 'dense/difficult')
- your purposes in reading it
- how familiar you are with the subject matter.

Trying to assess in advance how long it will take you to read a text will help you distribute and use your time effectively.

3.3   Study sessions

Apart from the question of how long overall you will have to spend reading a text, you need to think about how to divide up your time into study sessions. No doubt you would expect to get through a three-page article in a single study session, but you may have to spread a chapter of a book over two or more separate sessions. As we have just seen, that depends on your assessment of how long it will take to study the text. It also depends on your circumstances. But it is important to recognize that your span of attention is limited and you cannot expect to study intensively hour after hour. It is wiser to divide up your study time into several sessions during a week, if you can, rather than attempting a couple of very long sessions.

If your reading sessions are too short you will not have time to get properly into the frame of thinking required by the text before you break off. You might find two hours a reasonable span for a session, particularly if you are studying after a day of work. On the other hand, after only an hour of intense concentration you might need a short break, or to switch to another task. Take some time to 'observe' yourself and your reading habits. Think about what works best for you within the general contours of your life.

3.4   Setting targets

All this brings us back to the point made in Chapter 1 that as a student you have to act as your own 'manager', deciding how to invest your limited time and energy according to:

- what your overall goals are

- what your immediate priorities are
- whether the results you are getting are as good as you can reasonably expect.

It is all too easy just to plod on from one page to the next, hoping for the best but losing sight of what you were trying to achieve when you sat down to read. If you do that you will soon fall behind with your work, and you'll get depressed about it. So try to set yourself a goal for each study session (for example, the number of pages you will read tonight), and do your best to achieve it.

KEY POINTS

To 'manage' your reading effectively you have to keep:
- defining reading tasks for yourself and setting yourself targets;
- monitoring your progress; and
- re-setting your targets in the light of your progress.

3.5 What if you get stuck?

Sometimes as you read you will get stuck. When this happens don't sit staring at the page, going over and over the same few sentences. And try not to blame yourself unduly – it may be that the text is just badly written. In any case, don't despair, find an active way of tackling the problem.

Reading requires you to 'project' meaning into the words in front of you. When you are stuck it usually means that you have lost track of the argument and can no longer see the way ahead. So you have to find ways of re-constructing the argument in your mind. One way is to cast around for clues by looking elsewhere in the text. You can look back to the earlier parts – checking the title, the contents list and the introduction to remind yourself what the writer was setting out to discuss, and re-reading some of what you have covered to firm up the arguments again. Or you can look ahead a few pages or more to see what is coming up; or turn to the conclusion to see where the argument eventually leads. If you are still stuck you might look for clues in other books on the same subject, or in lecture notes, or you could phone other students to ask for help.

Another tactic is to use your pen. Write down the main questions you think the text is addressing, as we did earlier for Ellis's article. Try to summarize what you have read so far, particularly the part just before you were stuck. Try underlining words that seem important in the section you don't understand, and then see if you can summarize anything that is said in connection with those words. Your summaries may not be particularly good, but the process of writing them will help you get to grips with the text. Writing makes you put ideas in your own words, in terms that make sense to you.

KEY POINTS

When you are stuck, *attack* the problem.

● Look for clues in earlier parts of the text, or later on.
● Make detailed notes of the preceding section and the bit you are stuck on.
● Talk things over with your tutor or other students.

If you are still stuck, just skip ahead and see if you can pick up the thread again at a later point. Or leave the text altogether and start on another piece of work. Perhaps things will be clearer when you come back to it another time. Anyway, there is no point in sitting achieving nothing.

4 REMEMBERING

After you read the Ellis article, what did you write down as the two or three points that stuck in your mind? How much did you think you would remember a week or two later? How much *should* you be able to remember?

In Carol's answers she said: 'I think I'll remember the general information, yes. But probably not the names of the people who are quoted.'

I don't think she should worry about not remembering names. I didn't even try to. Why should we? We are not reading to find out about these particular people. We are reading to get hold of the central arguments in the text – about *why* women went to live in towns during this period.

Facts, figures and names

Should you try to remember facts, figures and names as you read?

It depends what you are reading for. Often the answer is no – you only need to get the general gist of the information. But if you think the details might be useful to hang on to, then *write them down*. Don't try to memorize them.

Having said that, when you are studying subjects such as languages, law or history you do have to do quite a lot of memorizing. In the case of history, it can be very important to remember the precise dates of particular events. Some people use rhymes, or mnemonics, to help them – 'In fourteen hundred and ninety two/Columbus sailed the ocean blue' is a well-known one. (But you can invent your own too.) And it helps if you try to remember an event and its date together, as one 'item', from the start – for instance, always saying to yourself 'the Battle of Trafalgar in 1805' or 'the Great Reform Act of 1832'. Once you have a few key dates for the period lodged in your mind they serve as landmarks. You can then 'position' other events in relation to them, in the context of the overall 'story' you are telling yourself. That way you keep the memorizing you need to do within reasonable bounds.

Even here, it is *more* important to understand the whole picture, to get an idea of *sequences* of events and to appreciate their meaning and significance. This is what is needed in essays and exam-answers. It is also easier to remember particular dates, events and historical figures within a meaningful framework.

Carol said she remembered three specific points from the Ellis article. Two of these were parts of the argument: the strength of opinion against women moving into towns at that time (the satirists' views, which Ellis dismisses); and the isolation women suffered in the countryside as a result of lack of transport and bad weather, a main plank of Ellis's own argument. She also remembered the references to literature, which Ellis uses to illustrate and support her argument.

What this shows is how we engage with ideas that are on our minds at the time, or that make a particularly vivid impression on us; and how these ideas tend to stay with us, bobbing about in our thoughts even though we have not made a point of remembering them. Carol thinks she'll never forget the bone-setter. In a sense this is 'real' learning – when we read things that appeal to our imagination or feed into our current thinking. We may not be aware of having 'remembered' them, but they strike a chord and set us thinking along new lines. However, it also shows that we cannot rely entirely on what we remember spontaneously. We need to make a special effort to attend to the main thrust of the author's argument and take down notes that capture the essential points.

Actually, how can you be sure how much you remember? Would it count as remembering if you found yourself referring to Ellis's views in conversation – or should you be able to sit down with pen and paper and write out all the main points she makes? The fundamental question is whether the article has made any changes to the way you think about eighteenth-century life, and the reasons for women's preferences and actions. If it has, then these changes will remain as substantial traces in your mind of the process of reading the article. You will be able to tell that this has happened if you try re-reading the article at a later date, because it will be much easier to read.

What is 'remembering'?

You should not aim to 'store' all the words of the text in your head. Even Ellis, re-reading her article now, would probably find things she'd forgotten having written. If even the author is not able to recall in detail all that she wrote, why should you want to?

Essentially, you want to be able to *think*, using the ideas and information presented in the text. You have acquired that thinking capacity when you have *understood* what you've read.

You know you have retained some of what you have studied when you can read the same piece more easily a second time, and when it's easier to read other texts on the same subject. It shows that your mind has retained some elements of the re-organization achieved during your original reading.

This re-organization is the most important kind of 'remembering'.

The point of reading, then, is to be able to understand what you read, and also to be able to *come back* to these ideas when you need them again. But holding ideas in your mind is not the only way of doing that. Your memory is too limited and too unreliable to serve as the main means for storing what you study. You can construct a much more reliable route back to what you have read if you make notes. You may need to do some deliberate memorizing just before an exam, but, for the most part, understanding is a more important aim than remembering.

KEY POINT

- Don't worry about your memory. Just write things down. It is what you understand that counts.

5 MAKING NOTES

Did you have a pen in your hand as you read the Ellis article? Reading is an *active* process of *'making' sense* as you read. One way of keeping your mind active is to use your pen.

ACTIVITY

If you didn't make notes as you read Ellis's article go back over it quickly and try to jot down some of the main points she makes.

When you have some notes, answer these questions.

1   What do you think is achieved by making notes?
2   What uses do you think you might have for the notes?
3   Where will you keep them?
4   Did making notes change your understanding of the article?

5.1   Highlighting and underlining

As I read through the article for the first and, especially, the second time, I was continually marking it with a red biro. I could just as well have used a highlighting pen. Figure 2.2 shows what paragraph 3 looked like after I had worked on it.

> Of course it was <u>not only women</u> who expressed a <u>preference for urban life</u>: many men would have agreed with the *e.g.* north-eastern landowner who contemptuously refused his mother's pleas for his return from London in 1720 with the rhetorical question 'Surely you don't think me such a fool as to prefer the charms of a stupid, dull, *versus* country life to the pleasures of the Town? But these pleasures were thought to be especially attractive to <u>women</u>, not simply because women were by nature self-indulgent and superficial (!!) but because urban life allowed them to gain the upper hand in the age-old struggle (!) to escape their natural subordination. What women sought in towns, <u>the satirists argued</u>, was <u>freedom from male control</u>. Such claims, however, reflected long-standing literary conventions and equally long-standing male anxieties rather than contemporary reality. It is <u>much more plausible to argue</u> that urban life attracted a disproportionate number of women not because they were trying to escape from or to subvert accepted gender roles but <u>because 'correct' female behaviour</u> ?? <u>was all too often</u> dysfunctional <u>in a rural setting</u>.

Figure 2.2   Sample of marked-up text.

ACTIVITY

Look carefully at my underlining and the other marks I made. Compare them with yours, if you made any.

Why do you think I underlined the words I did? Why did I use double underlining in some places? Why did I put some parts of the text in brackets?

I try to mark a text in ways that help me pick up the gist of things when I come back to it again later. The words I underlined in the first line simply remind me what the first part of the paragraph is about. I thought it was important, too, to identify the idea of 'Country versus Town', a main theme of the article. The // mark shows me that there is a change of direction at that point – from men's attitudes to country life to women's. In the next sentence I made the word 'women' stand out to remind me that they are the main focus of the article. I also double underlined parts of the final sentence because this is where Ellis tells us what direction *her* argument is going to take (that is, what questions the article is addressing).

Then I put the satirists' views, which Ellis does not agree with, in brackets, to separate them from the argument in the rest of the article (though in fact she returns to them in the last two paragraphs). The words underlined within these brackets remind me whose views they are and summarize what the satirists thought. The words bracketed in the final sentence again refer to the satirists' views, not Ellis's. I found this sentence difficult to follow on first reading and, since it is so important, I stopped to try and sort it out there and then. In fact I inserted the brackets and underlined Ellis's own case during the first reading to help me do that. I also put question marks against the term 'dysfunctional' then, because it is clearly important to know exactly what it means and I felt I didn't. Sometimes I circle terms like this as a reminder to think about them again, or look them up later. And I put in the exclamation marks simply to express my feelings – these are *my* markings and I can say what I like. I often make a few remarks of my own in the margins of a text.

As regards the article as a whole, I made most marks in the first five paragraphs and the last. Otherwise, I tended to underline a phrase here and there to remind myself of the *main points* being made, and picked out some of the illustrations that follow as 'evidence in support'. For instance, 'well-born women were much less mobile' (in paragraph 6); Montagu's 'bone-setter'; and 'Coke marooned'.

There are many other ways of marking this paragraph, and the article as a whole, that might be just as good or better. What my markings show is that the *act of highlighting* can be very *strategic*. It can be used to convey a lot of information. What's more, it forced me to pay close attention to the text and really *think* about the key points Ellis is making.

So there is no 'correct' way of marking up a text. You may have had good reasons for picking out quite different words. It depends what you are focusing on as you read. My markings are offered as a stimulus to make you think about:

- how *much* marking up you do; and
- *what* you chose to underline or highlight.

The value of highlighting and underlining

Do you feel like a vandal if you write in a book? It matters very much whether it's your book of course. But, if it is, remember that marking the text as you read, using a highlighting pen or underlining key words, is an extremely valuable way of

- focussing your *attention* on the text
- making you *pick out* and *think about* the main ideas
- leaving a trace on the page of the *sense* you have made of the text.

When you come back to a marked-up text you can tune in very quickly to the thinking you did on first reading.

Marking the text is a way of moderately increasing the time you invest in reading, while considerably increasing the pay-off – both in terms of what you understand at the time and what you can remember later.

You don't *have* to underline as you read, and certainly not all the time. It can slow you down too much and sometimes makes reading rather boring. In any case, not all texts require such detailed attention. On the other hand, if you scan back over material you have read but haven't marked, you may find that very little has stuck in your mind. Anyway, I find it boosts my morale to see my familiar markings on a text when I come back to it – offering direct evidence of the attention I have already given to it, and leading me to the main points.

If you really can't bring yourself to write all over books, then modern technology can come to the rescue. Those little yellow 'stickies' are very useful for writing down key points – just big enough, and they don't damage the page. Placed at the edges, they may also act as bookmarks or as a reminder of where you wanted to get to in your next study session.

5.2 Ways of making notes

When you want seriously to get to grips with the ideas in a text and 'make them your own' there is no alternative to written notes. For one thing, you don't always want to be hunting for books and articles you once read in order to see what you underlined. And, of course, you may have borrowed books from a library and have returned them. So you need a handier version of any material that is important. Making notes also forces you to pay even closer attention to the ideas in the text than when you underline, because you have to decide both *what* to write down and *how* to say it. Marking and underlining the text is a first stage in this process.

Whether your notes are particularly good or not, the very act of writing them forces you to 'make sense' of what you read. So, although note-making is hard work and quite time consuming, you are making an investment which adds a lot of value to the effort and time you are already putting into reading.

But what *kind* of notes should you make and how many? What do your notes on the Ellis article look like? They may be very brief, or take up a couple of pages. They may be written as sentences or set out in a diagram. There are many different ways of making notes. What works best for you will depend on:

- the way your mind works
- the kind of text it is
- what you want to use the notes for
- the time you think is reasonable to 'invest'.

For example, you might decide that all you need for an article like Ellis's is the reference and a single line on a card (see Figure 2.3).

Ellis, J. (1995) '"On the town": women in Augustan England', *History Today*, vol. 45, no. 12 (December), pp.15–25.
Reasons why women left the countryside for life in the larger towns, 1688–1820.

Figure 2.3   Example of a simple entry on a reference card.

You could then file this in a card-index box. This is the very least you should do: writing down a full, correct reference for what you read, as you read it, means you can find the article or book again in a library (see Chapter 6).

Or you could carry out the suggestion made in section 3.2 of writing down key phrases from the first sentence (or two) of each paragraph. However, that would not be enough on its own, because you wouldn't be able to make sense of the words at a later date. You would need to put more of *your own thinking* into it.

A sentence summarizing the main theme of the article would be helpful. Carol said that it is about 'Society's expectations of women in the eighteenth century'. This looks like a very broad theme. It is probably too vague to be helpful when she looks back at it. She would need to add something about migration into towns and the reasons for it. If you want a bit more detail you can make rather fuller notes, again on a card that can be stored in an index box, as in Figure 2.4.

Ellis, J. (1995) '"On the town": women in Augustan England', History Today, vol. 45, no. 12 (December), pp.15–25.

Reasons why women left the countryside for life in the larger towns, 1688–1820.
1 Country life no longer fulfilling/appealing to women, because:
 • household roles taken over by others
 • small social circle/difficult to socialize
 • few amusements.
2 Town life attractive, because:
 • more roles to play
 • more people of own status/easier to socialize
 • more occupations/amusements.

Figure 2.4 Card summarizing the contents of the Ellis article.

In my fuller notes, I made the decision to bring out the 'Country versus Town' theme by organizing them under two 'headings' clearly identified with a number. Under the headings are three bulleted points set a little way in from the margin, to show that each is a separate point and that each group of three is a sub-set of the main points 1 and 2. This layout does not directly reflect the structure of the original article. I have *re-organized* the main points into a pattern that makes sense to me – and one I'll probably be able to remember.

KEY POINTS

 ● Notes should *not* be a shorthand copy of the original text. They should be an attempt to lay bare the 'bones' of the text – especially those parts of it that are particularly *relevant* to your studies.

 ● Good notes reflect your own thinking. You need to reorganize the main ideas in a text and set them out in a way that makes sense to you.

But the notes in Figure 2.4 do not convey Ellis's full argument. Also, there is no record there of the 'evidence' she supplies to support her main points. For that you would need more detailed notes. Figure 2.5 shows some I made.

Ellis, J. (1995) '"On the town": women in Augustan England', History Today, vol. 45, no. 12 (December), pp.15–25.

Reasons why women left the countryside for life in the larger towns, 1688-1820.

1 **Context**

Female pop. of towns expanded ∴ inflow of women (see demographic research).

Why so keen on urban life? (see lit. refs. e.g. Etherege; 'satirists' views).

2 **Ellis's general argument**

Women esp. attracted to town, because:

(a) role expected in country restricted & difficult – ie 'dysfunctional'

viz., education for:
- household management   > done by profs.
- display: 'decorative', 'accomplished'; – but can't fulfil role (see 3 below) reflecting men's status

(b) town attractive (see 4 below)

3 **Country**

(a) small, scattered soc. circle   only 'correct' to mix with social equals (unlike men)

(b) travelling diffic. for women   – need carriage; poor roads & bad weather → accidents (e.g. 'bone-setter'; Coke marooned 4 months)

(c) few amusemts (unlike men)   – read, sew, write letters, walk = boring, unfulfilling

4 **Town**

(a) new role   – organizing balls, theatre, concerts

(b) easier to socialize, because
- more of 'correct' people in compact area
- more mobile, safely (i.e. pavements; lighting; transport easy)

(c) more amusemts   – (e.g. balls, etc.; pastry shops, circ.library, shops – see German visitor)

5 **Conclusion**

∴Women not attracted to towns ∵ wanted to 'escape from or subvert accepted gender roles', nor ∵ seeking freedom to indulge naughty desires (i.e. satirists' view).

Were attracted ∵ of mismatch between 'conventional perceptions of "correct" female behaviour' and 'the reality of rural life'.

Figure 2.5 Notes summarizing Ellis's argument, with illustration and supporting evidence.

Compare your notes with mine. What are the main differences? Do your notes include more detail than mine, or less? Does it matter? Are your notes clearer to you than mine? Are they laid out differently? What are the advantages of your layout and mine?

Can you understand all my abbreviations and symbols?

Although my notes are much shorter than Ellis's article, they probably capture all you need for most purposes. I have even quoted a few phrases in the 'Conclusion' that I think may come in useful. That's where I decided to summarize the satirists' views too, so that their ideas would not get mixed up in my attempt to explore Ellis's own line of argument. Otherwise, I have followed the structure of the original article and tried to make it clear to myself. In these, detailed, notes I have used a more elaborate hierarchy of main points: from numbers, to letters, to bullet points. And I have put illustrative material in brackets.

I have also abbreviated some words: 'esp.' stands for 'especially'; 'profs.' for 'professionals'; 'amusemts.' for 'amusements' (and I would have done much more of this if the notes had been just for me). I have used: = to mean 'equals' or 'is equivalent to'; ∵ to represent 'because'; ∴ for 'therefore'; > meaning 'increasingly'; and an arrow to mean 'leads to'. You can invent any kinds of abbreviation and symbol you like, so long as you are able to remember what they mean when you come back to them. It is important to approach note-making creatively and to lay out notes in a way that suits how you think.

Uncovering the 'skeleton' of an argument

Any text has just a few central ideas running through it. But you wouldn't be able to understand these ideas properly, or see why they matter, if a writer simply stated them baldly in the fewest possible words. So the writer puts flesh on the bones of the ideas, 'talking you through' and giving examples to show how they 'work' – as Ellis does.

Once you have understood the ideas, you don't need all the flesh any more. But you do need to hold the 'skeleton structure' of the argument in your mind. Making notes is a way to help yourself uncover this structure – the way the ideas are related – so that you end up with your own version of the author's argument set out in a way that makes sense to you.

Some people prefer to set their notes out as a diagram that shows the main ideas and their relationship to one another *visually*. The notes I presented in a written 'hierarchy' could be represented in a single *spray-diagram*. (Various terms are used – spider-diagram, mind map – but the principle is the same.) You write down the main topic in a few words and put a circle round it. Then you draw a line leading out from it for each major sub-topic and lines out from those for sub-sub topics. Figure 2.6 shows an example.

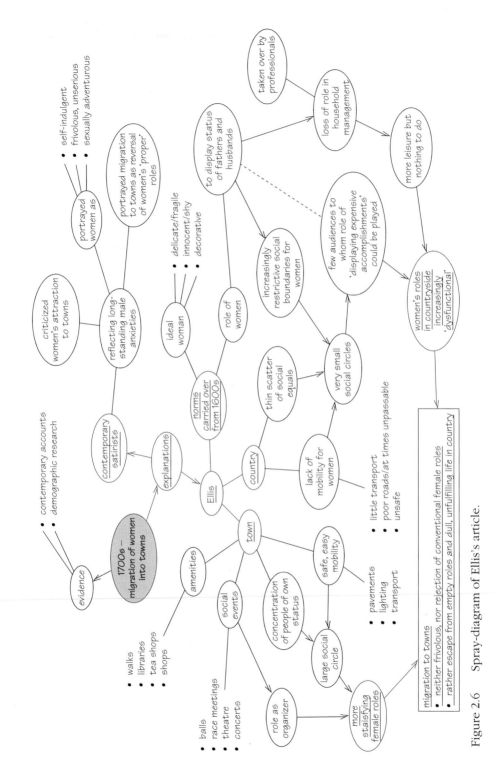

Figure 2.6   Spray-diagram of Ellis's article.

ACTIVITY

Take a little time to look at this diagram. Start with the shaded circle and follow the arrow to 'explanations'. Then you have a choice between tracing Ellis's own argument first (to town, or country, or norms of the time, and beyond), or the satirists' views. And so onwards.

Does this help you get a clearer idea of what the Ellis article is about, and of how her main points are related? Does it 'work' for you?

Perhaps the diagram looked a bit complicated and daunting at first sight. It's unlikely that you'd want to go into this kind of detail very often – though you might need to if you were writing an essay on an article you found difficult to understand, for example.

Anyway, the point of this diagram, and the 'hierarchical' notes earlier, is to demonstrate the *principle* of setting out ideas in a structured way – and to show that you can represent most of what is in a text in ways other than the sentences, and words, in which it is written. It is up to you to decide for yourself what kind of note-making pattern suits you best. You may need to experiment with a variety of methods to find out when the gain in understanding and remembering is worth the cost in time and effort.

What is the note-making 'skill'?

Note-making is not a single skill that you acquire once, for all times and occasions. It is a range of different activities: from jotting down a few points on an index card through to a detailed account of an argument – depending on your purposes. But the common characteristic is that you are *writing for yourself* rather than to an audience, so you don't have to worry about explaining yourself.

Making notes is more 'strategy' than skill. Being good at it involves reading texts in an *active* way – thinking, 'What is this about?', 'What questions is it addressing?', 'What am I making notes *for*?' and 'What do I want to remember?'

It requires you to be *flexible*, sometimes making detailed notes and at other times very sketchy ones. You should keep looking back at your notes asking yourself, 'Are they doing the job I want?', 'Could I be using my time more effectively?'. Then you need to adjust your approach accordingly.

5.3   What is the point of note-making?

What do you think you achieve by making notes? What was your answer to Question 1 in the Activity on page 51? Here are some of my ideas.

(a) Focusing your attention

Making notes is an excellent way of stopping your mind from wandering as you read. Jan (in Chapter 1) should have pitched into underlining and jotting things down and stopped worrying so much about what to write. (Notes can come out any old way if necessary. Special techniques take time to develop.)

(b) 'Making sense'

As you make notes you are forcing yourself to look for the sense of the words in the text – to make them *mean* something. In other words, you are making yourself formulate the ideas in the text in a way that makes sense to *you*. And to do this you need to use your own words, not just copy phrases and sentences from the original.

(c) A form of 'external' memory

The notes you make act, in effect, as a kind of extension to the memory capacity of your mind – enabling you to have ready access to a far wider range of ideas and knowledge.

(d) A symbol of progress

Notes provide you with evidence of the work you have done, so they can make an important contribution to keeping up your morale.

(e) Preparing an essay

Making notes which draw together what you have learned from your various study activities is an essential part of constructing an essay (see Chapter 5).

(f) Pulling the course together

As you study a course and range over different topics and different texts, your mind tends to become cluttered with disconnected bits and pieces. You can create order and make your ideas less confused and more useable by making notes that summarize a section of the course, even if they are just a set of headings.

Making notes on notes

Sometimes it is useful to bring together notes you have already made and make a new, condensed version (that is, notes summarizing earlier notes).

You are particularly likely to make notes of this kind as part of your revision for an exam (see Chapter 7). But it also helps you pull things together at other stages of a course – for example, when you have finished work on one topic and are about to move on to the next.

This kind of note-making is a great help to your learning because it makes your mind create order at a higher level of thinking.

Having stressed all the positive points about note-making, it is important to add that it is not a panacea. You can do too much of it and end up making your studies tedious. The pleasure of exploring new and interesting areas of reading is one of the main attractions of studying. If note-making undermines that pleasure it is counter-productive. It can make studying *more* satisfying, when it helps you sort out the meaning of what you are reading and when it creates a tangible 'product' from your labours. But it can also hold up your progress and dull the attractions of studying. The last thing you want to do is turn all your reading into a chore. The trick is to find the right balance. You have to weigh up carefully *when* to make notes, what *kind* of notes, and in what *detail*.

5.4   What will you do with your notes?

If making notes is a way of 'extending your memory', then clearly you need to work out some kind of system for storing them so that you can find them again easily. As a start, get hold of some folders and some boxes, and make shelf space for storing them. You will then need to develop a filing system. It is easy to end up with large piles of notes which are such a mess that you never can face trying to find what you want. When you are starting out it is hard to believe that you could produce enough notes to create filing problems. But you will waste a lot of the time you invest in making the notes if you don't also invest some towards working out a simple and effective filing system.

Notebook or loose-leaf?

Some people use a notebook for all their notes and draw a line across the page after each session. You could use a different one for each major topic in a course of study – colour-coded if you like. It can be very useful to have everything in one place and in sequence. As you progress through a course you build up a summary of its content.

On the other hand, a loose-leaf folder has the advantage of flexibility. Again, you could use a different coloured folder for each main topic. You can add pages, include assignments when you get them back, and change the order of your notes around if it helps. But will you be disciplined about keeping it up to date and well organized?

Having stored your notes, what uses are you likely to put them to? As you make them you might imagine that one day you will sit down and read carefully through them all. Perhaps you will. On the other hand there tends to be a shortage of suitable times for doing that. Your course will keep driving you forward into new areas. There is always another topic to study or another essay to write. Going back over old notes is seldom as urgent, or as attractive, as advancing to something new – unless you have a specific purpose in mind such as looking for material for an essay, or pulling together ideas for an exam. Often, it is the fate of notes to accumulate dust.

So there is little point in making mountains of them. You are much more likely to use your notes for reference purposes than to read them in full. Make them with this in mind – short, succinct and well-structured. It doesn't necessarily matter if you *never* go back to them. The process of writing them is valuable enough in itself.

6 CONCLUSION

Reading is one of the central activities in most courses of study. The purpose of it is to make you *learn*, but learning is not a passive process. You don't just let ideas wash over you. You have to *make sense* of ideas as you read, and then put them to *use*.

KEY POINTS

Reading for study purposes is a *set of practices* which you develop to enable you to *engage* with the text. These practices include:

- defining your task as you set out to read (setting a target)
- underlining or highlighting the text while reading, as appropriate
- making notes, as and when appropriate
- stopping to look ahead or back in the text when you lose your way
- monitoring your progress from time to time
- changing your approach as necessary.

If you are a beginning student, it is worth *experimenting* with a range of different ways of doing things, so that you have a wider base of experience from which to work towards developing a robust, flexible style of studying. To read effectively you have to be able to work out *what you are trying to achieve* and *how well you are progressing*. It is not easy to make those judgements. That is what becoming a skilled student is all about.

CHAPTER THREE

DIFFERENT WAYS OF STUDYING

1 INTRODUCTION

In Chapter 2 we looked at working from printed texts – at *reading* and *making notes*. Along with *writing essays,* these are the core study processes in the humanities. But of course there have always been other ways of studying and, in recent times, a variety of new ways have developed. We shall be looking at some of them in this chapter.

Below is a list of the kind of study activities your course might involve you in. Read through it to see which of these things you have done before and how often. Which do you think you are quite skilled at, and which would you need to practise?

A range of study activities (in no particular order):

- reading texts and making notes
- planning and writing an essay
- attending a lecture, a seminar discussion or tutorial
- studying from an audio-cassette
- listening to an educational programme on the radio
- studying illustrations of paintings and artefacts; 'reading' and sketching plans of a building
- listening to and analysing a piece of music
- absorbing the details of a case-study (for example, in law)
- reading and interpreting the meaning of a poem, play-text or novel
- watching an educational TV programme or video
- using a computer to 'talk' to other students or to analyse a text
- searching in a library for assignment material
- practising the grammar of a new language, or learning new vocabulary
- going to a gallery, theatre, museum or historical site.

These different ways of studying can all make a valuable contribution to your learning. They also allow you to switch between different kinds of activity, to keep your mind alert, or find a new way forward when you are stuck. Varying your activities makes studying more interesting.

As we saw in Chapter 1 (section 5), learning at higher levels is about much more than just remembering facts. It involves trying to *make sense* of new ideas, *thinking* them through, and learning how to *use* them. Reading is an excellent way of doing the first of these things. You can approach new ideas on your own terms and work at your own pace. Provided the text is written clearly enough, you can get a long way just by studying on your own. This is particularly true if your understanding of a subject is fairly well developed. Then you can pick up the latest book in a library, take it home and absorb new ideas by yourself. But reading may not be enough on its own when you are just starting out on a subject. If it were there would be no need for courses of study.

The advantage of engaging in different types of activity is that it enables you to tackle *all three* aspects of learning, and from a *variety of angles*. You learn a wide range of ideas, different ways of thinking and of arguing. In the process, you develop a well-rounded and secure understanding of your subject. As a modern-day student you need to be comfortable with many more ways of studying than just working from books. Here we will explore a number of the other activities on the list above, looking at what they offer and the skills and techniques they require of you. I have grouped them in three broad clusters:

- ways of studying that make learning a *collective* activity – learning with other people rather than by yourself;
- ways of studying by *listening* and *viewing*, as opposed to reading;
- ways of studying that emphasize the '*doing*' side of learning.

KEY POINTS
- Nowadays there are many ways of studying, each of which helps your learning in different ways.
- This variety makes studying more interesting and helps you learn in depth.
- To take full advantage of this variety, you need to understand the benefits of different study modes and to develop appropriate skills.

2 LEARNING WITH OTHER PEOPLE

Studying involves many hours of private work but it also has a social side. We don't *only* learn in the isolation of our own rooms, in quiet concentration. As human beings we survive by living in society with others. And because our societies are complicated and flexible, we depend on learning enormous amounts from each other. We do the bulk of this learning through talking to each other.

Learning by talking

Conversation gives you access to *other people's* thoughts and helps clarify *your own*. As you talk, ideas that defeated you when you studied alone suddenly take on new meanings. You find you can think in a more free-flowing way and achieve insights you would never have arrived at left to yourself. Sometimes, in the effort to make your point, you find yourself saying things you didn't even know you thought. In short, *talking* helps you to *think*.

So exchanging ideas with other people is an important way of helping you to learn – to *take in* new ideas and *think ideas through*. But it is not all plain sailing. When you are reading, the great advantage is that you can move at your own pace. The meaning of the words does not run ahead of your thoughts. But the drawback is that *you* have to shoulder the whole burden of pushing the meaning along. If you get tired or confused, the process of understanding grinds to a halt. With the spoken word it is the other way round. The advantage is that speech has its *own* forward momentum; you have the opportunity to be carried along a line of thinking by the momentum of discussion. Making meaning isn't just a private process going on inside your head, it 'happens' as a social event you take part in. The burden of making meaning and of driving it forward is shared with other people. The drawback is that when other people are doing the speaking, meaning can sweep along independently of you. You may not always be able to keep pace, so that you are left floundering at times.

Becoming accustomed to working with other people also plays an essential part in putting your new knowledge to *use* beyond your course. For example, in many jobs it is important to be a skilled communicator, whether with specialists in your area or people outside it. You may have to collaborate with others or work in a team, thinking and talking alongside people from different backgrounds. It is not necessarily enough to understand something yourself. You also need to be able to explain it clearly to other people and, in turn, listen to what they say so that you can connect their ideas with yours.

As a student working alongside others, then, you have to have your channels open to other people. Your aim is to develop what have been called the 'communicative virtues'. This means:

- *tolerating* other people's points of view
- *respecting* the differences between people
- being *willing to listen* to others, in the spirit that you might be wrong
- being *patient* and *self restrained*, so that others can have a turn to speak or act.

KEY POINTS

Learning about a subject is not simply a private, mental activity. It also has an important 'collective' side, because:

- talking with others helps you understand your subject better
- you need to be able to communicate well with others in order to make use of your knowledge and understanding.

2.1   How studying with others helps

Working with others helps you learn and helps you put your new knowledge to use. It can also help you in other ways too: to keep going when things are tough, and to meet study deadlines. It can give your confidence a boost, and, through getting to know other students, bring you extra support and friendship. We'll look first at the learning gains.

Sorting out your ideas

It helps to learn alongside other people because studying is often confusing, especially in the early days. People sometimes say they used to know what they thought, but now they have started studying they're not sure any more. Why is this?

The problem is that as you are developing new ways of thinking and new ideas, you are also trying to think in those new ways while the ideas are only partly formed. At the same time you carry on thinking in your customary ways, using the ideas you already have on the subject. So it's easy to get your wires crossed. But, sometimes, as you hear your tutor and other students talking, suddenly a key idea will come right into focus. All at once you 'see' what has been baffling you for days. You may even feel a bit stupid for having struggled with it so long. That is how learning goes. You spend ages preparing the ground – exploring the nature of a problem, looking at it this way and that – developing and shifting your thinking. Then, as your mind is still groping for comprehension, you reach a critical point. Your framework for thinking is sufficiently developed and meaning begins to flow.

Frameworks for thinking

Making sense of new ideas involves a kind of chicken-and-egg dilemma (which comes first?). One one hand, you cannot make much sense of new ideas in a discussion in your subject area until you understand its *frame of reference* – what *questions* the discussion is trying to address. On the other hand, you cannot really get hold of what the important questions and issues are until you have begun to engage with some of the the the new *ideas* themselves. Learning is not just a matter of furrowing the brow, concentrating the mind and working systematically through a series of ideas from A to Z. It is more a matter of circling around, picking up the gist of what is going on in the subject.

As you spend time exploring a subject area, you gradually come to understand its frames of reference – you become more aware of what its purposes are, what questions are the important ones, and how ideas and arguments are meant to 'work'. Once you understand who is speaking to whom, about what, and why it matters, ideas begin to fall into place and to *mean* much more to you. You have acquired an appropriate *framework for thinking* within the subject. When you don't have a grasp of this frame of reference, it is quite possible to follow a discussion about something – to understand it in terms of your existing ideas – yet not see what the *point* of it is.

Teachers and writers often just *assume* that we can see the point or significance of what is being said and done. They assume that we already have the appropriate 'framework for thinking' in place. They don't start off by explaining *why* they are discussing a particular topic, or addressing this question rather than that. They just pitch in. As experts, they tend to speak from 'inside' the framework of the subject – which is exactly where you eventually want to be.

You may have been a bit uncertain about Ellis's frame of reference when you were reading her article about why so many women left the countryside and went to live in towns during the eighteenth century (see Chapter 2). Once you see that the *debate* as to why women migrated arises out of a disagreement between what the 'satirists' claim and what Ellis wants to say – that this disagreement *is* the frame of reference for her argument – then the *ideas* Ellis explores (about women's roles in country and town) really start to make sense and to *mean* something. But you may not have grasped the frame of reference on first reading and, meanwhile, you had to do the best you could to grapple with the ideas. Indeed, until you do understand the frame of reference you might not realize that Ellis is putting forward an *argument* at all. You might think her account is simply a description of the past and wonder what the *point* of it is.

But historians never simply describe the past. They study what *evidence* we have of past times (not the past itself) – seeking it out from a whole range of sources, such as documents, paintings, buildings, literature – and then present you with their analysis and interpretation of what happened and why. Studying history is not just a matter of remembering 'facts'. The point is to understand the past – to *make sense* of it. Historians debate the past: they argue with each other over ways of understanding and explaining events and changes. As a student, you have to engage with their *arguments*, compare their *explanations* and 'weigh up' the *evidence* they offer to see whether you find their conclusions convincing. Once you understand that, you have an appropriate *framework for thinking* about any historical topic you study.

Whatever your subject is, it is a difficult job to grasp the appropriate frame of reference and keep it in place as you study. A *group of people* can help each other in this process of 'making sense'. We have seen that when you are thinking by yourself you have to do two things at the same time: you have to hold in mind the frame of reference (what issue you are trying to weigh up, for example the debate at the heart of Ellis's article), while you work through the content (the *new ideas* themselves, about women's roles). It is easy to lose track of one while you concentrate on the other. You can spend so long trying to make sense of a particular idea (conventional expectations of women, for example) that you 'forget' what the point of it is and how it contributes to the larger question the text is addressing. However, when you are discussing things with other people, you *share* the job of holding on to what the discussion is all about. That means you can have a quiet think about women's roles in the country for a while, then 'tune in' to the discussion again to remind yourself what it's about and where it's going.

In other words, *together* you can often keep enough of a frame of reference in place to push your understanding of a new topic further ahead than you could on your own. As you hear others trying to sort out their ideas, you glimpse new ways of understanding the subject. For instance, you might suddenly see that what Ellis is doing is constructing an argument, so that the whole article takes on a new meaning and significance. And in the process of making your own contribution to the discussion, you are re-working your ideas. So, when you are back studying on your own, you can come at things from a fresh angle.

When you hear your tutor and other students speaking in terms of these ideas you may find they take on a new force. You begin to see that there is more to understand here than you thought at first. And you begin to see new possibilities for *using* the ideas. But can you use them? When you try, you may find that they dissolve or slip from your grasp, or that they emerge in a garbled way. It is only when you have been using the ideas in debate for some time that you get onto reasonable working terms with them. Later, when you come to write an essay, you struggle again to achieve even further control of the ideas as you use them to answer a question. By the time you have done all that, these ideas will have acquired extra layers of meaning and have become integrated into a range of other, related, ideas you have in your mind. They become 'active' – ideas *you use* to help you make sense of things and think about them. They are not just 'out there' on the page, to be memorized. They have become part of the way you think and understand. They may even come to seem rather 'obvious'.

At that point you have achieved a major reorganization of your mental apparatus. This is *real* learning – far more important than memorizing facts or dates – and it is helped along by collective ways of studying.

Learning the language of the subject

We saw in Chapter 2 that learning the 'language' is part of becoming knowledgeable in your subject. You pick it up as you read texts and practise using it when you write essays. But it is a great help to have the chance to 'speak' it as well, and to hear it spoken by others. As you become a fluent speaker you become more confident in your subject, and you gradually come to *think* in its terms. In the process, it is very helpful to hear how people who are already expert in the subject speak: to 'pick up' the way the discourse works. Listening to a lecture can be a good way of doing this – although these days lectures have a rather bad name: they have too often been used as the main way of communicating information, and have acquired the reputation of being tedious and boring.

However, when a talk on a topic is well delivered you have the opportunity to hear the language of the subject 'as it is spoken', over an extended period and without interruption. This helps you see how ideas fit together in the subject, how arguments work, and how particular terms are actually used. And the 'expert speaker' is also able to demonstrate what these ideas and arguments amount to – what they *mean* in the context of the debates currently going on in the subject, and why those particular questions and issues are significant. In other words, the speaker does the job of keeping a frame of reference about the ideas firmly in place as you listen.

Because the speaker does this work for you, it is often easier to listen to a talk on a new topic than to learn about it from a book. When you read, *you* have to be able to 'project' meaning into the words on the page. That is, in order to understand what you read you *already* have to have some idea of what the words *might* mean. What can you do if the only clues are in the very text you are trying to read? On the other hand, when people speak *they* inject meaning into their words. This makes it easier for you to understand the gist of what is said.

This need to pick up the 'general gist' of what is going on in a subject area is why the spoken word is helpful when you are learning new ideas. Lectures, group discussions, TV and radio programmes and audio- and video-cassettes are all very valuable in giving you a chance to 'sit in', as it were, and 'overhear' ideas in action. Even if you sometimes get lost or confused, you can still make valuable progress in:

● hearing how the *language* of the subject is used

● hearing the kinds of *questions* that are asked

● getting a sense of the types of *argument* that are used.

All these things help when you return to your solitary reading, because they give you clues as to the kind of sense you should be making from the printed text.

Other benefits of studying with others

ACTIVITY

I said earlier that working with other people can help you in other ways too. Think back to Jan and Nathan in Chapter 1, when they went to an art gallery with some fellow students and chatted together afterwards at the bus stop. These people could have gone to the gallery alone, so what is the value of going in a group?

Why do you think such an outing might be valuable? Write down a few benefits you can think of.

Here are the benefits I thought of.

● You see things you wouldn't have noticed otherwise. Your whole level of consciousness and sensitivity is raised by the discussion going on between you: new ideas and insights are sparked off.

● You become more aware of your own ideas and tastes as you hear other people's, and realize that their reactions are different.

● Your curiosity and your motivation to look for things is fuelled by the energy and enthusiasm the group generates.

● It's interesting and fun to be able to discuss your ideas with people who share your enthusiasms.

● You get to know other students. You realize that they find some aspects of studying a struggle too, and this makes you feel better about your own difficulties.

● It's easier to stay in touch with people once you have been together as a group and got to know them. Later, you can talk things over or ask for help when you are stuck.

We have already talked about the first two advantages, which are to do with how working with other people can help you learn. We will look at the other benefits in more detail.

Keeping yourself going

As well as helping you to learn, working alongside others can help keep you going. As with Jan and Nathan's outing, discussing things with other people who share your enthusiasms boosts your own interest. It might even *create* the interest that is so essential to your progress. More formal meetings, such as regular tutorials, can give you an extra incentive to keep trying to reach your study targets. And if you do fall behind with your work, they may help you catch up. Talking to others can help you readjust your sights, and work out how to cut corners when you need to.

Once you have friends among your student group you can contact them in difficult times. You can discuss strategies for tackling the work ahead and perhaps even collaborate sometimes. Studying does not have to be competitive. You may be able to share out tasks on a project, or compare outline plans for an essay, or read through each other's work and make helpful comments. Or you might collaborate in a purely practical way, such as setting up a child-minding exchange. Networks of support can make the everyday challenges of study more manageable. When you run into a crisis, as most people do from time to time (pressure at work, moving house, domestic complications, and so on), these networks may make the difference between struggling on and dropping out altogether.

Boosting your confidence

As soon as you start talking things over with other students, you realize that they find many aspects of studying just as difficult as you do – and it makes you feel better to know that you are not alone. Of all the benefits students claim for contact with others, this is the most common. When you are working away on your own it is very easy to lose confidence in your abilities. You doubt your intelligence, your self-discipline, your memory, reading skills, powers of concentration, and your motivation. But when you contact other students (whether by meeting in a group, talking on the phone or sending messages by computer) you discover that everyone has similar doubts. This helps put your own worries into perspective. Making contact with others is the surest way of giving your confidence a boost.

Meeting people

Finally, meeting interesting people is an end in itself. Studying often brings together people from a wide range of backgrounds who share a common interest. Sometimes the friendships you make turn out to be the most rewarding part of taking up study.

KEY POINTS

Working alongside others can bring many benefits.

- Talking with others can help you make sense of ideas you are struggling to learn.
- It also helps you learn to 'speak the language' of the subject.
- Studying in a group keeps up your interest in a subject and helps you keep pace with the course.
- When you get to know other students you can help each other out in practical ways.
- Sharing study worries with others helps boost your confidence.
- Studying is a way of meeting interesting people.

2.2   Group tutorials

Some people find the idea of the cut and thrust of group discussion very appealing – getting the chance to air your views and hear other people's – really getting to the bottom of things. Others think of it as a complete waste of time. What could be more dreary than being trapped in a room with a bunch of posers and bores, all banging on about their pet themes? In fact, most tutorial sessions fall somewhere in between these extremes.

Tutorial, seminar and *workshop* all refer to ways of studying in groups. Since different terms are used in different places, I will simply use the term 'tutorial' to mean any kind of session of, say, one to two hours in which a tutor works with a group of between five and twenty-five students. They are not only discussion groups. A tutor may run a tutorial as a 'trouble-shooting' session, asking students about their study difficulties and then either working through some problems with the whole class, or dividing the students into groups who share similar difficulties and circulating between the groups helping them find solutions. Or, the tutor might choose some tricky sections of a study text to go over with the class, or circulate a document, poem or illustration for the group to analyse and discuss.

Whatever goes on, the point is that during tutorials you have access to a scarce resource – the time of an expert – in a setting where you can participate actively along with other students. There is the opportunity for direct engagement between the tutor's expertise and the learning you are currently concerned with. But that can only happen if you are *actively* involved. You have to be ready to ask questions, and willing to participate in tackling problems and sharing your ideas with the group. You also have to be prepared to share tutorial time with other students, playing a constructive part in helping to solve *their* problems. Often you learn as much from listening carefully to your tutor dealing with another student's difficulties as from having your own sorted out. And sometimes you learn even more by trying to help others. So a tutorial should be a genuinely *collective* process in which the whole group pools its resources and works together to help everyone become more familiar with the ideas and skills developed in the course.

When tutorials work well, a group of students can, together, advance their level of thinking. We saw how during a discussion individual students might achieve thoughts they could never have arrived at on their own, because the group shares the responsibility for keeping the 'frame of reference' in place as everyone tries to grasp new ideas. When the same group of people meets regularly, so the *group's* handling of the subject matter 'evolves'.

Collective progress

A study group which meets over a period of time gradually develops a *shared understanding* of the subject matter. The discussion doesn't go back to first principles each time. It builds on the achievements of previous meetings. This means that as your own thoughts on the subject matter are becoming gradually more developed, through working on the course, so the 'shared understanding' within the group also becomes more sophisticated – and the collective frames of reference that the group constructs during discussions become more powerful. The result is that you are able to take part in discussions which come increasingly close to the level of the ideas you are reading in texts.

The combination of *private reading* and *regular discussions* is an immensely powerful one. The level of debate within the group benefits enormously from the efforts students have made individually to grapple with ideas in texts; and, at the same time, the advances in collective understanding within the group give a huge boost to private reading – by supplying far richer meanings to 'project' into the words on the page.

But study groups do not always work in this 'ideal' way. Discussion is a flexible process, which can accommodate a wide range of needs and interests, but it is also unstable. It can veer from stimulating and illuminating to dreary and confusing and back again. In this sense it is a 'high risk' mode of study. At best discussion offers a great deal, but at worst it can seem a dreadful waste of time. It is sometimes hard going, as you grope your way through tangled thickets of confusion, but then it is suddenly exhilarating when you glimpse a new way of thinking. You need to understand the unpredictability of group learning if you are to make proper use of it, so that you don't expect too much or too little.

One source of stimulation, but also of tension, is that discussions define themselves as they go along. When you start out on a chosen topic the options are boundless. But as you explore one pathway you close off the possibilities of others. Every minute you spend on one issue is time denied to others. So there is always uncertainty about how long the group should spend following any one line of discussion and what would be the best direction to take next. Indeed, members of the group will have different views about that. And they will be unsure about what right each group member has to influence the direction of the discussion. So the flexibility which is a core strength of discussion is also a problem. It is never absolutely clear what is and what is not a useful contribution to the discussion, or where the debate as a whole is supposed to be heading. The 'intellectual agenda' is always uncertain.

The 'social agenda' is even more tricky. When several people are engaged in a single conversation there is immediately the problem that *somebody* has to speak (or the conversation will stop), but only *one* person can speak at a time. How is the group to determine *who* should speak and *when*? Taking turns is too 'mechanical'. It would work against the whole idea of following a train of thought, or arguing out the differences between two points of view. But anything else means that the members of the group must make judgements about the value and the timeliness of their contributions. Some people are much more optimistic about this than others. Some tend to doubt the value of *anything* they might say, and prefer to take the 'safe' option of staying silent. Others are quite happy to throw in their thoughts without worrying about how relevant they are. So a group can establish a very uneven pattern of contributions. This is unsatisfactory for the group as a whole, because its members do not benefit from hearing everyone's views. But it is particularly bad for those who are not getting a chance to try out their ideas.

To establish and maintain a *social* and an *intellectual* agenda for a discussion someone needs to 'manage' the process. Usually, the tutor takes overall responsibility for this. But a tutor cannot manage a discussion without help. For example, it is in no-one's interests when one or two students are allowed to dominate the whole discussion, but it is very difficult for the tutor to prevent this without taking over and dominating the discussion. A tutor can't *make* the other students talk. A direct question to someone who is rather shy, for instance, shines the spotlight too suddenly and too brightly and creates embarrassment rather than encouragement. In the end tutors have to rely on students coming forward to make contributions. They also value help in drawing out the less confident students and keeping a check on the more enthusiastic ones. In other words, a good group discussion relies on *active participation* and a sense of *shared responsibility*.

'Philosophizing'

The opportunity for group discussion is particularly important for students of philosophy because 'philosophizing' is something you *do* in dialogue with others. The best way of learning how to conduct a philosophical argument is to practise doing it. Usually, philosophical discussions involve close attention to particular ideas that the group needs to get clear. In the process, what people say is scrutinized in detail: statements are taken apart, questions are raised, objections and counter-arguments are put forward. So you have to be very careful about what you say and how you justify it – indeed, that is a main *point* of learning to philosophize.

At first, this kind of discussion can be daunting. Some people in the group may seem to see it as a 'game', in which the 'winner' is the person who scores the most 'points' in argument. If the topic is something you feel deeply about (an ethical issue such as abortion, for example), and your ideas are getting the treatment, you may feel that it is also *you*, as a person, who is being probed, criticized and found wanting. Try not to; and don't be reduced to silence by others in the group who may be more aggressive or appear very confident. Remember that you are not in a competition with anyone: the purpose of the discussion is to help you learn how to argue a case well or, if you are sincere, to try to get at the truth of something. Unless you keep contributing you will not learn.

Any study group discussion is a challenging social process. Like Nathan in Chapter 1, most of us are eager to speak effectively but at the same time we are concerned not to appear foolish. So we feel ambivalent, particularly in the first meeting or two. It is easy to form the impression that the other students are cleverer, more articulate and more confident than you are. But most of them are thinking exactly the same about you! In the early days they are much more concerned about what you think of *them* than about the quality of what *you* say. Remember too that you have as much right as anyone else to make demands on your study group's time. Tutorials are part of the study package you are paying for. They are not set up as an ordeal to 'test' you: they have been arranged precisely to help you learn. So don't sit on the fringes of the group – push your chair right in, so that you can see everyone and hear what they are saying. Get your money's worth.

In any discussion you are likely to be confused at times – unsure what the discussion is about or what someone has just said. This may make you feel rather inadequate. Don't let it. You may be quite right. The whole group *may* have lost its bearings or the person who just spoke may not have made much sense. These things often happen. Simply saying that you don't understand is a helpful contribution because other people will probably be worrying about the same thing.

Ask the simple question, give the 'obvious' answer

You don't need to wait until you have something 'really important' to say before speaking in a tutorial. If you raise the stakes that high you will only create problems for yourself. For a start, it will be a long time before you attempt to speak. As you wait, poised for the right moment, the discussion will move on to other topics, so that when you finally say something it is no longer clear what you are referring to. And you will also be so wound up by the significance of the occasion that you may say too much or speak too quickly, and other people will find it hard to follow you. They will then have difficulty responding to what you have said and working it in to the flow of the discussion.

Rather than entering into this cycle of inhibition, it is much better to set your sights lower. Just ask the simple question, give the obvious answer and suggest the straightforward example. What seems obvious to you may not be to other people and, in any case, it may be just what the group needs to help identify a problem and sort it out. You can make a very useful contribution simply by saying 'What do you mean by that?', 'Can you give us an example?' or 'Will you please explain that again?'.

Being a quiet student

Don't worry if you don't speak a lot. There isn't much time, and some people are just more talkative and thrusting than others. You can get a lot from a debate by listening closely and 'participating' silently, agreeing or disagreeing in your mind. And it certainly isn't true that people who participate the most always know the most. So don't feel bad if you find yourself cast in a fairly minor role – though you should try to join in *some* of the time.

In a tutorial it pays to be frank about what you need help with. It is tempting to ask 'safe' questions, about things you almost understand, so that you do not appear 'weak' to other students and your tutor. But a tutor needs to know what the *real* problems are, otherwise he can't help with your deeper confusions. If you are open about your difficulties he can focus on identifying and sorting them out much more effectively. In any case, the chances are that if you are confused about something other students will be too. When you don't understand an explanation, say so. If you let the tutor think you have understood when you haven't, then he will pitch later explanations at too high a level. And don't worry about taking up the tutor's time. It is his job to help you, and it is up to you and the other students to make sure the tutorial covers what you need.

You will benefit more from your limited tutorial time if you *prepare* for it in advance. Try to be reasonably up to date with the course work – even if you only skim through the relevant parts beforehand – and spend a little time thinking about what you need help with. Remember to take the relevant study materials with you. But don't be put off attending a tutorial if you have fallen behind with your work. As we have seen, it can help you catch up. Finally, if for any reason you are unable to arrive on time for the meeting, or have to leave early, don't feel you have to miss the whole session. Tutors understand that this is unavoidable sometimes. Just let them know beforehand if you can, and arrive and leave without fuss when you have to.

KEY POINTS

For tutorials:

- try to do some of the relevant reading beforehand (and take the course texts with you)
- don't worry about what other people might think of what you say
- don't be afraid to ask a simple question or give the 'obvious' answer
- share in the responsibility for keeping the group going
- remember that it's your study session, so aim to get the most from it.

2.3   Self-help groups

So far I have talked as though a discussion group is necessarily led by a tutor. But there is no reason why you shouldn't arrange your own study groups with other students. A self-help group can be any size from two upwards. You can meet at a place and time of your choice and set an agenda to meet your own needs. You may find a regular self-help group just as useful as tutorials, but it will take a little organizing.

You will need to set firm agendas for your meetings and probably to appoint a chairperson. No-one likes to appear too self-important, particularly when you don't know each other well. So it is sometimes difficult to find anyone who is prepared to take the responsibility for making decisions about when and where to meet and what to discuss. But if you are going to have a successful group, *someone* has to stick their neck out and accept the role of 'leading' the group (perhaps on a rotating basis?). Otherwise good intentions get nowhere, discussion turns into chat, and people stop attending.

KEY POINTS

- Self-help group meetings are an excellent idea.
- They need organizing, so work out early on how you will share out the role of 'leader'.
- Set an agenda for each each meeting and try to stick to it.

2.4   Day schools and residential schools

If you are studying part-time, as an alternative to regular tutorials you may be offered less frequent but longer study sessions. The occasional day school does not give you the same opportunities for developing friendships and team spirit as tutorials, but otherwise the benefits are similar and you spend less time and money travelling to and fro. However, a residential school is more demanding of your time and money, whether it lasts for a weekend or a week, so it is worth thinking a bit about its purposes.

The greatest benefit of attending a residential school is that it allows you to become completely immersed in your subject for a while. When you have been studying on your own, at the same time as coping with a busy life, to work 'full time' on your subject for a even few days can give an enormous boost to your progress and your morale. An Open University residential school, for example, also offers students what may be their only chance to use expensive equipment (such as a language laboratory or advanced computing facilities), and to gain access to primary source material and data-banks. In some subjects, it offers the opportunity to study with a tutor who is a specialist – 'philosophizing', for example, in discussion with an expert. When numbers of people are gathered together, and there is enough time, large-scale activities become possible. For instance, students of music may hear specially arranged recitals; access to galleries and specialist libraries can be arranged for groups studying art; and literature students can work together to stage a play. A site such as a university campus allows regular access to a good academic library, which some students may not normally be able to get to easily. It is very valuable, too, to mix with a variety of tutors who can offer a wide range of knowledge and insight.

These are some of the 'formal' benefits of residential schools. But there are other equally important informal ones. If you study mainly on your own at home, it can be hard to establish a sense of being a 'real' student. Your studies may seem like a slightly unusual hobby tacked on to your 'normal' life. A few days in a residential school helps you to acknowledge your studies for what they are, a very important part of your life. You recognize that you are a member of a large body of people who share a serious interest in studying. You 'live' alongside them and you work together intensively. As a result, many students find that a residential school is the high point of their course, and that it transforms both their approach to their studies and their understanding of the subject.

2.5   Learning with others 'at a distance'

We have been looking at forms of face-to-face contact with other students and tutors, but nowadays there are many other ways of keeping in touch.

One-to-one telephone tutorials

The obvious use for the telephone is to contact another student or your tutor for some advice. But it can also be used more formally, as an alternative kind of tutorial for those who cannot attend group meetings. Clearly it is not a full substitute because the 'collective' dimension is absent. And the telephone is a restricted medium of communication in that you cannot see each other's facial expressions or gestures. It is not possible to sketch a diagram, for instance: your tutor cannot see where you might have gone wrong, just as she cannot show you how to put things right. You need to put some time into planning this kind of session in advance. A series of one-to-one telephone tutorials is very time-consuming for tutors, so each call must be businesslike. You need to draw up a list of points you want help with and make sure you have any course material to hand that you will need to refer to. You and your tutor can negotiate this agenda beforehand, by mail if necessary.

Group telephone tutorials

These days telephoning does not have to be one-to-one. You can be linked to other students and your tutor by a 'conference call'. At one time it was hoped this technology would lead to the telephone equivalent of regular study group 'meetings'. However, the system is frustratingly prone to faults so that it can take some time to get everyone 'linked up', and some of the contacts may be lost periodically. Also, although in theory group telephone tutorials enable you to benefit from collective work, it is actually very difficult to achieve the constructive, flowing kind of discussion you can experience face-to-face. When there are a number of participants each has to get into the habit of announcing his or her name before speaking, and this alone makes for stilted dialogue. Turn-taking is also much more difficult because you cannot see who might be preparing to say something as the current speaker finishes. Since you cannot point or write, it can be hard just to follow what other people are saying. You need to be very clear about what point you are raising; for example directing listeners to the precise page and paragraph in the appropriate text. Group telephone tutorials are expensive and require skill and discipline. But they are certainly better than no contact at all.

Electronic mail and computer conferencing[*]

These are in many ways the best alternatives to face-to-face contact nowadays. If your computer is connected to a computer network, you can send electronic messages (e-mail) to other computers linked to the network. This means you can send a message to other students or your tutor at any

---

[*] I am grateful to Simon Rae of The Open University's Academic Computing Service for his help with this section and with section 4.2.

time of day or night. For example, if you were very puzzled about something you could send off a request for help straight away. You could send it to just one person or to the whole group. If one of them happened to be 'logged on' to the network at the time, you might receive a reply within minutes. Or it may be a few hours, or a day or so, before they log on, read your message and reply to it. Either way, you can be confident that your message will reach them. If for any reason it does not get through, your computer will usually let you know.

You may then decide that you need expert advice, but do not want to disturb your tutor by phoning at midnight on a Sunday. So you can send her an e-mail, and it will join the queue in her 'in-tray'. She will deal with it when she next 'logs on' to look at students' messages. You can 'attach' documents or diagrams to your e-mails. In some courses students send their essays by e-mail and get comments back that way too. It is a particularly important means of communication for students studying through distance education because it is both rapid and reliable.

A *computer conference* is an extension of the e-mail idea. But instead of messages being sent from one person to one or several others, *all* messages are sent to *everyone* who is a conference member. It works rather like a shared notice-board. People stick up messages, and whoever reads a message and wants to reply posts their reply on the 'notice-board' next to the original message. Several people may reply to the same message, and then reply to a reply. In this way, a number of 'conversations' spring to life which everyone in the conference can read and join in if they want to.

A conference can be made up of your student group and tutor. So if you get stuck as you are working, instead of wondering who to ask you can simply post a question on the conference 'notice-board' for everyone in the group to see. One or two students may offer replies which solve the problem. Or they might reply – 'Yes, that's giving me trouble too' – and add extra questions of their own. When your tutor reads your question and the replies that have been posted, he may decide that the question has been answered well enough. Or he may offer additional advice. Computer conferencing is excellent from the tutor's point of view because he only has to say things once for the whole group, rather than answering a number of separate e-mail messages or telephone calls.

So the computer conference works like a continuing conversation, spread out over days, with people dropping in to 'listen' at any time and 'speaking' when they choose. A group can have several conferences on different topics running at the same time. There might be a conference set aside for discussing assignments, where students talk about plans for the next essay or how the last one went. The tutor can 'drop in' to find out what students are concerned about and offer advice. Often there is a conference just for 'chat', where people can talk about whatever they like and get to know each other.

Computer conferencing, then, offers similar opportunities for working collectively and for friendly support as face-to-face tutorials. But *time* is the big limitation. When everyone is able to contribute as much as they like – with no-one 'managing' the process – the amount of reading matter to get through can soon become overwhelming. In fact, some conferences do appoint a 'manager' who edits the contributions. But in any case, agreed rules and some self-discipline are needed to make computer conferencing work well.

'Netiquette'

The good manners of e-mail and conferencing on the network are known as 'netiquette'. A computer conference is a kind of 'social space' – communally shared, but not located in a particular place and time. Unlike most social spaces it is not influenced by people's physical attributes (their appearance, manner, gestures, or accent). Most people enjoy the freedom this 'anonymity' offers. But a few enjoy it too much – saying things and using language they wouldn't normally when they are in direct contact with others.

People do of course make judgements about each other, according to their writing style, spelling, typical concerns and such like. And they have developed ways of signalling their meaning, when there might be some doubt about it. For example, this symbol :-) is called a 'smiley' and signals a joke or an amused reaction to something (tilt your head to the left as you look at it).

Like any social space, this electronic one has to develop its own 'culture' so that people can understand each other and get along together. That involves some rules, for instance about how to address people in the conference and what kind of language is acceptable.

Conferencing and e-mail can be used alongside each other. E-mail offers *private* communication, whereas a conference is *public*. You might, for example, put a question to your tutor privately. But then, if it emerges that your problem is widely shared, your tutor may ask you to copy the question into the conference so that everyone can see her reply. She might even send an e-mail asking permission to 'save' your question onto disk to feed into next year's conference. Once the computer connections exist there are countless ways of using them.

KEY POINTS

If you cannot attend face-to-face tutorials regularly there are various other ways of benefiting from 'collective learning':

- you may be able to attend the occasional day school or residential school
- or you can share in contact 'at-a-distance', through various forms of modern communications technology.

3 LEARNING BY LISTENING AND VIEWING

When you can study print in your own time and at your own pace, why should anyone want to listen to people talking, or watch films?

Why listening and viewing are important

One trouble with studying through print alone is that what you see on the page is 'finished'; neat, precise and polished. This gives a false impression of the way academics think. Their thinking, like everyone else's, is often fuzzy and goes forward in unpredictable leaps. The seamless arguments and elegant phrases you see on the page give you no idea about all the false starts and crossings out that were involved in the writing. So you don't get much feel for the *thinking process* that lies behind the words and symbols you read.

This is why it is helpful to be 'talked through' the arguments in a text. Watching or hearing someone analyse a painting or take a philosophical argument apart makes the underlying thought processes much clearer. You hear how the analysis is 'said', and become aware of the unwritten logic behind a move from one point in the argument to another. It even helps just to hear how words and terms are pronounced. In these ways, a teacher can give living meaning to ideas which may at first seem remote. You begin to see connections between the formal, printed words and active, creative processes of thought. The academic language of the text starts to become a working language that you can use to think and speak with.

3.1 Lectures and talks

For a long time lectures were the main mode of direct teaching in higher education. The 'traditional image' of studying at university is of rows of students frantically getting down notes as the be-gowned figure at the front strides back and forth for an hour delivering his thoughts at a great pace – or, while mumbling to the blackboard, covers it with obscure words and hieroglyphics. Afterwards, students were expected to make what they could of their jottings. So the lecture has acquired the reputation of being a mindless, tedious and inefficient way of learning. Critics have argued that a lecture simply 'presents' knowledge to 'passive' listeners, who anyway cannot concentrate for more than twenty minutes and can scarcely remember anything afterwards. What is more, the lecture is said to pander to students' immature yearning for security: their desire to be *told* things by an authority. It does not encourage people to *think for themselves* about what they are studying. In the current jargon, it is not 'empowering'. Lectures, they conclude, should simply be abandoned.

But it is wrong to think of the lecture mainly as a way of 'transmitting' knowledge. It is *not* a good way of delivering a lot of detailed information.

Texts of all kinds are much more accessible and reliable as sources of information than hastily scribbled notes taken from a lecture: the information is set down correctly, you can study it when you are ready to take it in, you can spend time working things out, and you can return to it when you need to. Lectures are a way of helping you to *understand* the ideas you study in texts. And a lecturer can demonstrate various skills 'in action', such as how to analyse an historical document, a poem or piece of music.

So lectures are a good way of helping you to *think*. Far from depositing a pile of information in your head, the effect of a particularly powerful lecture might be to shake up all your thinking on a subject. You may end up with a lot of new questions in your mind. And these questions may be exactly what you need to help you make more sense of things when you return to your texts. This kind of lecture helps you to 'get inside' the subject you are studying. Listening to it, you are far from a 'passive' recipient of recycled 'knowledge'.

Lectures, talks and learning

The lecture comes into its own in helping you to understand how the ideas in a subject work. The speaker can 'project' meaning into the academic language for you. The sense of the words is expressed through tone-of-voice, facial expression and gestures and, most of all, the context in which they are used. Devices such as diagrams, slides, sound, and notes on a board can also be brought into play. By orchestrating all these different means of communication, the ideas you are grappling with in the course can be presented to you much more *explicitly* and *forcefully* than in a book. In turn, you have to participate by making the effort to follow the argument. While this isn't easy, the lecturer can at least 'talk you through' it from beginning to end, without interruption. Even if you cannot understand it all, and even if you miss some of what is said (because your attention wanders from time to time), you can still pick up a sense of how the whole argument is supposed to work.

All this applies to shorter, more informal talks by teachers too – for example, the contribution a tutor might make at the end of a tutorial discussion. He may take some of the ideas that have been floated and show how they can be made to work in terms of the questions and arguments that are central to the subject matter. In other words, the teacher can take the *ideas produced within the the classroom discussion* and show how they work *within the more formal discourse* of the subject.

This makes lectures and talks an excellent counterpart to reading and discussion. *All* these approaches are helpful when you are studying unfamiliar material.

KEY POINTS

Nowadays in the arts and humanities, the strength of the lecture is not as a source of information but as an opportunity to:

- be talked through the thought processes that lie behind the ideas and arguments in books
- be shown how arguments and explanations 'work'
- be shown how to apply skills and techniques of critical analysis
- hear how the language of the subject is used.

Getting the most out of a lecture

Listening to a lecture sets you three challenging tasks to do at the same time. You have to:

- *attend* to and *make sense* of a line of argument
- *think* about what is said
- *make notes* of some kind.

Of course you can't actually do more than *one* of those tasks at once. The best you can do is switch quickly from one to another. But in a way, trying to cope with this mental juggling act is helpful. By putting you under pressure, lectures make you take leaps and short cuts. You are forced into making what sense you can of the subject quickly and, as a result, you learn to 'think on your feet'.

But how can you juggle these three tasks? Clearly, you can't afford to stop *attending* to the lecture for very long or you will lose the drift of the whole argument. However, you are bound to miss *some* of what is said, because listening 'intelligently' will mean you stop and think (as you make connections with ideas already in your mind). You have to find a workable trade-off between listening and thinking. This is where selective note-making helps. Deciding what to write down focuses your attention on the subject of the lecture while also making you think. But the notes have to be brief, or the note-making process itself becomes a distraction. You have to strike a balance between the quality of your notes and the speed at which you can write.

Styles of note-making

There is no 'best' way of making notes during a lecture. Some people scribble away all the time and produce several pages while others take down only a few key points set out diagrammatically. Both approaches can be very effective. It depends on *why* you are attending the lecture, the *kind* of lecture it is, and the way *you* work and learn best.

If lectures are your main source of information then you probably have to write down a lot to make sure of getting what you need. But if they are backed up by hand-outs and textbooks, you may need to make very few notes. If the lecture is delivered in a monotonous way, and is packed with detailed information, you may find you have to write a lot just to keep yourself alert. On the other hand, when the lecturer is lively and your imagination is sparked off by striking examples, you may learn most by concentrating on listening and just noting down occasional points and topic headings. In the end, though, the main factor is *you*.

What kind of listener are you?

Do you go off into daydreams in lectures? Or do you feel anxious about whether you are understanding enough? Do you feel confident that a few phrases will be enough to remind you of the points you need to hold in mind, or do you find it too difficult to decide which points are important as the lecture is in full flow? Do you worry that if you stop writing you will miss something crucial?

ACTIVITY

Think about your experience of any lectures in the past. Have you been able to make sense of your notes afterwards? Have you actually got round to reading them, or do they just pile up in your folder?

What kind of note-making do you think suits *your* style of listening?

If writing a lot helps to reduce your anxiety and keeps you actively 'working', rather than letting things wash over you, then that is the right approach for you. But be aware that if you try to write *everything* down you will learn very little during the lecture itself, and there will be a lot of work to do afterwards. Will you actually find time to make use of very full notes? On the other hand, if you decide you only need brief notes, how will you know what to select and write down?

Selective note-making

The beginning and the end of a lecture are particularly important times for note-making. At the start you need to make notes of the topic and the purpose of the lecture. And at the end you will want to summarize the main points that have emerged. So for the first and last ten minutes you might expect to make quite full notes, while allowing yourself to be more relaxed in between. During the lecture you may need to note only a few words and phrases, or draw a diagram, to remind yourself of the key points. But do include any examples or illustrations the lecturer provides because they will remind you of the arguments and explanations she has given. And note down the names of major writers who are mentioned and the dates of their work. This will help you to build up a sense of who the main figures are in your field and to make connections between the lecture and what you read in course texts. Occasionally there may be a point you want to get down in detail, so that you can make proper sense of it afterwards. Also note down questions or comments as they occur to you. After the lecture, these will help you reconstruct what was going through your mind at the time.

Styles of note-making

Selecting what to write down and positioning it on the page imposes a structure on what you hear in a lecture. This structure helps you to *understand* and *remember*. So don't be stingy with your paper. Spread your notes out and use lines, arrows, brackets and boxes to emphasize divisions between points and links between ideas. You might also make a separate space for your own remarks and queries, for example putting them over to the right-hand side of the paper [or enclosing them in square brackets]. Some people find it helpful to draw their notes as a spray-diagram, with the topic of the lecture in the centre circle and lines branching out for each sub-topic as it arises. (See Chapter 2, section 5.2, for examples of different ways of note-making. There you will see that a very simple but important technique is to develop your own shorthand.) But don't expect your lecture notes to have as much structure and clarity as the notes you make when you read. In lectures, the emphasis is on speed.

Improving your record of the lecture

When you have invested an hour or more in attending a lecture, it is usually worth spending a bit more time afterwards tidying up your notes and checking that you understand them. It helps if you can compare your notes with another student's. What you get out of lectures is determined not only by what you do *during* them, but also by the work you put in *beforehand* and *afterwards*.

KEY POINTS

- When you attend a lecture, be clear in your mind as to *why* you are there and *what* you want to take from it.

- Try to do some relevant reading before the lecture (however brief), so that your mind is ready to make sense of the topic.

- Develop flexible techniques of listening, thinking and note-making which you can adapt to the kind of lecture it is.

- Take account of your own listening habits, and work out a note-making strategy that helps you to concentrate.

- Don't feel you have to write down 'everything'. Listening is the main job. Pick out the main themes and key points of the lecture.

- After the lecture, check over your notes and tidy them up.

3.2 Broadcasts and cassettes

Many courses now make use of TV and radio programmes, video and audio-cassettes. Indeed, if your subject is communications, the media or film, then they themselves are the *objects* of your study. Equally, if you study modern history you might use archive film (of the Second World War, for example) as a primary source. Here, however, we will look at uses of the audio-visual media as secondary sources in arts and humanities subjects.

Clearly, learning from audio-visual media is a very different experience from reading a book or listening to a lecture. So what skills do you need? If you are asked to watch a programme on Classical Greek architecture, or religious rites, or the history of the discovery of penicillin, is it enough just to watch and listen and absorb?

● Is there a difference between studying, and casual viewing or listening?
● What are you supposed to be able to *do* with what you learn from these programmes?

TV and video

If you have ever seen a TV programme on architecture you will know how well the camera can explore the façade of a building, 'zooming in' on the smallest decorative features and showing you them in detail. The camera can also give you the 'experience' of being inside the building, as it moves around and through the rooms, revealing the way the different spaces 'work' and how they relate to one another. These spaces and relationships are very hard to imagine just from looking at plans and photographs of a building. It is this sense of being able to explore the world directly – the *dynamic*, multi-layered quality of TV and video – that can make a special contribution to your learning.

Learning from 'being there'

By combining high-quality pictures and sound, TV and video give you a sense of actually 'being there' and seeing things directly. The 'real world' seems to be very powerfully present. You don't have to struggle to hold your focus on the subject matter (as you often do when reading a book). All your most basic processes of perceiving and experiencing the world are brought into play more or less effortlessly. Meanwhile, the voice-over, discussing and explaining what you see, has a ring of 'authenticity'. (Of course it's true, you can actually see it.) This is a very powerful combination. It seems you scarcely have to think at all. Is this learning, or is it just seeing and absorbing? Is there a difference?

It *is* learning in that you have the chance to see aspects of your subject in a new way. But it is not very profound learning unless, when you switch off, you are able to recreate that way of seeing for yourself. The difficulty lies in connecting what you are 'shown' with what you already know, in such a way that you can *use* it effectively. It is the studying and thinking you do before and, particularly, afterwards that transforms *viewing* into substantial *learning*.

On the face of it, TV ought to be a very easy medium to learn from. Yet students don't always find it so. It's easy enough to *watch*, but it's often hard to be sure just what you have *learned*. As you watch and listen, the TV programme does all the work of holding a strong 'frame of reference' in place for you, and at the same time it makes ideas 'concrete' or dramatizes them, so that things seem 'obvious'. Then the programme ends, the frame of reference is gone, and the clear understanding evaporates. At worst, TV's capacity to take over all the work of 'framing' our thoughts leads to a habit of passivity: of simply accepting what we see – basking in a sense of having understood – instead of making the effort to understand for ourselves. The combination of sound and vision is so powerful that we are swept along by it and we 'forget' we are being presented with another person's point of view or *version* of things, just as in a book or a lecture, and that we need to think critically about what we are being told.

If you really want to *learn* from TV you have to find ways of 'making sense' for yourself of what you see and hear. You can do this by:

- preparing for the programme, by reading programme notes and skimming relevant course material beforehand

- jotting down a few notes as you view (but only a few or you will be distracted)

- afterwards, taking some time to summarize the main points of the programme and what contribution it has made to your understanding of the subject (that is, re-creating your thoughts, *without* the supplied frame of reference, for *yourself*)

- trying to make use of what you see on the screen in your essays.

People also find it difficult to *study* television programmes for more mundane reasons, such as simply being unable to watch at the time of transmission or forgetting to tune in at the right times. Or sometimes there are conflicts between family and friends over channel choice. It may be hard to watch uninterrupted or in the right 'atmosphere' for serious study. In a lecture, the formal setting and the ritual of entering and sitting in attentive silence help to create the frame of mind you need for studying. Sitting in the living room, where you usually watch TV for entertainment, with other people coming and going and the phone ringing may make it very hard to concentrate sufficiently.

However, that aside, studying TV can bring many benefits. For example, it is particularly good at helping you understand the dynamics of complicated *processes*, in which many things go on at the same time. It can illuminate your understanding of a community's religious beliefs, for instance, by showing you their services, practices and celebrations 'in action'. This provides a different *kind* of knowledge from a written description of processes and events such as these: broader, more rounded and multi-layered. These impressions remain – at a deep level – part of the intellectual apparatus you use for making sense of things, just as your own direct experience of the world provides insights and knowledge. The difficulty is connecting up this kind of insight with 'academic' knowledge.

Written knowledge and aural/visual knowledge

The discourses of the academic world are built upon the strengths of the written word, which provides opportunities for detailed and unhurried analysis and for 'freezing' propositions in a timeless way. TV, on the other hand, is a more 'plastic' medium for representing the world and communicating ideas and, as such, it provides opportunities for complex and dynamic ways of understanding. However, these do not necessarily engage easily with the more formal and rigorous discourses developed through writing. Whether the newer media will eventually give rise to academic discourses of equivalent weight to print-based ones (or even supersede them) is impossible to say. But for the time being, you as a student are left with the problem of 'translating' the insights and understandings gained from TV into written forms of argument.

TV is also very valuable for showing elements of *performance* in the arts, particularly in music and drama. Televised concerts and plays may be the only way some students can experience 'live' performance – though obviously it is not the same as the direct experience of a concert hall or theatre. Other kinds of dramatization can provide *case-study* material, in a subject such as law for example. Here, some 'experience' of court procedure may be helpful, or a demonstration of an interview between client and solicitor can be used as the basis for classroom analysis and discussion. TV is also the only way in which many of us can 'see' objects and places that are *removed* from us in space or time – works of art in galleries all over the world, buildings and their locations, the design of an ancient city. Furthermore, if you were studying the Parthenon in Athens for instance, you would be able not only to see it as it is now, from a number of different angles, but also with superimposed computer-generated images of the original structure and decoration, while a spoken commentary explained what you were looking at. With such exciting possibilities available to us it is a wonder that TV and video are sometimes seen as mere 'adjuncts' to study at higher levels.

But in fact, as we have seen, it isn't as easy to learn from TV as it might seem. When images, information and arguments are presented simultaneously to your eyes and ears, there is so much to think about that it is hard to attend closely to any one of them, or to stop and think, or make notes. And when the programme is over, so much has happened that it can be difficult to pin down exactly what it was about. Also, the knowledge has a 'fluid' quality which is an advantage when the subject is a complicated process, but means that the details soon begin to fade from your memory. You really need something written down as well – either printed 'programme notes', or your own notes – to help 'fix' the knowledge in a more simplified, encapsulated form. Then you can look back over things and investigate the ideas for yourself.

If you study with the Open University, the TV programmes are usually accompanied by printed notes with 'exercises' to help you make connections between 'screen knowledge' and 'print knowledge'. Perhaps in future, if course assessment involves interacting with screen images on computer, a more fluid 'holistic' mode of understanding will predominate. For now, though, you have to learn to 'translate' the insights gained from moving images into the more specific and detailed forms of written words and symbols.

Video-cassettes

To help absorb the richness of audio-visual messages, many students record TV broadcasts onto cassettes so that they can watch the programmes more than once and 'stop and start' whenever they want. Instead of watching a seamless presentation for 20–30 minutes at a stretch, in which the message and its delivery are controlled by others, *you* control the buttons. The stop–start video facility enables you to replay sequences of the programme, taking things in your own time and at your own pace. This helps offset the 'intensity' of the medium since you can switch the programme off to think and write notes, and you can replay a difficult section until you have grasped the point. You can also return to the programme to find material for an essay. The catch is that these processes are time-consuming. When you are estimating the time you need for this kind of activity, allow at least twice the playing-time of the cassette.

Increasingly, though, teaching material is prepared for video-cassette rather than broadcast. These video sequences may be of any length and often include exercises that help you interrogate what you see and hear. You may be asked to stop the tape part way through a case-study interview, for example, and to jot down notes of the main points. Or, at some points you may be asked to stop viewing and read a couple of pages of a textbook or study an illustration before continuing. These kinds of exercise are a great help in translating what you learn from the screen into academically useful terms.

Sometimes video sequences are very short. You may see only 5–10 minute 'snippets' to stimulate group discussion during a tutorial. That way, you can all compare your interpretations of events and ideas while keeping the 'evidence' in front of you – by replaying, and stopping at appropriate points. This is a very effective way of helping develop skills of analysis, interpretation and argument.

Or, if you study modern languages, you may find that the whole course is based on video rather than print these days. The 'spine' of the course may be a series of videos that show native speakers in action. You hear the language in the contexts in which it's actually spoken – at the railway station, in the shop or business meeting – and also pick up related facial expressions, gestures and aspects of the culture. You can stop and start the video to practise speaking yourself. Then you may be directed 'out' to books that supply explanations of relevant points of grammar and vocabulary. When a course is 'video-led' it is even more important to work out ways of viewing that allow you to concentrate without being interrupted.

Radio

Of all academic disciplines, the arts and humanities have taken most naturally to radio – indeed, some people complain they have colonized the medium. Whole channels are devoted to music, plays are broadcast regularly, there are reviews of current art exhibitions, theatre and books, and talks of all kinds – from philosophical discussion and aural history programmes to chat about the latest novels. Daily, there is a feast of experience to be had.

In education, radio has made *discussion* and *analysis* its own. Radio talks share many of the characteristics of lectures, and fulfil similar functions (see section 3.1). For instance, they enable you to hear academic discourse as spoken by experts – who, in this context, may indeed be world-renowned figures in their field. The difficulties involved in simultaneous listening, thinking and note-making are similar too. If anything, though, radio speakers are under even greater pressure than lecturers to pack a lot into a short time, and also to make their talks or discussion high-powered and impressive. Without the social context of the lecture and the presence of the speaker you may find it more difficult to follow the arguments they present. You should make a point of reading any programme notes beforehand and, afterwards, try to write a summary of the main points that emerge.

Educational radio programmes tend to be broadcast at even more 'unsocial' hours than TV – often after midnight or very early in the morning. Probably the last thing you want to be doing then is sitting with pen in hand trying to make sense of a high-flown discussion. So it is even more common for students to record radio programmes onto audio-cassette.

Learning from radio

When you are listening to debates between experts it is a positive advantage that radio is a less intense medium than TV – that less is happening simultaneously. It is much easier to concentrate on an argument when you do not have to attend to visual images at the same time, and it is easier to sit with a pad in hand and make notes. A philosophical debate, for instance, can be very arresting when you have nothing but the words to focus on. There are other ways of making a virtue of the absence of 'interfering' visual images too. Poetry readings can play directly on your imagination, as can serialized novels and play-readings. And music performances on the radio make you concentrate on what you *hear*. In fact, radio encourages you give your whole attention to just what the speaker or performer intends.

Other benefits flow from the fact that radio is a relatively cheap and technically uncomplicated medium. In the context of distance education, it is often used to broadcast 'magazine-style' programmes which keep you up to date with new developments in your subject and course, or in touch with the thoughts and feelings of teachers and other students. You can get people into a studio one day and have the programme ready to broadcast the next. This gives these programmes an immediacy and raw authenticity which the glossy TV version lacks. If you are a home-based student you tend to miss out on a lot of very useful background 'know-how' about your course, which full-time students pick up on the grapevine in between lectures or in the bar. Radio programmes of this less formal kind can help fill that gap. For students who cannot attend group meetings they can also help to create a sense of 'belonging' to a lively academic community.

Audio-cassette

As with TV and video, so with radio and audio-cassette. You can tape radio broadcasts onto audio-cassette and play them back at times that suit you. This brings similar benefits; of being able to take things at your own pace, stop to think and make notes, or replay difficult parts as often as you need. You may not want to go over every programme in a detailed way, but the fact that you *can* allows you the freedom to listen with full attention knowing that you can choose what else to do afterwards. Audio-cassettes are also much more portable and flexible than videos, so you can listen in breaks at work, as you do household chores or drive along in the car. They open up new areas of study time.

However, when audio-cassettes are designed to be used interactively, with instructions to stop and complete exercises, you cannot study them on the hoof. You need pen, paper and, usually, some of your course material in front of you. In some subjects audio-cassettes are an invaluable way of 'talking you through' quite complicated processes of analysis. Because only your ears are involved in the business of listening, your eyes are free to fix on a detailed plan of a building or classical site, an historical map, an illustration of a painting or sculpture, or a short poem. You can scrutinize the illustration in detail while, on tape, the teacher discusses it and directs your attention to particular parts of it. When this is done in a text, you have to read the discussion and keep switching your attention back and forth between it and the illustration, which may be on a different page. Using audio-cassette, you can focus fully on the illustration as you listen. Then you may be set follow-up questions to work on after the cassette is switched off.

Again, the drawback is that studying audio-cassettes can be particularly time-consuming. Because this is such a flexible and effective teaching medium, cassettes often include frequent stops and quite lengthy exercises. When they do, your study plans may need to allow three times the cassette playing-time. However, you will usually find this investment of time very worthwhile.

KEY POINTS

- To gain full benefit from TV and radio broadcasts you need to prepare in advance by reading programme notes and skimming relevant sections of course material.

- With TV it is hard to take notes as you watch, but you will learn more if you write down key points afterwards.

- With radio you can take notes as you listen, though some follow-up work will help to consolidate your learning.

- Learning from TV and radio is transformed if you can record the broadcasts and replay them in your own time, as often as you want.

- Cassettes include learning exercises; and you should simply follow the instructions. Allow sufficient time to study them, but guard against letting time run away with you.

4 LEARNING BY DOING

All learning is an active *making* of sense. But there are elements of most arts and humanities subjects in which other kinds of 'doing' are central. This is particularly true of the performance arts: taking part in a play or playing an instrument in an orchestra are prime examples of learning by doing. Going on a dig is an integral part of the study of archaeology, and in modern languages it is essential to learn to speak the language appropriately in real-life situations. We have also seen that studying philosophy involves the active process of 'philosophizing', and that being a historian means seeking out evidence, for example in archives and parish registers. More generally, there are certain kinds of activity that *all* students can expect to engage in at some time or another. The most important is learning through writing, which we will explore in Chapters 4, 5 and part of 6. Others, which we look at here, include: making a presentation; using a computer to search for information, analyse text and explore a range of source material; and making visits, to galleries, historical sites, museums and so forth.

4.1 Making a 'presentation'

A device sometimes used in study group meetings is for one of the students to prepare a short talk on a particular article or book, and speak for around fifteen minutes at the start of the session to get the discussion going. In some settings, delivering a 'seminar paper' is a rather more formal task than that. But, either way, in principle it should be fairly straightforward. However, students sometimes feel overawed by the responsibility, and by the prospect of speaking to a group of people on an unfamiliar topic. In fact finding a 'public speaking voice' takes practice, even for such a small public, so it isn't surprising if you are unsettled by the idea. Here are some basic guidelines for making your presentation go well.

The most important principle is to avoid being too ambitious. In fifteen minutes or so you are not going to be able make more than two or three main points well. If you allow feelings of anxiety to push you into preparing a lot more, you will end up burbling and no one will understand a word. Whatever your topic, begin with a brief summary of what it is about and why it is of interest in order to set the context for your listeners. Keep it simple. Remember that although *you* have been thinking a lot about the subject, the other students haven't. They need things spelled out carefully. As you get on to your main points, use examples to illustrate them so that people can see what you are getting at. Prepare a diagram if it makes things clearer, and circulate copies of any illustrations you want the group to look at as you speak.

Don't write out what you have to say in longhand and then read it out word for word. You will bore your audience. And, worse, you will not learn the skill the exercise is designed to teach – taking hold of the ideas and academic language you are learning and putting them to use in making your own argument. Instead, having done the preparatory work, write three or four simple headings on a card or overhead projector transparency, with a few 'bullet points' under each one. Then talk your way through. Speak simply and clearly and, above all, speak *to* the members of the group – try to make 'eye contact' with some of them. Remember, for everyone else your presentation is just another session. They are not concerned to know how hard you have worked or how clever you are. All they care about is whether they can understand what you say.

> **KEY POINTS**
>
> When you have to make a presentation to other students:
> - don't be too ambitious – keep it short and simple
> - use examples to illustrate the points you make
> - speak directly to your audience, from notes on a card or overhead projector transparency.

4.2 Computing

Using computing is an increasingly important way of learning by 'doing' in arts and humanities subjects. Computers are enabling us to gain *access to information,* to techniques for *textual analysis,* and offering new possibilities for *multi-media study.* As we saw in section 2.5, the potential for rapid and reliable communication among students and between them and their tutors, using e-mail and computer conferencing, is also of great benefit, especially to students in distance education. And computers are transforming study methods and patterns through word-processing facilities (see Chapter 5).

So, despite their expense, computers are becoming popular because they can make you much more efficient at many of the things students have always had to do and they also open up possibilities for studying in new ways. (You do not necessarily have to buy one. You may be able to use a computer at work, or rent one.) To become proficient you will have to set aside time to learn three things:

- how to set up the equipment itself (the hardware)
- how to work the operating system (Windows, DOS, the Mac interface)
- how to use the features of your software packages.

The first two are the most important to begin with. You might spend some time finding your way round the equipment and operating system, and learning how to 'format' discs, create documents and move text around. When you are on top of the basics you can take the more sophisticated features a bit at a time. The 'Help' facilities may provide all the help you need, but there are also very useful guide books. And, luckily, most people who already know what they are doing are only too happy to instruct you.

Access to information

A place where you are very likely to come across a computer is in any large *library.* Nowadays library *catalogues* are increasingly held on a computer system. This has transformed the activity of hunting for books, journals and articles – one of the basic processes of studying and of academic research. It is now possible to carry out searches for source material much more quickly and flexibly than before. Beyond that, computer networks can also *connect* you to sources of information. Instead of ordering books from a library or using them there, you can 'download' a copy of a book from an electronic library and either print off a paper copy or read it on your own computer screen.

Through your computer you can also gain access to the masses of information now available on the *Internet*; some put there by institutions and some by individuals. You log on to the network, find your way to the source of information you want, and wait for it to 'down-load' onto your computer. Anyone who is linked to the network can make information available. The snag is that there is no guarantee as to its quality or accuracy. Also, it is difficult to find your way around this electronic labyrinth, so that 'surfing the net' can become a costly and time-consuming distraction. In fact, when you are a newcomer to an area of study there is a lot to be said for concentrating on a limited amount of well-structured, carefully explained material rather than thrashing about in a sea of information. However, as tools are developed for 'searching' out information in the Internet, it will become more useful as a source of information. Increasingly, it will be used as a medium for delivering 'education' to people who may be linked to the network from virtually any point in the globe. You will no longer be restricted to courses available in your own country. Eventually, you may even be able to enrol in 'The Global University'!

Textual analysis

Once a text is put into digital form for the computer, it is possible to 'tag' certain words and phrases electronically. Then, if you have the appropriate 'software' package, you can point to these words and be taken to a different screen which provides information about them. This can be very helpful in the case of texts which contain 'antique' words and references to past customs, beliefs or events that the modern reader is unfamiliar with.

Other software may enable certain kinds of *textual analysis* which were extremely time-consuming if not impossible before. You can do various kinds of analysis in seconds that would take weeks or years of time if done 'by hand', especially in long, complex texts such as novels. For example, you can count the frequency with which particular words are used, making lists of synonymous words in a text and using them to invetsigate the themes or allusions that run through it – finding all the references to the colour red in a novel for example, or various uses of irony. Using a KWIC (Key Word in Context) text analysis package, you could see whether the references to the colour red occur in relation to particular characters, or places, and whether they act as metaphors. You could also find out which characters are assigned which words in what contexts. Then you can go on to think about what that might reveal about the characters, and their differences from or similarities to other characters in the novel. Or you could list the words that are used

CHAPTER FOUR

WHAT IS GOOD WRITING?

1 THE IMPORTANCE OF WRITING

1.1 Why write?

Of all aspects of studying, writing is probably the most challenging. That is because when you write down an account of your ideas for other people to read you have to explain yourself particularly carefully. You can't make the mental leaps you do when you are in conversation with others or thinking about something for yourself. To make your meaning clear, using only words on a page, you have to work out exactly what you think about the subject. You come to understand it for *yourself* in the process of explaining it to others. So writing makes you really grapple with what you are studying. In other words, it forces you into a very deep and powerful kind of *learning*. That is what makes it so demanding. When you write you are really putting ideas to use.

In previous chapters I have talked about how to 'take in' ideas from books, articles, TV and so on. But I said then that it is only when you can *use* these ideas to say something for yourself that you have really 'learned' them. Ideas only become a properly functioning part of your thought-processes when you can call on them as you *communicate* with other people. It is very valuable to debate issues with other students in discussion groups (see Chapter 3). But an even more exacting way of using ideas in argument is to do it in writing.

A key part of using ideas effectively is to be able to write clearly and persuasively. In our society this is a very valuable skill. It puts you on a much better footing with other people if you can present your point of view forcefully in writing. Perhaps you started out on your studies with the idea only of learning more about art, music or history, but you may discover that one of the most valuable things you gain is the ability to write much more effectively. Whether you start with a rather weak writing style or a fairly well-developed one, there is always plenty of progress to be made.

So writing tends to be both the most demanding and the most rewarding part of any course of study. And, because it contributes so much to what you learn, you have to put a lot of your time and energy into it.

1.2   What is an essay?

The different arts and humanities subjects make their own particular demands on you. You may have to do various kinds of writing – diaries, logs, project reports, case-studies – or even write creatively. In this chapter, though, we are going to concentrate on the essay because that is by far the most common form of writing in arts and humanities subjects.

The word 'essay' originally meant 'an attempt' or try at something, but now it usually means a short piece of writing on a specific subject. It is a *complete* piece of writing that can stand alone – it must make sense to the reader 'in itself'. You are given an essay title or question, which sets out the isues you need to address, and a word limit of around one or two thousand words – possibly a bit shorter to begin with. You work from the title, putting together an *argument* that leads the reader towards a conclusion. Your tutor marks your essay, making comments not only about *what* you have said but also the *way* you have structured and written the essay. These 'criticisms' are meant to help you develop both your grasp of the subject and your powers of expression. So an essay opens up a teaching–learning dialogue between you and your teacher. In fact, it does still have some of the original sense of 'trying your hand' at something, with the idea that you can get better at it through practice.

Your tutor will usually grade your essay too, so that you can see where you 'stand' in relation to whatever standards apply to your course. This means that, over time, you can see what kind of progress you are making. However, you should not see essay-writing simply as something to be endured because your work must be assessed. It is an *essential* part of the learning process. When you look back over a course you have studied, you will find that the topics you have written about are the ones you understand most clearly and remember best.

KEY POINTS

Writing essays is a very important part of studying because:

- it deepens your *learning* of the subject you are studying
- you learn to use ideas to *argue* a case
- it enables you to enter into a dialogue with your tutor through which you can *extend* and *refine* your thinking, and your *writing skills*
- it enables your tutor to *assess* your progress.

1.3   Developing your essay-writing ability

To develop your skill in writing essays you need to address two basic questions.

- What does a good essay look like?
- How do you set about producing one?

We will look at the first of these questions in this chapter and the second in the next.

Reading guide

There is a lot to think about in this chapter, particularly if you work carefully through all the examples and activities, which are mainly in section 2. I suggest you take the chapter in five stages:

1   Up to the end of section 2.1
2   Section 2.2
3   Section 2.3
4   Sections 2.4 and 2.5
5   Sections 3 and 4.

Alternatively, simply stop reading closely when you feel you have gone far enough for your present needs. Just skim through the rest of the chapter looking at the boxes. You can come back to it at later points in your studies when you are ready to work on new aspects of your writing. Learning about good writing is not the kind of thing you can do in one 'go'. It is something we all need to keep working at.

2   WHAT DOES AN ESSAY LOOK LIKE?

One of the curious things about learning to write essays is that you are seldom offered much insight into what you might be setting out to produce. You know only too well what *your* essays look like and what your tutor says about them, but you don't know what else you might have done. For instance, you have very little idea what other people's essays are like and what comments *they* get back. Perhaps you are told your essay ought to be 'more structured' or 'less subjective', but how are you supposed to know what a more structured or a more objective essay would look like? Your tutor passes judgement on your essay by comparing it with lots of others, whereas you only get to see your own.

2.1　Looking at other people's essays

One of the best ways of developing your essay-writing ability is to see how other students respond to the same essay title as you. It is not that you want to copy someone else's style. It's just that you need to broaden your understanding of what is possible when you are answering an essay question.

'Self-help'

If you are studying with other students you might arrange to meet from time to time to read and discuss each other's essays. If you can't meet, you could exchange essays by post. This is *not* cheating. It is a way of gaining insight into the strengths and weaknesses of your own writing by comparing your approach with other people's. Anyway, you probably wouldn't be able to copy their styles even if you tried. And why would you want to when it is *your* writing you are aiming to develop?

The idea of letting other people see your work is a bit daunting at first. Your writing feels like a 'private' matter, between you and your tutor. But, once you take the plunge, other students can often be as helpful as a tutor in giving you ideas and opening up new possibilities.

That is just what we are going to do here. We'll look at a couple of short essays about the Joyce Ellis article you read in Chapter 2, so you'll need your photocopy of the article in front of you. And if you didn't make copies of these two essays earlier, you need to do so now (see pp.106–7) The writers were adult students in a 'return to study' course, who were given this task:

Write a short essay (of no more than 500 words) on the following:

Did eighteenth-century women migrate to towns mainly because of the attractions of the towns, or mainly to escape from life in the countryside? Discuss in the light of Joyce Ellis's article.

Read the essays by 'Philip' and 'Hansa' on pages 106 and 107.

1   As you read, mark any places where you have difficulty grasping the point, and write any other thoughts that come to you in the margins. Pencil in any alterations you think could usefully be made. (If possible, work on photocopies of the essays.)

2   When you get to the end of the essays, take a sheet of paper and write two headings: 'Strengths' and 'Weaknesses'. Note down the good things about Philip's essay and the weak points. Then do the same for Hansa's.

3   Try to weigh up the quality of these essays.

Do you think that one of them is better than the other? (Can they be good in different ways?)

Overall, do you think that they are good essays or poor ones?

How much of that is to do with the quality of the ideas in them and how much to do with the way the ideas are presented?

4   Finally, can you draw any general conclusions about the qualities a good essay should have? (Look back over your answers to 2 and 3 above.)

Write down your conclusions.

Before you begin, read the box below about '"Judging" writing'.

'Judging' writing

This is a demanding activity and it will take you some time. You may not want to do all of it at this stage. However, it is *worth doing*. It will be time well spent because you need to develop your ability to see what works in writing and what doesn't. It is not helpful to try to learn formal 'rules' of writing. Rather, you have to become a reasonably good judge of real pieces of writing, including your own. 'Marking' other people's work helps you understand what you should be aiming for in your own writing.

Here are the two essays. Philip's was handwritten and came with a note. Part of it reads: 'Writing this is a learning experience because I am starting late in life to going back to be re-educated. But I feel more than willing to attempt the challenge…'

Philip's essay

On the Town. "Woman in Augustan England" 1680–1820

Joyce Ellis presents to us a portrayal of woman living around the eighteenth century. The women who lived a fairly comfortable style of life belonged to a class of society where the father or husband would be a land-owner, these males were orientated to country life and all it entailed so they expected their wifes or daughters to fit in to a standard of life they felt gave a certain status to the country way of life. These were under-privileged women as the boredom of country life could become frustrating to them, does it not make you see a resemblance to the modern day young woman, she can combine marriage, raising children, and holding on to a carreer as well.

With society becoming more wealthy it was possible for the fathers and husbands to provide an even better standard of life for their wifes and daughters, more servants could be provided to do the work and this left the woman more time than ever to develop the social skills of the era, but this in turn led to extreme frustration among woman of that class. The country was no place now to exercise these new skills they had been taught, for one thing females outnumbered males at that time, also few chances arose to meet and mingle with crowds of people, but most importantly the demands of propriety meant that their conduct should be impeccable at all times any error would be seen in such a limited environment so therefore woman began to long for the urban or city way of living, if even for a short period so that they could deploy the art of socializing and mingling with a greater amount of society

Towns offered woman a great variation of respectable ways in which to carry out the social skills, indeed many women have gone down in history as being great experts as organizers of social events thus enhancing their husbands standing. In a town or city, women could meet with many more of the female sex than they did in the country, they could exchange views and learn new ideas from each other, also they could meet with more of the male population as the citys had theatres concert halls, and many places where both sexes could mingle together respectably. In many ways going into urban life from the countryside was beneficial to woman of the upperclass.

This transition was not without a certain amount of jibes from the male population against the women of that time, who looked on them as being inferior in many ways, and considered those who chose to get away from boredom of the country as being improper in outlook.

Nevertheless woman, whether wealthy or poor need the stimulus of company and the need to escape from routine and boredom and so will continue to seek for the things that will be in their favour.

Hansa's essay

Did eighteenth century women migrate to towns mainly because of the attractions of the towns, or mainly to escape from life in the countryside?

Eighteenth century society expected women to have accomplishments such as the ability to embroider, play the piano and sing. They were supposed to be fragile, delicate and innocent; they were taught at smart boarding schools or by private tutors, social skills to fit them for the role expected of them at the time, as 'embodiments of their husbands' and fathers' status'.

Life in the country during this period of history offered little scope for the indulgence of these skills owing to the sparcity of the popuation and the difficulty of transport, as women from the higher ranks were constrained to mix only with their own kind.

Thus the lives of these well born ladies were immensely boring. It was not considered fitting that a woman should take any part in the management of a country estate, or in the country pursuits of riding, hunting or fishing as enjoyed by the men and she was therefore reduced to spend her time reading or writing letters. However, in an urban environment, it was acceptable that women could socialize on a much wider scale and even organize and plan social events, an added dimension to their very constrained lives. Because of this, and because an urban environment offered women so much more scope, not only to display their accomplishments but also to indulge their own desire for sociability, amusement and companions', the female population of England's towns expanded dramatically.

In view of the somewhat prescribed role forced upon women in the eighteenth century by the male dominated society which formulated social mores, it was inevitable that women would be attracted to the towns where the skills that society required of them could be more widely indulged and more fully displayed. In the towns there were more people of the same rank, so that women could socialize on a wider scale, and as there was public transport they had greater mobility. They therefore fled from the country in order to escape the restrictions and consequent boredom placed upon them by the very limited pastimes that a high ranking women in the eighteeenth century was permitted to indulge.

In effect, I think that the high ranking women of the eighteeenth century were neither mainly attracted to the towns, or escaping from the countryside, what they were seeking to do was to fulfil the very limited role with which society had burdened them as fully as was possible.

We will look at of each of these essays in turn, so that you can compare your thoughts with mine.

2.2 Analysing Philip's essay

The title

The first thing I noticed about Philip's essay is that although it begins with a title it is not the one he was given. This immediately creates two problems.

1 If I were Philip's tutor I would find it difficult to weigh up his essay against the challenge he was actually set.

2 The title he has made up is not a good one, so it weakens his essay from the outset.

Philip's title doesn't pose a *question* for him to answer. So I began reading without any sense of what he is trying to say. He has given himself a broad theme, but no purpose. An essay never asks you just to 'write what you know about the topic' – it always requires you to present an *argument* of some kind. Often, as here, the purpose is to answer a question. Other essay titles may ask you to discuss a particular point of view, or compare and contrast two points of view. But however the title is worded, it is always meant to pose a 'problem' which your essay should then set out to argue about and solve.

Philip neither starts with a problem to solve, nor finishes with a solution, so there is a rather aimless feel to the essay. It's reasonably interesting, but it isn't going anywhere in particular. This makes reading it a lot harder. Since, as a reader, you have to 'project' meaning into the written words, if you're not sure where the words are leading it is much more difficult to follow. A good essay is never just a string of sentences. It is a journey from the question in the title to the answer in your 'conclusion'.

Philip's lack of clear purpose is the biggest weakness of his essay. We see it at the end of the first paragraph, where he throws in a comment about modern young women. The comment doesn't mean much to me, but in any case it has little to do with the topic. *Everything* you say in an essay should contribute in some way to answering the question in the title. This is the great value of having a problem to solve – it gives you a way of deciding what to put in and what to leave out. It also helps you to organize what you put in, so that it builds up towards your conclusion. Because Philip does not have a clear purpose, he drops in stray points that don't lead anywhere. And in his last paragraph he is left making vague remarks about women in general – needing company and seeking things 'in their favour' (couldn't this be said about men too?). So the essay fizzles out, without doing justice either to the themes of Ellis's article or to Philip's own ideas. All of this is quite understandable in a first essay. But it points up the crucial importance of recognizing that an essay is meant to be an *argument*.

Yet in spite of getting off on the wrong foot by not sticking to the title, Philip's essay has a lot in it, as we can see if we pull it apart. Here is the basic content of his essay set out in note form. Check the notes quickly against his essay to see if you agree that I've captured the gist of what he says.

The content of Philip's essay

Paragraph 1: Introduction – social context

1 Ellis – a portrait of C18 women whose fathers/husbands were of land-owning class.

2 Men were country-oriented → expected wife/daughters to fit into high-status rural life-style.

3 Women were under-privileged [?], owing to the boredom of country life.

4 *Contrast* with modern woman – who can combine marriage, children and career.

Paragraph 2: Tedium of country life

1 Increasing wealth → rising standard of living → more servants → women more time for skills → extreme frustration.

2 In country, women couldn't exercise skills:

– females outnumbered males [?]

– few opportunities to meet.

3 Strict rules of social propriety, very visible → conduct impeccable at all times.

4 Longed for urban life – even for short spells – to be able to socialize.

Paragraph 3: Attractions of town

1 Towns → variety of respectable social options, including active role in organizing.

2 More women to meet – exchange views – learn new ideas.

3 More meetings with men – theatre, concerts – both sexes could mix respectably.

4 In many ways beneficial to women.

Paragraph 4: Male interpretation of women's migration to towns

1 Male jibes at women's migration to towns.

2   Viewed women as inferior in many ways. ·

3   Saw escape from boredom of country as 'improper'.

Paragraph 5: Conclusion – Women's need for company and amusement

1   Women need company and escape from boredom

2   → will continue to seek things in their favour.

Setting out the essay like this shows us a number of things.

Structure

We can see straight away that Philip's essay has a structure. Each paragraph deals with a new aspect of the topic and the sequence of paragraphs has a clear line of development. In the first paragraph Philip sets up the general background; then he explores the repellent side of country life, followed by the attractive side of town life; then he notes male attitudes to the women's migration to towns; and in his final paragraph he draws a general conclusion. This is an excellent outline plan for a short essay. He hasn't entirely carried it off, as we shall see in a moment, but there is nothing wrong with the basic structure.

> **KEY POINTS**
> - An essay needs to be *structured*.
> - Partly this involves organizing the points you want to make into *groups*, and giving a *paragraph* to each group.
> - It also involves arranging the paragraphs into a meaningful *sequence*, leading towards your conclusion.

Arguing a case

Philip clearly has a sense that he is meant to be arguing a case. Perhaps the best bit of argument comes at the start of paragraph 2. If you look at the notes you'll see that I have used arrows to show how the argument works. He says that increasing wealth led to a rising standard of living, which meant that more servants were employed, which led to women having more time to polish up their social skills, but that this 'in turn' led to frustration because country life no longer gave women enough opportunities to exercise their skills. This is very purposeful writing. He drives us forward through the logic of his argument.

As paragraph 2 continues, Philip tells us *why* women didn't have the opportunity to exercise their social skills in the country, saying first that women outnumbered men (though I'm not sure where he got that from) and then that few chances arose for meeting others. At this point the logic is still clear – we have just been given two reasons why opportunities to exercise social skills were limited. But he then moves on to the oppressiveness of the rules of 'propriety'. It isn't obvious whether that still has to do with the exercise of social skills. Perhaps it is added simply as another source of the 'frustration' Philip mentioned earlier, but if so the connection is not made. It reads as just an item in a list of points, not as part of a clear sequence. This lessens the impact of the build-up of the logic. That's a pity, because the last point is about women longing for city life where they could exercise their skills, which would have followed on very nicely from the points about not being able to do so in the country. We end the paragraph with the sense that there were 'a bunch of reasons' why women were fed up with country life, instead of a sharp focus on the irony of having increasingly sophisticated skills but dwindling opportunities to use them. Just read the paragraph again to see if you agree.

KEY POINTS

- An argument is a series of points arranged in logical sequence, with links made from one point to the next.
- Putting in points that distract from the main flow of the argument diminishes its impact.

Linking points together

Looking at the flow of Philip's argument as a whole, we can see that it gets off to a weak start – it lacks a title to give it a clear framework and purpose, and the opening sentence does not engage the reader.

Openings

There is a lot to be said for brisk, direct opening sentences in an essay. You need to set the reader's thoughts off in the right direction, so there is no virtue in a lot of formal 'throat-clearing'. The first sentence should grab your reader's attention. It should be related to the essay question and it should be doing important work for your argument. But it doesn't have to be fancy.

It is often said that in your 'introduction' you should say what you are going to do in the essay (then do it in the 'middle' part of the essay, and then say what you have done in the 'conclusion'). But this kind of writing to a 'formula' is tedious to do and pretty dull to read.

After the opening sentence, the first two proper points in paragraph 1 (see my notes) actually do a good job of getting things going. Unfortunately, point 3 does not follow on particularly well and point 4 is simply a distraction. Yet broadly, once he gets going, you can see that in the first two paragraphs Philip is telling a 'story' about how and why women's roles in the countryside changed over time, and what this meant to them.

At the end of the second paragraph he concludes 'so therefore woman began to long for the urban or city way of living...'. This *leads* us into the next paragraph, and to the topic of women's role in the town. He begins the fourth paragraph with 'This transition...' which connects *back* directly to what he has said in the last sentence of paragraph 3. And by using the linking word 'Nevertheless' at the start of the last paragraph, Philip shows he knows he should be making a connection there too, even if he hasn't quite worked out how to pull the whole thing together at the end. So he has a good general sense of the need to connect each stage of his argument into a flowing sequence.

But although Philip links up the *stages* of the argument well, he doesn't always organize the main points he wants to make *within* each stage into a meaningful sequence. As we saw, in the second paragraph he does not manage to weave the idea of the demands of propriety into the flow of his otherwise purposeful writing. Here's how the main points about women's role and their life in the countryside might be re-organized into a connected, logical sequence.

Life in the countryside

1 Points about rising standard of living, etc. (which Philip handles well) → these women lost their household function.

2 As a result, they had more time to develop accomplishments and fulfil a 'decorative' role.

3 But the demands of propriety meant they could mix only with their own kind (unlike their menfolk).

4 This particular population was sparse. Lack of transport and bad weather prevented women from mixing socially and so fulfilling their role in rural society.

5 Instead they were restricted to pastimes in and around their homes, such as needlework, letter writing, reading and walking.

Here a clear line of argument is being developed within the stage of the argument that deals with life in the countryside.

> ### KEY POINTS
>
> - You have to *develop* an argument in *stages* towards your conclusion.
> - This means you have to *link* each stage to the next, so that the reader can follow the *direction* your argument is taking.
> - And, *within* each stage of the argument, you need to organize your *main points* into a logical *sequence*.

Bringing in your own ideas

At the end of paragraph 2, Philip makes his point about the busy lives of modern young women. (Presumably he means to draw a contrast, rather than suggest a 'resemblance'.) Why did I suggest that this is not a good idea? Doesn't it show initiative to bring in a few ideas of your own? Is essay-writing meant to be just repeating back what you've read in books and articles? This is a tricky issue. Certainly you are meant to think about what you write and to say things as you have worked them out for yourself. It would be very dreary indeed simply to repeat back what you have read, and you wouldn't learn much. On the other hand, your thinking is meant to be based on the ideas and information you have been reading about in your studies. The essay is an exercise in 'engaging with' these arguments and ideas, and trying to put them to use. This helps you to learn in depth. It is also an exercise in being disciplined in your writing – saying exactly what you intend to say, and only what you can justify saying. It is not an open invitation to write down your thoughts to see what your tutor makes of them.

There are three problems with Philip's attempt to introduce the comparison with modern women.

- If he is going to bring in something from outside the Ellis article he needs to *justify* it. He can't just drop in a remark in passing and expect his reader to accept it without question.

- Because Philip's observation is not drawn from what he has read in Ellis's article, it opens up a whole new area – it *raises questions* about what kinds of generalizations can be made about women now, what kinds of comparisons can reasonably be drawn between then and now, and what kinds of evidence might be relevant to making this case. He simply does not have the space to tackle all this.

- In any case, it is beside the point; it is *irrelevant* to an argument about the reasons why eighteenth-century women migrated to towns (the task set by the original question).

You are not forbidden from bringing in ideas of your own but you have to do so cautiously, and always take the time to back up your case so that your reader doesn't just dismiss it out of hand. Your reader is only interested in well thought out arguments based on good authority or good evidence, not just anything you happen to want to say. Generally, as a newcomer to a subject, it is best to concentrate on trying to do an intelligent job of working with the arguments and information you have been reading about. Your own originality of thought has plenty of opportunity to shine through.

This even applies to the terms you use. For example, Philip says in paragraph 1, 'These were under-privileged women...'. 'Under-privileged' is not a term Ellis uses, and it sounds pretty odd given that she is talking about wealthy society women. Privilege was what they did have. 'Socially cut-off', 'under-stimulated', or 'under-employed' are all terms that might more accurately be used. But it is wisest to stay close to the terms that authors use, unless you know a lot about the subject. After all, what grounds has Philip for placing these women in a particular category other than what he has learned from Ellis? She will have chosen her terms carefully, based on her own detailed knowledge of the subject and on the terms in use amongst other experts. Writing essays is also learning to use the 'language' of the writers in the field you are studying.

KEY POINTS

- Dropping thoughts of your own into your essay, in passing, tends to raise lots of complicated questions that you cannot deal with.

- Any ideas you do bring in need to be explained and justified.

- If you just focus on working with the terms and ideas you have been studying, your own thoughts will work their way in anyway. You don't need to make a special effort to bring in extra ideas of your own.

Arguing to a conclusion

If we ignore the bits where Philip strays off the subject, how well does his argument work? Does he make a good case? Well, I think even Philip was feeling a bit doubtful about this, since by the end he seems to be running out of steam. The conclusion is tame. He obviously hasn't realized that his closing sentences need to pull together what he has said earlier, and present an answer to the question in the title (as given). Rather, he seems to be casting about for something grand-sounding to finish off with, so he makes a general point about women's needs.

Yet, as we saw, there is some quite vigorous argument earlier in the essay. So what does it all add up to? The general gist of his argument seems to be this:

- Men of the land-owning class enjoyed country life and expected their women folk to 'fit in'.
- But women found country life stultifying and frustrating.
- Town life offered them many more opportunities (so they migrated there, though Philip doesn't actually say so).
- The men mocked them for migrating, or criticized their impropriety.
- But women will do what they need to.

In the end, he presents the women's migration as a straightforward clash of interests between them and their menfolk. The upshot is that women refused to bow to pressure or criticism from the men, and looked to their

also outlines what it is she is going to say. So, by then, we can see both *what* she proposes to do and *why*. In short, she has set up a 'frame of reference' within which we can understand the purpose of her argument. (Bear in mind how important frameworks for thinking are for readers; see Chapter 3, section 2.1.)

This 'frame' is missing in both Hansa's and Philip's essays. If Hansa gave us some idea of the scale of the migration, and a few pointers to the debate she is engaging with, we would be able to follow her argument through to its conclusion more easily. For example, she might add something like this to the end of her first paragraph:

> They were also expected to live for long spells in their family homes in the countryside. When these women began to migrate to towns in large numbers, satirists of the period presented this as a wilful desire for 'freedom from male control' and a chance to enjoy frivolous pastimes.

There are many different ways of doing this kind of frame-setting. The point is that nowhere in her first paragraph does Hansa make a link to the title of the essay (and hence to the conclusion she is leading towards). She has her argument in her head, but she doesn't remember to set up a frame of reference within which her argument will make sense to us. Remember, an essay is a *complete* piece of writing; it must make sense to readers 'in itself'. So you have to explain yourself 'as if' the reader is someone who has not read the texts you have been studying and has no special knowledge of the subject.

KEY POINTS

You have to remember that your readers need some kind of frame of reference for your argument. You need to find a way of setting a context for your argument at the start, so that you set your readers' thoughts going in the right direction. They need some sense of:

- *why* it is worth paying attention to what you are saying
- what you are arguing 'against'.

Making judgements

The essay title, then, invites the writer to engage in the debate between Ellis and the satirists. This involves coming to some kind of judgement between the arguments on the two sides. As we saw, Philip does not really commit himself. Insofar as he makes judgements, they are about the parallels between the situation of eighteenth-century women and women now, and between eighteenth-century women's actions and those of women in general. I found these views:

- *irrelevant*, in that they do not contribute to his argument – they do not connect with either the official essay title or his own made-up title;
- *inappropriate*, in that we have not been reading about these other women, so we have no information or arguments to go on in responding to Philip's observations.

> ## Making judgements
>
> We make judgements about what we read all the time. Indeed, we read other people's writing *in order* to think our ideas through more thoroughly and to extend them. Unless we have some ideas of our own we can't 'make sense' of what we read. And our ideas 'inform' our judgements.
>
> However, when you present your judgements in an essay they have to be *relevant* to the question you are discussing, and *appropriate* in terms of the sources of information and authoritative debate available to you. You must try not to make assumptions as you develop your argument. Ask yourself 'what if my reader disagrees with me?'.

Hansa, on the other hand, does commit herself. In taking Ellis's line against that of the satirists, she brings her own judgement to bear. But does she manage to present her judgements 'relevantly' and 'appropriately'? In the first three paragraphs she very properly keeps her judgements to herself and sticks to outlining the women's general circumstances, and the opportunities available to them in country and town respectively. But then in paragraph 4 the gloves come off:

> In view of the somewhat prescribed role forced upon women in the eighteenth century by the <u>male dominated society</u> which <u>formulated social mores</u>... (underlining added)

Hansa is saying that this society was dominated by men; that men made the social 'rules' and, presumably, 'forced' them upon women. The relationship between men and women at the time is certainly *relevant* to the essay question. But is it *appropriate* for Hansa to make such a statement as if it is based on her own knowledge of the facts – when actually, if she got it from anywhere, we know that it was from Ellis? At least, she should refer to the source of her information, saying perhaps, 'As we see from Ellis's article, this was a male dominated society...'

But she would have difficulty doing that because Ellis does not say this explicitly anywhere. Ellis does not actually use the term 'male dominated', nor does she explore the question of where the rules of correct female behaviour 'came from'. So Hansa is not making a statement based on fact here – this is a judgement, based on her interpretation of Ellis.

What Hansa says, then, is inappropriate for two reasons:

1 because she writes *as if* she herself has knowledge that she does not have;

2 because she presents what is a *judgement* as though it were fact.

In effect, what she presents us with are her own *assumptions* about how eighteenth-century society worked.

Hansa's personal judgement comes through again right at the end of the essay when she talks about women being 'burdened' by their role. Again, she presents this as if it is obvious and well established that 'society' placed a heavy and oppressive load on these women. I dare say some of their servants would not have found their way of life such a burden. So, again, this 'pronouncement' jars. It feels as though we are being dragooned into seeing things from Hansa's point of view, without having been given good reason to.

So although Hansa has brought in her own judgements in a way that is relevant, she has not quite handled them appropriately. But then in a first essay it is quite an achievement to have engaged so well with Ellis's arguments. I doubt if it will take Hansa long to develop the ability to present her case more convincingly.

Referring to your sources

One of the best ways of putting together a convincing argument is to make direct use of your source material – in this case, Ellis's article. Neither Hansa nor Philip does quite enough of it. Hansa does some in her opening paragraph, when she refers to the particular accomplishments women acquired – playing the piano, singing, embroidering – and, in the last sentence, quotes from Ellis briefly. In her second paragraph she also identifies the different pastimes men and women had in the countryside. (Philip does none of these things in his opening paragraphs.) They need to make the Ellis article a more tangible presence in their essays because Ellis is both the *authority* for their arguments and the *source* of the *information* they present.

For instance, we saw that it would have been helpful for Hansa to be able to rely on Ellis's authority when mounting her argument about male domination. Had Ellis in fact argued this explicitly, Hansa could have used Ellis's terms and also quoted her words. In this way Hansa could both have *explained* herself clearly and offered *evidence* in support of her argument. She might also have illustrated the attractions of the towns by referring to some of the detail Ellis provides; rather than vaguely referring to 'social events', she could have made specific mention of the theatres and concert halls (as Philip does). This would help us to 'see' why women were attracted to the towns, and would not take up many more words.

'Referring' to a text

When you are asked to 'discuss' an essay question 'in the light of' or 'with reference to' a course text such as the Ellis article, you not only have to explain the ideas but also bring in some of the *detail* of the text to *illustrate* what you mean to say. You also need to refer directly to the text to back up or *justify* the main points you make; you have to use 'examples' and snatches of quotation from the text as *evidence* to support your points. And you must always take care to be *accurate* when making these references and quotations.

At present, Philip's and Hansa's arguments appear to arise too directly out of their own 'knowledge' and this is unlikely to be convincing to their readers. It is a vital part of writing skill in the humanities to be able to weave quotations and other references into your essays, so that you convey a sense of direct engagement with the texts you have been studying.

KEY POINTS

An essay should stand on its own as a *complete* piece of writing. You cannot assume that your readers have any 'special' knowledge of the subject you are writing about, nor that they have read the texts you have been studying. You have to *refer* to your source material in order to:

- *explain* the points you make
- *illustrate* them (give examples of what you mean)
- provide *evidence* to support your arguments (justify them).

2.4   Other aspects of writing

Now we will look at the *way* Philip and Hansa wrote and presented their essays. Did you find them both easy to read? As regards Philip's, my answer is, 'yes and no'. It is sometimes easy because he has a fluent way with words. But it is often difficult because he does not use enough punctuation to help us make sense of his words, and because of certain mistakes he makes. I found Hansa's essay easier to read. Her writing is more technically correct and more assured than Philip's. But I think that sometimes it is too formal and elaborate.

ACTIVITY

Look back at the essays and the notes you made about them. Look at the way Philip and Hansa *express* their ideas. Did you pick out any mistakes in their sentences, punctuation or spelling? How important do you think it is to spell words correctly?

Sentences

We can see that Philip knows what a sentence is because he writes some perfectly good ones. For example:

> In many ways going into urban life from the countryside was beneficial to woman of the upperclass.

This sentence begins with a capital letter and ends with a full stop. It has a subject (urban life) and a main verb (was). As any sentence is, it is a self-contained 'unit of meaning'. It makes sense read out on its own. The only thing wrong with it is that 'upper class' should be two words rather than one. Also, although it is not wrong to say 'woman', it sounds odd because we normally say 'women'.

But what about this one? (Read it out loud.)

> With society becoming more wealthy it was possible for the fathers and husbands to provide an even better standard of life for their wifes and daughters, more servants could be provided to do the work and this left the woman more time than ever to develop the social skills of the era, but this in turn led to extreme frustration among woman of that class.

It sounds long and rambling. But in fact all it needs is two full stops and a couple of minor corrections (to 'wifes' and 'woman') to turn it into three pretty sound sentences, as follows.

> With society becoming more wealthy it was possible for the fathers and husbands to provide an even better standard of life for their wives and daughters. More servants could be provided to do the work and this left the women more time than ever to develop the social skills of the era. But this in turn led to extreme frustration among women of that class.

Writing sentences

Every sentence needs a *verb* – a 'doing' word – and (almost) every sentence needs a *subject* – a person who, or thing that is 'doing'. Take this sentence: 'She popped the question'. 'She' is the subject (because she was 'doing' the popping) and 'popped' is the verb (because that is what she was doing). If you are not sure whether you have written a sentence, a simple test is to ask 'Does it have a subject and a verb?' – in this sentence 'it' is the subject and 'does have' is the verb.

It is quite possible to use grammar effectively without knowing the rules in a formal way. Many people can 'hear' whether a string of words is a sentence or not because it 'sounds' complete when it is. They don't have to stop and think about whether it contains a subject and a verb. If you find it isn't obvious to you, even when you read your work out loud, then you need to get some help with grammar (by going to a local class or getting a book about it). You will find it very difficult to develop your writing style until you have a good feel for what a sentence is.

At first sight it looks as if writing in sentences may be a big problem for Philip. Yet he *does* have a sense of where a break is needed – but he tends to use commas where he needs a full stop and capital letter. The sentences are there; he just hasn't *marked* them as sentences. I doubt if he needs to worry too much about this. With prompting from a tutor and plenty of practice – and especially through reading his essays out loud – his sensitivity to sentences will develop spontaneously. But the local library or bookshop would be a good place to ask about courses and books if need be.

Hansa's writing is much more assured. But, as I said, some sentences strike me as over-formal and elaborate. Take this one, for example:

> Because of this, and because an urban environment offered women so much more scope, not only to display their accomplishments but also to indulge their own desire for sociability, amusement and companions', the female population of England's towns expanded dramatically.

Too many points that are important in their own right are squashed into one sentence here. The construction is extraordinarily complicated: 'Because A…, and because B…, not only C…but also D, E and F, the female population…' It would read more easily if she removed the central part – 'not only to display...amusement and companions'. (Incidentally, she does not need the apostrophe after the 's' in 'companions'.) There would still be more than enough to think about. Also, more emphasis would be placed on the last part of the sentence, which is actually the *main point* of it. As things stand, we arrive at 'the female population…' over-burdened and out of breath, as it were.

In sentences such as this Hansa's meaning is so condensed that it gets lost. She is trying to say too much. Her sentences are over-elaborate and her meaning too densely packed. If she wrote more directly, in simpler sentences, her meaning would be clearer and she could give more emphasis to the points that are most important.

Keeping it simple

A sentence is a self-contained unit of meaning. An essay is constructed by putting these units in sequence, one after another. Meaning should flow from one sentence to the next, carrying the argument forward.

If you sometimes do not make proper sentences, or you make them too dense and complicated, your meaning becomes unclear. Your reader cannot follow you because the flow of meaning is interrupted. Until you have a lot of experience you should write fairly short, simple sentences that carry your meaning forward in a reliable way.

In the main, aim to make one point in each sentence. If a sentence delivers two points, consider splitting it in two. A reader may want to agree with one point but not the other, so it is useful to have them set down separately. Then your reader can examine the logic of each one more easily.

Punctuation

Some of the sentences we have looked at are harder to understand than they might be because they are not very well punctuated. Punctuation marks are the 'stops' in a sentence that divide it up into parts. They make it easier to follow the meaning of the words. For instance, it is easier to read this sentence of Philip's if we put a comma after 'wealthy':

> With society becoming more wealthy, it was possible for the fathers and husbands to provide an even better standard of life for their wives and daughters.

Punctuating

Punctuation is the system of signals you give to your reader to show how the grammar of the sentence is supposed to work. The basics are the capital letter at the start of a sentence and the full stop at the end. You use commas to mark off any sub-parts of the sentence. Other punctuation marks are:

semicolon ;	marks a pause which has more emphasis than a comma but less than a full stop; also often used to divide up items in a list
colon :	signals that a list is to follow
brackets ( )	always come in pairs and go round an 'aside' – a point which is not part of the main flow of a sentence. If you read 'through', missing out what is in the brackets, the sentence should still make sense
dash —	can be used similarly to brackets, but you can use just one to signal a shift to a related point
hyphen -	links words together (as above, in 'sub-parts')
apostrophe '	indicates letters missing (as in 'don't' and "phone'); also indicates belonging to (as in 'Philip's')
inverted commas ' '	discussed in Chapter 5, section 5

question mark ? and exclamation mark ! are pretty obvious. You will very rarely need to use an exclamation mark in an essay.

We all make mistakes in punctuation as we write. So it is important to check through the first draft of your essay with this in mind. When in doubt, read the sentence out loud, perhaps even in an exaggerated way, and 'listen' to where you make little pauses as you speak it. Often, you need to put in a comma at those points.

Consistency

A common problem with sentences is not making all the parts match up. What is wrong with this sentence of Philip's, for example?

> So therefore woman began to long for the urban or city way of living, if even for a short period so that they could deploy the art of socializing…

The mistake is that 'woman' should be followed by 'she' not 'they'. 'Woman' is *singular*, whereas 'they' are *plural*. (He should also put a comma after 'period', and change 'even' to 'only'.) Similarly, in her fourth paragraph Hansa refers to '*a* high ranking wom*en*'. You have to make up your mind whether you are talking about one thing or lots of them.

Another kind of matching up is making the items in a list the same kind of word. Instead of writing 'sociability, amusement and companions' Hansa should say 'companion*ship*'. The first two words are abstract nouns, so the third word in the list should also be an abstract noun. Also, some words take partners: 'not only…but also', for example, and 'either…or'. When Hansa writes in her conclusion 'women…were *neither* mainly attracted to the towns' she should add '*nor* escaping from the countryside'.

Another common slip is to have tenses of verbs not matching. Look at this sentence of Philip's:

> The women who lived a fairly comfortable style of life belonged to a class of society where the father or husband would be a land-owner.

'Lived' and 'belonged' are in the past tense. So Philip should use the past tense of the other verb in the sentence; 'would *have been*', rather than 'would be'. (Incidentally, a 'class of society' is not a place so he shouldn't say 'where'. He should have said '*in which* the father…'.)

Tenses

The tense of a verb indicates the *time* the action takes place. For example, 'I laugh' is happening in the present. 'I laughed' is what happened in the past, and 'I will laugh' is set in the future. (There are of course other tenses too.) The main thing is to be *consistent* in using them. Decide whether you are discussing the past, present or future and then stay there, unless you have a good reason for making a change.

Some of these may seem small points. But I am not nit picking, nor being critical for the sake of it. Inconsistencies such as these get in the way. They slow your readers down and distract them from taking in the meaning of your sentences. Reading is hard enough, without having our attention diverted along the way.

Choosing the right words and phrases

Both Philip and Hansa occasionally use words and phrases that don't really do the job they want. We saw, for instance, that Philip uses the word 'resemblance' when actually he means 'contrast'. Here are some other examples from his writing.

	Philip's words	*More accurate words*
Paragraph 1	'portrayal'	portrait, account
	'orientated to'	fitted for
Paragraph 2	'a greater amount of society'	a wider society
Paragraph 3	'variation of'	variety of
Paragraph 4	'certain amount of jibes'	many jibes

And in Hansa's second paragraph I'd say it is more correct to refer to the 'exercise of' skills than to the 'indulgence' of them.

Choice of words

When you are writing you have to use the words that come to you. You would never get started if you stopped to worry over each one. However, when you are reading over what you have written you should check that you have used words that convey the meaning you intended. The exact meaning of the words you use is more important in writing than in speech.

In the long run your sensitivity to the shades of meaning words carry will increase. But as you study, the best thing to do is just get on with your writing – with a dictionary at your elbow.

Writing style

As we have seen, Hansa tends to use whole clusters of words and constructions that are a bit over-formal rather than wrong. She seems to be trying to impress her reader. For example:

> They therefore fled from the country in order to escape the restrictions and consequent boredom placed upon them by the very limited pastimes that a high ranking women in the eighteenth century was permitted to indulge.

Normally, we would use a word such as 'allowed' rather than 'permitted to indulge', which sounds rather pompous. And, strictly speaking, we 'indulge *in*' pastimes. Also, 'restrictions' may be 'placed upon' people, but we don't usually say that about 'boredom'. Boredom is something we experience or suffer. It would be altogether simpler and more straightforward to say:

> So they fled from the countryside to escape these restrictions, and the boredom that resulted from having so few pastimes.

Sometimes Philip, too, seems to be striving to impress by using formal language instead of simple, direct terms. For instance, in paragraph 3 he talks about women being able to meet '...many more of the female sex' when he just means 'other women'. And at the end of paragraph 2 he says, '...so that they could deploy the art of socializing and mingling with a greater amount of society', when it would be more direct to say '...so that they could put their social skills to use, and mingle with a wider society'. Similarly, 'This transition was not without a certain amount of jibes from the male population against the women of that time...' could simply be put as 'Some men mocked these women for making the transition...'. Perhaps Hansa and Philip are assuming that they have to sound 'academic' for their tutors.

On the other hand, Philip uses a phrase from popular speech when he says that these women have 'gone down in history' as experts at organizing social events. This is definitely not an academic turn of phrase since it implies that there is one history we all agree about – a kind of 'hall of fame' for society's all-time 'stars'. (Note that Ellis herself does *not* say this; she is very precise. What she says is that women 'sometimes took a leading role' in planning certain social events such as race meetings, balls, theatre performances and concerts.) Phrases like Philip's may seem to give a flourish to your writing, but they are not appropriate in an academic essay. They are not precise enough, and they tend to raise more problems than they are worth. In any case, a flourish is not quite what you are after. What you need is a lively and compelling style that is at the same time simple and direct.

But who exactly *are* you writing for? How can you develop an appropriate style and tone of voice unless you can 'picture' your reader?

'Speaking' to your reader

Writing is a very special form of 'conversation'. As you write, you are talking to someone you cannot see and who does not reply. But you know he or she is 'listening' and reacting mentally to what you say. *You* have to take all the responsibility for deciding *what* is to be said and *how*, and for sustaining the other person's interest. You are also responsible for establishing a *relationship* between you and the 'listener'.

This is one of the trickiest things about writing. You have to convey a sense of who you are assuming your reader is and how you expect he or she to approach your words. You also have to convey a sense of who you are claiming to be – from what position you are 'speaking'. Are you speaking as an expert on the subject of discussion, as a witty entertainer, as a patient explainer, or what?

There are two issues here. You have to develop a sense of your 'audience' and of the right 'tone of voice' in which to write.

1   A sense of audience

Who should you assume your audience is when you write an essay? Is it someone who is very learned and critical, or someone who knows nothing and couldn't care less about the subject? Although your tutor is the person who actually reads your essay, he or she is not your 'audience'. The standard advice is, 'Write for the intelligent person in the street'. In other words, assume that your reader has not read the books you have been studying, but that she or he is interested in the question posed by the title of the essay and is capable of picking up your arguments quickly, provided you spell them out clearly.

2   Your writing 'voice'

Who are you to present yourself as? Basically you are expected to be a calm detached observer, pointing out to an equal (who happens not to be informed on this subject) some arguments that are relevant to a question you are both interested in (that is the question in the essay title). It is not easy to find a comfortable writing 'voice'. It may take several essays before you can settle on a satisfactory one. One of the main reasons for getting stuck at the start of an essay is trying to work out where you are 'coming from'. Sometimes you have to make several shots at your opening before you can find a voice with which you can proceed.

Essay presentation

Both Philip and Hansa presented their essays neatly, with no crossings out or obvious slips of the pen or type. And they make very few spelling mistakes. Philip puts 'wifes' for wives, 'citys' for cities and 'carreer' for career, and Hansa 'sparcity' for sparsity.

Spelling

People often worry about how important it is to spell correctly. Do you lose marks for bad spelling?

In principle, no you don't. You shouldn't actually lose marks. But it is hard for a marker not to be influenced by very weak spelling (or grammar, or punctuation). It detracts from the general impression your essay creates.

If you are really poor at spelling, don't worry that it will prevent you making progress. But don't be entirely relaxed about it either. You should make the effort to look words up in the dictionary when you are not sure about them. And it is a good idea to make a list of the words you often get wrong and try to learn them. However, it isn't worth trying to memorize great long lists of them. In general, the more you read and write the more you will develop a sense of when a word 'looks right' and when it doesn't.

If you use a word-processor for your writing it can be a great help in improving your spelling. You just instruct it to do a 'spell check' and then make a point of looking out for the mistakes you make regularly, so that you can try to memorize the correct versions.

It is important to present your essay well. Otherwise, it suggests that you don't care enough about your work to read it through and make corrections before handing it to someone else to read. And your tutor is bound to find it harder to make sense of what you are trying to say if there are too many mistakes in it. Tutors usually make allowances for the occasional blunder, but, if you want your writing to have its full impact, you must read it through carefully and correct any errors that you spot.

KEY POINTS

The *way* you write is as important as what you say. So when you are writing you must try to:
- use properly formed and mainly simple sentences
- punctuate them in a way that makes your meaning clear
- pay attention to grammar, making all parts of sentences consistent
- be precise about the particular words and phrases you use
- address your reader appropriately
- present your work with care, reading it through to correct spelling and other mistakes.

We have seen that, although there are good things in Philip's writing, there are quite a number of ways it could be improved.

To test yourself out on the points we have talked about, go back to Philip's second paragraph, starting from 'The country was no place…' and put in some punctuation and any other alterations that make it read more easily.

Here is my attempt, with the reasons for the changes I made given below. (New words appear in red.)

> The country was now no place ~~now~~ to exercise these new skills. ~~they had been taught.~~ [For one thing, females outnumbered males. ~~at that time~~] Few chances arose to meet and mingle in society. ~~with crowds of people. but~~ Most importantly, the demands of propriety required that ~~meant that~~ women's ~~their~~ conduct should be impeccable at all times. Any error could be seen in such a limited environment. So ~~therefore~~ women began to long for the urban ~~or city~~ way of living, if only ~~even~~ for a short period, so that they could put their social skills to use ~~deploy the art of socialising~~ and mingle ~~ing~~ with a wider ~~greater amount of~~ society.

Changes

- 'Now' interrupts the flow of 'no place to exercise these new skills', so I moved it to earlier in the sentence.
- When Philip wants to identify which 'new skills' he is referring to, he can either say 'these new skills', or 'the new skills they had been taught' – he doesn't need both, and it sounds awkward.
- Start a new sentence after 'taught'.
- Comma after 'thing' because it's a preparatory phrase before the main sentence starts. No need for 'at that time' because he has already said 'now' in the previous sentence. But my square brackets indicate that this sentence should really come out altogether – Ellis does *not* say this.
- New sentence at 'Few'; 'crowds of people' isn't quite right for gatherings of people of this rank – 'in society' or 'socially' captures it better.
- No need for 'but'– just start another sentence at 'Most'.
- What the demands of propriety imposed on women were 'requirements' not 'meanings'. 'Women's' instead of 'their', since readers might be losing track of who 'they' are by now.
- New sentence at 'Any error'. And 'could' is better than 'would', since not every error might be spotted.
- New sentence at 'So'. Doesn't need both 'so' and 'therefore'. Needs the plural 'women'. Doesn't need 'urban' and 'city'. Good to put a comma after 'living', and after 'period' – since 'if only for a short period' is a side point.

The rest we've already discussed.

How do these compare with your improvements ? It doesn't matter if yours are different. Many of these changes are more a matter of taste and judgement than 'right and wrong'. The main point of the exercise was to focus your attention on the details. Your aim is to achieve directness, simplicity and a nice flow to what you write. You will gradually develop a feel for what works best and when, and your tutor will probably have plenty of suggestions to make.

2.5   How good are Philip's and Hansa's essays?

There are no *absolute* standards against which the quality of an essay can be judged. It depends on the course you are studying – its content and aims, and the level at which it is pitched. Your tutor will tell you how your essays stand within the context of your course. What we *can* do is outline the strengths and weaknesses of Philip's and Hansa's essays. In the second question of the Activity on page 105 I asked you to think about this and to make your own lists. Have another look at them and see how they compare with my judgements.

Philip's essay

Strengths

- a reasonable understanding of the general issues Ellis deals with
- a good basic structure
- some good sequences of argument
- a promising feel for language
- fluency of expression

Weaknesses

- the wrong title and consequently a lack of focus
- argument is loose-knit in places – some points are not relevant
- occasionally misrepresents Ellis
- uncertainty regarding the overall argument, so arrives at a weak conclusion
- poor punctuation
- the language is artificial at times – striving for stylishness, instead of clarity

Overall, Philip's essay shows plenty of promise. He develops some useful ideas and has the makings of an effective writing style. However, there are some points to work on. If I were his tutor writing to him, this is what I would say.

Dear Philip,

Well done for getting yourself over the hurdle of sending in your first essay, especially as it's such a long time since you last did this kind of writing. The essay shows a lot of promise. You obviously worked hard with the Ellis article and you have done a good sound job of getting your thoughts together for this essay. The structure is very solid and, what is more, you have a nice fluency to your writing which gives you a good base to build on.

Where you have come a bit adrift is in not working with the exact title you were set. This made it hard for you to come to a strong conclusion at the end. Also, as you will see from my notes on the script, there are some places where your line of argument could be strengthened. And you will need to spend a bit of time working on your punctuation, as well as a few other points of grammar and choice of words. None of these should present a major difficulty – they will gradually come right with practice. Just make a habit of reading my markings and notes carefully and then work out how you can make things read more easily.

Broadly, you are doing exactly the right thing – which is to pitch in and work as best you can with the ideas you have been reading about. As you keep doing this you will find your style getting sharper and your grip on your subject more secure. Keep up the good work.

Hansa's essay

Hansa's essay would get a higher grade than Philip's. But, like his, it has both strong and weak points.

Strengths

- subtle understanding of Ellis's argument
- excellent focus on the question in the title
- generally sound structure
- some very fluent writing in places
- plenty of attack in the opening – pacey first paragraph
- good sense of how to draw a conclusion

Weaknesses

- one weak point is in her paragraphing
- in places, language over-formal and sentences too densely packed
- needs to clarify her line of argument (that is, reorganize a little)
- could pay even more attention to signalling how the argument is developing
- doesn't quite set up the frame of reference within which she is arguing

If I were Hansa's tutor, I would write to her in congratulatory and encouraging terms. This is a very creditable job of getting to grips with quite a subtle article and an essay title which demands a bit of careful thought. Hansa has studied well and attacked her essay with insight and flair.

This comparison of Philip's and Hansa's work shows that essays *can* be good in different ways. And it shows that when we make judgements about the quality of an essay, we need to think about *both* the quality of the ideas in it and the way these ideas are presented. After all, the ideas only really 'exist' in the form we see them on the page.

As I've suggested, judging one essay against the other I'd say that Hansa's is better than Philip's. That is mainly because she addresses herself to the essay question she was set, and puts together a reasonably well-connected argument that leads to an answer to it. Along the way, she shows that she has a good grasp of the ideas contained in her source material.

Re-working Hansa's essay

Now we have looked at Philip's and Hansa's essays in such detail, what have we learned? Perhaps the best way to answer that is to write another version of the essay, building on all the things we have discussed. In fact, I have taken the basic content of Hansa's essay, tidied it up and shuffled it about a little to bring out her argument more strongly. (However, as we shall see in Chapter 5, this is not the only possible way of structuring an argument in answer to this question.) I have also woven in some of Ellis's terms, and more reference to her article, to show what is meant by 'referring to your source material'.

ACTIVITY

Read the version below and compare it with Hansa's. Then look quickly back through all the Key Points boxes in this chapter to see whether what we said should be done is achieved here.

Did eighteenth-century women migrate to towns mainly because of the attractions of the towns, or mainly to escape from life in the countryside? Discuss in the light of Joyce Ellis's article.

In eighteenth-century society, women of the higher ranks were generally seen as 'embodiments of their husbands' and fathers' status'. This role placed tight restrictions on what they could do and whom they could meet. They were expected to appear fragile and innocent, yet highly civilized. This involved having 'accomplishments', such as the ability to embroider, play the piano and sing, which they were taught at boarding schools or by private tutors. And 'propriety' demanded that they mixed only with people of a similar social status.

However, life in the country gave these women little opportunity to fulfil this conventional role. The homes of the upper ranks of society were scattered across the countryside. 'Suitable' transport was often unavailable, and in bad weather it was either impossible or dangerous to travel on the unpaved, unlit country roads. Consequently, they could only occasionally mix socially. Meanwhile, they could no longer take part in the management of the household and country estate as increasing wealth resulted in those roles being carried out by servants and professionals. Nor could they engage in the rural pursuits enjoyed by their menfolk – riding, hunting and fishing. So these highly trained and sophisticated women were often left with unfulfilling, boring lives – passing their time in and around the home sewing, reading, writing letters and taking short walks – unable to display their accomplishments, or keep themselves usefully active, or find much amusement.

By contrast, in an urban environment many people of similar rank lived in a much smaller area. There was a variety of social venues, and good transport and street lighting, so that women could mix in 'respectable' society frequently and in safety. Indeed, some created an active role for themselves as planners and organizers of events such as balls, race meetings, plays and concerts. At these and other social gatherings they had plenty of scope for displaying themselves and their accomplishments, while also enjoying the amusements of shopping and taking tea with companions, and amenities such as circulating libraries. During the century, the female population of England's larger towns expanded dramatically.

This migration was presented by satirists of the day as evidence of women's improper desire for 'freedom from male control' (as well as their 'natural' frivolousness). However, Ellis believes this to have been far from the case. It was, she argues, a society in which women's lives were largely defined by their relationships and duties to their menfolk, whether in the country or the town. But town life, at least, offered these women some satisfaction, in enabling them to play out their essentially 'decorative' role to good effect. In the countryside that role was for the most part an empty one.

So, in flocking to the towns, high-ranking women of the eighteenth century were neither mainly attracted by the pleasures of the towns nor trying to escape from the boredom of life in the countryside. Mainly, they were seeking to fulfil their conventional role as fully as possible.

3 WHAT IS A GOOD ESSAY?

So far, we have been analysing essays in a practical way, looking at the strengths and weaknesses of some actual examples, rather than at formal rules or abstract ideas about essay-writing. Now, though, we need to summarize.

I suggest this because I think you already have a fairly good idea of what effective writing is. I don't think the point of a chapter like this is to tell you much that is devastatingly new. It is to bring into sharper focus what you 'know' already, and to help you apply these intuitions as you develop your own writing. It is one thing to be able to see when someone else's writing is ill-planned and confusing, but quite another to be able to pinpoint why and to avoid making the same mistakes yourself. So have your notes on the final part of the Activity on page 105 in front of you and compare them with mine which are set out below.

KEY POINTS

Criteria of good essay-writing

When a tutor reads your essay, she or he will be asking the following questions.

- Have you answered the question in the title?
- Have you drawn on the relevant parts of the course for the main content of your essay?
- Do you show a good grasp of the ideas you have been studying in the course?
- Have you presented a coherent argument?
- Is the essay written in an objective, analytical way, with appropriate use of illustration and evidence?
- Is the essay clearly written and well presented?

3.1 Answering the question

An essay can be good in almost every other way and yet be judged poor because it ignores the question in the title. Strictly speaking, I should say 'it ignores the issues presented in the title' because not every essay title actually contains a question. But, in fact, there is usually a central question underlying an essay title, even when it takes the form of a quotation from a text followed by the instruction 'Discuss'. And you need to work out what that underlying question is, because this provides a sharper focus for your 'answer'. But, in any case, it is generally a good idea to ask yourself 'Have I answered the question?'. That's because you are never just asked to 'write all you know' about a subject, or simply describe something. You are set a specific problem to think about in the light of what you have been studying.

Your task is to argue a case in relation to the question posed in the title. Everything you say in the essay should be relevant to that task. It isn't enough that a point you make is interesting to you (as we saw with Hansa's interest in women's oppression). You have to convince your readers that the point has some bearing on the title and is therefore worthy of their attention.

That is why it is a good rule always to write the title of the essay across the top of your opening page. It reminds you what you are supposed to be doing and where your readers are starting from when they begin reading your essay. And you must always stick exactly to the title you are given – not devise a modified version of your own, as Philip did. A tutor faces a demanding job commenting on and assessing your essay. The job is made possible by setting it up in a tightly defined way, so that it is clear what has to be done to show a certain level of achievement. This is the purpose of the title and the reason you have to work to it at all times. Tutors can be quite impatient if you insist on demonstrating a whole lot of knowledge you haven't been asked for.

3.2 Drawing on course material

Unless you are taking a course in creative writing, essays are generally meant to help you consolidate what you have been studying. You are not asked to answer the question in the title 'off the top of your head' nor on the basis of some prior knowledge. You are expected to take the essay as an opportunity to scan back over what you have been reading or doing and select relevant material from that. The tutor who marks your essay will already have in mind a range of course material that could be used in answer to the question. Your ability to make good, relevant selections from that material is part of what she or he assesses.

If you miss out some of the important ideas and information, or make the occasional strange selection, it may not matter provided you make good use of other relevant material. But if you try to answer the question entirely from knowledge drawn from outside the course, you may run into trouble. In effect, what you are doing is focusing attention on the fact that you *haven't* used the relevant material in the course and the *new* knowledge available to you. Also, it is often very difficult for tutors to evaluate your account of material they are not familiar with. They are unlikely to have time to read, view or listen to your sources. So, you may find you receive a higher grade for an essay that *is* based on course material, even if it has been put together hastily, than for one on a topic you *think* you know much more about.

3.3 Showing a good grasp of ideas

To show your grasp of the ideas you have been studying you have to express them for yourself, *in your own words*. Your tutor will certainly be looking out for signs that you understand the centrally important issues. For example, Philip showed that he understood the significance of Ellis's point about women's loss of a household management role. But he was very vague about the effects this had on women's lives in the countryside, which suggests he hadn't really sorted out that part of his argument. His tutor would see that he needs help with it. Your tutor has to be able to see your thought-processes at work in this way in order to give you the kind of advice and support that will help develop your understanding. So what you must avoid doing is using other people's words.

Plagiarizing

When you are writing an essay you are often working with ideas and terms you are not familiar with. This makes it difficult for you to produce a clear, coherent argument and you may become anxious about whether you will 'get it right'. To be on the safe side, some students are tempted to 'lift' sections of words from textbooks and articles and put them in their essays without using quotation marks or acknowledging the source. In other words, they try to pass these words off as their own. This is known as 'plagiarism'.

Tutors are usually very familiar with the difference between the way students write and the way experienced authors write, and soon notice when a student lurches between an 'expert' and a 'beginner' style. A particular giveaway is when most of the words are as in the original except for one or two (changed for purposes of camouflage), which stick out like sore thumbs because they are in a different style. Another is when smoothly flowing sections of writing are interspersed with short, inelegant linking phrases. It seems that most people write particularly badly when they are trying to stitch together someone else's words. Because you are not in control of 'making' the sense as you write, plagiarizing actually makes your writing worse.

This approach will not get you good marks. Indeed, when tutors spot what is going on (which is not difficult) they will tend to assume you understand very little and mark you down. Worse, you do not develop your own writing style. If you become locked into the sterile and tedious business of parroting other people's words rather than expressing thoughts for yourself, then you are likely to remain a beginner for a long time. And you will not learn much about the ideas in the course either.

There is only one way to learn to *use* ideas in writing and that is to practise expressing them in your own words. They may not come out very well to begin with but, like a learner in any field, you have to be prepared to make mistakes sometimes. It is through letting your weaknesses show that you learn how to do something about them, and allow others to help you learn.

3.4   Presenting a coherent argument

Presenting a coherent argument is closely linked to 'answering the question'. The essence of an essay is that it sets out to be an argument about the issues raised in the title. Even if you have a lot of good material in it, it will not be judged 'a good essay' unless the material is organized so that it hangs together. This implies two things:

1   You need to sort out your points into groups so that they can be presented in a *structured* way, giving the essay a beginning, a middle, and an end.

2   You need to keep a *thread of meaning* running through your essay. Each sentence should flow on from the previous one, with adequate *signposting* to help your reader follow the moves you are making.

Presenting a coherent argument is also closely linked with 'showing your grasp of ideas'. One of the reasons why your writing tasks are set in the essay form – the form of an argument – is because that makes you *use* the ideas you have been studying to *say* something. Anyone can copy material from books. The point of an essay is to make you *think*. When you present a coherent argument you are showing that you can *take hold* of the ideas and *organize* them to do some work for you.

Perhaps you were a bit puzzled when I said earlier that Philip and Hansa both argue quite well, in view of the criticisms I had made of their arguments. What I meant was that they both have some sense of what an academic argument should be like. Most important, they show they know that arguing in an essay is not the same thing as 'having an argument' in everyday life, when people tend to confront each other – often being stubborn, emotional, irrational, and making wild generalizations. An argument in an essay aims at the very opposite of these things. The writer must be objective, precise, logical, and concerned to back a case with evidence.

Philip and Hansa sometimes write in a vague and woolly way, but at other times they are quite precise – accurate in what they say, and careful to use the right word. This shows they know it matters which words you choose in making a particular point, even if they don't always find them. And they connect up the stages in their argument well enough to show that they are aware they should present their ideas in a reasoned or logical sequence, not spray them around any old how. Even if they do not use enough evidence from Ellis's article to illustrate and support what they say, they use enough to show they know this matters too. In other words, they both give signs of recognizing what it means to write an academic essay, and this is fundamental to everything else.

3.5 Taking an objective, analytical stance

One of the things I said an essay should be is 'objective'. What does that mean? Being objective about something means standing back from it and looking at it coolly. It means focusing your attention on the 'object', on *what* you are discussing, and not on yourself and your own (subjective) feelings about it. Your ideas should be able to survive detailed inspection by other people who are not emotionally committed to them.

An essay should argue by force of reason, not emotion. You must make deliberate efforts to develop a style of writing that is cool, dispassionate and fair to all sides. That means you yourself must be open to doubt and criticism. Your arguments should be presented in the spirit that your reader might not agree with them. And if you want to dispute a claim someone else makes, you are expected to have analysed that claim carefully, to argue your case and provide evidence for your point of view, rather than setting out to criticize or cast doubts on your opponent's character or motives. You should be respectful to other writers. You should assume that you are writing as a member of a community of equals, all of whom are intelligent, open-minded, fair people. You should write on the assumption that your readers are also members of that community, and that they will be interested only in your *reasons* for thinking what you do. They will not be interested in you as a person, or in your ideas because they are *your* ideas.

3.6 Writing clearly

A final point that emerged from our analysis of Philip's and Hansa's essays was that a good essay is easy to read. Grand-sounding phrases and elaborate sentences do not make an essay impressive. Clarity and economy are what count. Such ease of reading is achieved at several levels.

Technical considerations

Handwriting

At the most basic level, ease of reading depends on the quality of your handwriting (unless of course you type or word-process your essays). It is only fair to your tutor to try to make your writing as legible as possible. This will take time and care. But when you have spent a long time putting an essay together, it is a waste if what you say is misunderstood just because your writing is misread. It is also prudent to take care. It would be an angel of a tutor who was not a bit impatient at having to spend ages trying to make out your handwriting. If it is really dreadful you will have to get someone to tell you which letters are hardest to read and practise straightening them out, rounding them more, or whatever. Having said that, most tutors have resigned themselves, in the course of duty, to becoming expert at deciphering all kinds of scrawl. They will usually do their best not to be too influenced by it. (Actually, a lot of students complain that they can't read their tutors' scribbled comments on their essays, so this is not a one-way street.)

Layout

Again, in an obvious way, your essay is easier to read if it is set out neatly on the page. You should use lined A4 paper and leave generous margins for your tutor to write comments. Write on one side of the paper only – this makes it much easier to cross-refer from one section of the essay to another. Make sure you leave spaces between paragraphs. This is all straightforward stuff, but the point is that you should 'stand back' from your finished essay and look at it as an 'object' you have created. Does it look inviting to read? It is surprising how many essays have words squashed onto every square centimetre of the page. Be 'page-proud' and generous with space. Unless your essays look as if *you* care, why should anyone else?

Grammar, punctuation and spelling

As we have seen, these contribute enormously to ease of reading. The whole point of punctuation is to help the reader approach your words in the right way, and the rules of grammar are what enable the reader to construct the sense intended by the writer. Mistakes in either make the reader stop to work out what is being said. Poor spelling can also cause frequent interruptions. Meanwhile, the reader 'loses' the thread of your meaning. None of these abilities is easy to improve quickly, and all fall beyond the scope of this book. But if you think you are particularly weak in them you should seek help. Take comfort from the thought that your tutor will usually try to 'read through' to your intended meaning, and will also try to help you improve.

Language

Your language should be direct rather than fancy. Don't strive for effect. You should always go for short and simple sentences where you can – especially when you are building up a basic essay-writing style. You can play with more elaborate words and grammatical structures later, when you have established a secure basic technique. Don't beat about the bush; pitch straight in to answering the essay question in a direct, purposeful way.

Fluency

Try to make your essays flow from one sentence to the next. As we have seen, this is partly a matter of *structure* and partly of *signposting*. It is vital to think of your essay in terms of its overall structure – to move points around, and cut and trim, in search of a clear sequence for your ideas. Then, having worked out a structure, you have to 'talk' your reader through it, emphasizing the key turning points in the essay, summarizing where you have got to, showing how each new point follows from the last, and finally bringing it all to a conclusion.

Explaining

You need to be able to think of things from your reader's point of view. The reader cannot see into your mind so you have to explain your points quite fully and carefully. You need to give examples to illustrate what you are talking about and to justify what you say. In other words, you need a sense of your 'audience' and you have to work out how to 'speak' to these readers in the right 'tone of voice'.

4 CONCLUSION

Finally, a few key messages to take from this chapter. One is that there is no great mystery about what good writing is. We can recognize it just by reading it. The difficulty is how to produce it, which is what the next chapter is about. However, since there are different aspects of writing well, you will find it useful to return to the 'Criteria of good essay-writing' on page 136 from time to time to consider how your writing is developing. When you are about to submit an essay to a tutor, or after you get it back with comments on it, you can check through the list to see what progress you are making on each front.

Another point you might think about is that, in the processs of reading Philip's and Hansa's essays, you have had a glimpse into the role your tutor plays. As you saw, it isn't easy to read other people's writing and make sense of it. Nor is it easy to pinpoint what their strengths and weaknesses are. There are two lessons here.

1   Be sympathetic to your tutor and present your work as well as you can.

2   Don't be too upset or too irritated if your tutor misses your point, or if he or she offers advice you don't think is appropriate or makes comments you don't think are fair. It is almost impossible to get things right all the time.

Last, take away the knowledge that *you don't have to get your writing perfect before submitting it.* The essays we have looked at are nowhere near perfect, but they are fine as early attempts. In fact, there isn't such a thing as 'perfect' anyway. There are many different ways of writing a good essay. These students did exactly the right thing by simply 'having a go'. You have to assume that your first attempts will not be wonderful and just get on with it. A good learner in any field is prepared to make mistakes.

CHAPTER FIVE

HOW TO WRITE ESSAYS

1 INTRODUCTION

In Chapter 4 we looked at *what* you are trying to produce when you write an essay and now, in this chapter, we turn to the vital question of *how* to go about it. Most people find writing hard. The adult students who wrote the short essays you saw in the last chapter said that writing them took a lot longer than they expected. They also said they found the task difficult. I am not saying this to alarm you, but to cheer you up when *you* find it difficult. You are not alone if you find writing takes a long time and never seems to go smoothly. If you get stuck, it is *not* a sign that you are a poor writer or that you are necessarily going about it the wrong way – maybe you just haven't had much experience of this kind of writing.

Looking on the bright side, writing can also be *extremely rewarding*. Very many of our interesting thoughts drift away from us before we really formulate them properly. Looking back, it is as though those thoughts never existed, so it can be very satisfying to preserve at least some ideas on paper. And the discipline of writing often has the effect of shaping your ideas into a clearer, more coherent form. This is also a source of great satisfaction. The fact that you are working your way through this book suggests that you are interested in the realm of ideas. So I would guess that the rewards of writing ideas down are likely to appeal to you.

To strike another positive note, since you now know for certain that writing essays is always a challenging and demanding activity, you can *prepare* yourself by working out a sound strategy. That way, you can enjoy the satisfactions of writing without feeling overwhelmed by the challenges. It is all too easy to become tormented by the kind of doubts and frustrations Nathan experienced in Chapter 1, but you don't *have* to be as helpless as he was in the face of them. There are many ways of taking a more active and constructive approach to writing, so that you can drive on through to the end of a task. The purpose of this chapter is to explore them.

I should point out at the start that there is no single approach to writing that suits every writer, or every kind of writing task. But it would be a long and tedious chapter if I tried to cover all the options. Instead, I shall follow a particular line of thinking and present a basic writing strategy, which I assume you will modify to suit your own style of studying and your own purposes. Even the process of rejecting some of my suggestions will help you firm up your own approach.

Reading guide

As with Chapter 4, there is a lot in this chapter. If you want to divide up your reading, I suggest you take it in the following three stages:

1   Section 2
2   Sections 3 and 4
3   Sections 5 and 6.

2 THE CRAFT OF WRITING

How do you imagine really experienced writers go about their writing? Do you picture them sitting in front of a blank sheet of paper or word-processor screen, just letting the words spill out? Do you think of them as 'inspired' to compose those words in beautifully formed sentences all ready to be sent off to the publisher? This is an image we all have lurking somewhere at the back of our minds. But writing isn't like that. And it certainly isn't with the kind of 'expository' writing you do as a student, which involves analysis, description, explanation and argument. Putting well-formed sentences onto paper ready to send off to your tutor is the *last* of a number of stages in the process of putting together an essay. Before that a great deal of thinking and preparatory work has to be done.

It is helpful to think of writing as a 'craft': to have in mind someone like a furniture maker setting out to make a table. First he or she has to conceive a design for the table, then choose the wood, prepare it, measure it, mark it, cut it, shape it, make the joints, and finally put it together. And even then it still has to be smoothed, waxed and polished. Writing essays may not be quite such an elaborate process (or you may not have time to let it be), but it is something similar – requiring you to work methodically through a whole series of closely linked activities. If you just sit down when you have finished reading the course texts and try to write a whole essay in a single sweep, you will get nowhere. The job is too big. You *have* to break it down into stages. Then you can take it stage by stage and work your way through to the finished product.

Learning the craft of writing

Each of the stages involved in essay-writing is important in its own right. And each requires you to develop your own techniques.

If you are to fulfil your potential as a writer you need to give careful thought to each stage, experimenting with different approaches and looking back over your successes and failures to refine your strategy.

You can't expect to be in control of every aspect of essay-writing straight away. At first you just have to get on and do some writing without worrying about it too much. However, when your writing is not going as well as you'd like, you will find it very useful to be able to think about the *separate stages* involved. These are:

● thinking about the essay title

● gathering together material for the essay

● getting some ideas onto paper

● organizing the material

● writing a first draft

● reviewing your work in the light of the essay title

● writing a final draft.

We'll look at each of these stages.

2.1   Thinking about the essay title

It is best to take a good look at the essay *title* a few days before you intend to get down to serious work on the essay. This is useful in two ways.

● It helps you make sure that you cover all the necessary ground in your preparatory reading.

● Having the title floating about in the back of your mind for a few days helps you to clarify what the question is asking, and to work out a strategy for approaching it.

Then, you need to study the *wording* of the title in detail. A very useful technique is to highlight or underline what you think are the *key* words or phrases.

ACTIVITY

Underline the words you think are particularly important in the essay title we worked with in Chapter 4. Add any other marks that might help you focus on the essentials.

Did eighteenth-century women migrate to towns mainly because of the attractions of the towns, or mainly to escape from life in the countryside? Discuss in the light of Joyce Ellis's article.

I would be inclined to underline and mark up the title as follows:

Did eighteenth-century women <u>migrate to towns</u> // **(a)** <u>mainly because</u> of the <u>attractions of the towns</u>, or **(b)** <u>mainly to escape</u> from life in the <u>countryside</u>? <u>Discuss</u> in the light of Joyce <u>Ellis's article</u>.

The markings draw my attention to the following points.

1   The segment *before* the dividing mark // (that is, 'Did eighteenth-century women migrate…') is the 'stem' of the question; the whole question is about *why* these women migrated.

2   The marks (a) and (b) make clear that I am given *two* possible answers to that question – both of which are underlined – and remind me that I must discuss *both*.

3   The word 'or' suggests that these answers are alternatives – *either* (a) *or* (b).

4   The word 'mainly' is underlined in both places because it implies that, even though these are alternative answers, both may be true to some extent; my task is to say whether one or the other was *more* important. (This means that I don't *necessarily* have to come down on one side or the other in the end – I may want to give a rather different answer.)

5   The word 'Discuss' suggests that there are arguments *for* and *against*. This, too, indicates that my essay should look at *both* sides of the question. If I end up wanting to propose a different answer, it must not *take the place of* discussion of (a) and (b), but come out of that discussion.

6   Finally, I must remember that I am not asked to discuss my own views on the matter. I am to pay particular attention to the arguments that are discussed in *Ellis's article*. I may want to bring in some additional material of my own, but I must be certain to give the arguments in the article pride of place.

Having done that, I can now focus more sharply on some of the things my essay needs to give attention to. I can see that the words in the title put quite a tight frame around what is to be in the essay. I am certainly not being given free rein to follow up any themes that happen to be dear to my own heart.

KEY POINTS

- Thinking carefully about the *title* is a vital part of producing a good essay.
- It is very important to look carefully at *each* of the words, or phrases, in turn. Otherwise you can easily waste a lot of time writing about things that will bring you very little credit.

2.2   Gathering together material for the essay

When you start to work in earnest on an essay, your first task is to go back over what you have been studying recently to check what might be relevant to it. One reason why it is useful to have read the essay title some time in advance is that you can hold it in the back of your mind *as you work* on your course material. Then, when you come across something that might be useful, you can make a note of it at the time. But, whether or not you have already made some notes as you studied, you will need to go back over relevant parts of the course making notes specifically for the purposes of the essay.

Figure 5.1 shows some notes I made towards answering the question on the Ellis article. If I were making them just for myself they wouldn't be as full and I would use many more abbreviations, but they have to make sense to you too. However, you will see that they are more *selective* than the notes I made in Chapter 2 (p.56) because this time I *only* need what is *relevant* to the essay title.

Evidence of migration

Demog. research: female pop. of larger towns 'expanded dramatically' = migration (net inflow)

'Evidence' from contemporary literature (e.g. Etherege, satirists)

Reasons for migration

1	According to satirists –	women rejecting male control; by nature self-indulgent
2	According to Ellis –	women's role had become 'dysfunctional' in country

Women's 'conventional' role

•	embody men's status = correct behav. ('propriety')	fragile, innocent; trained for accomplishments/ display; only mix with social equals
•	lost earlier, wider role (in home/estate management)	incr. wealth → tasks done by servants & profs → more leisure

Arguments 'against' country

1	Company restricted	few =s within travelling distance
2	Travel difficult	lack of transport, bad roads, bad weather (e.g. Coke)
3	Few activities/pastimes	sewing, reading etc. (no country pursuits, unlike 'active' men)

i.e. can't fulfil conventional role/life constrained and boring

Arguments 'for' town

1	Easier to socialize (display skills)	more = s in smaller area; more mobile, safely
2	More events/amusements	theatre, concerts, shops etc. (Roche)
3	Wider role	organizing social events

i.e. can fulfil 'proper' role/life much less restricted and more fun

---

Figure 5.1   Notes from the Ellis article taken specifically for the essay.

The importance of note-making

The stage of writing down notes for an essay makes a very important contribution to your studies in general. While you are searching through your course material to pick out what is useful for the essay you are forced into thinking hard and purposefully about the content. *Choosing* what is relevant and what is not makes you focus very sharply on *what a text is about*. This process of selecting produces some of your most intensive *learning*. So you need to allow plenty of time for this aspect of essay-writing.

A basic mistake Nathan had made, when we came across him in deep despair in Chapter 1, was trying to start writing *without* a set of notes around him that already contained a lot of the material he needed for the essay.

KEY POINT

- Don't try to start writing an essay until you have collected together plenty of *notes* drawn from the course material.

2.3   Getting ideas onto paper

In writing notes for an essay, you have already begun the process of putting ideas onto paper. However, up to this point the main emphasis has been on getting hold of what *other* writers have said. Once you have gathered your material together, you need to switch to thinking in terms of what *you* are going to say. You certainly don't want to 'copy out' what you have taken from others. That would contribute nothing to your understanding of the subject or your ability to express ideas. It would also be boring and gain you very little credit. Instead, at this point you need to put the notes you have made to one side for a while, and develop your *own* thoughts about how to approach the question you have been set.

For this you need a pen in your hand, and some bits of paper which you *know* will not be part of the final essay. That means you won't worry about what you write on them. You need to tell yourself that what you are about to write is *not final* – that you will quite happily scribble all over it, change it all around and eventually throw it away. So just jot down *lots of thoughts* relating to the title without worrying about what comes out, or in what order. Write down points *for* and *against* – perhaps a whole sentence if one comes to you in a nicely rounded form – and any *extra questions* that the essay title throws up. It doesn't matter if these jottings make no sense to anyone but you. You will only use them for a day or two, as your essay takes shape, so it is perfectly all right if they are bitty and undeveloped. Look, for example, at Figure 5.2.

Did eighteenth-century women <u>migrate to towns</u> // (a) <u>mainly because</u>
of the <u>attractions of the towns,</u> or (b) <u>mainly to escape</u> from life in the
<u>countryside</u>? <u>Discuss</u> in the light of <u>Joyce Ellis's</u> article.

Question is, (why) did they <u>migrate to towns</u> – mainly (a) or (b)?

     Ellis says, because couldn't carry out their <u>role</u> in
       countryside → not really (a), nor (b)?

                                  v. boring

(BUT, sounds as if <u>did</u> want to escape from ∧ life in country, and town life
was far more <u>attractive</u>???)

Satirists say, because wanted to be free of men's control and have fun
→ both (a) and (b)? (Which <u>mainly</u>?)

(NB need to sketch out reasons why country 'boring' and town life
'attractive'.)

But can't just assume they did migrate?? – what's the <u>evidence</u> for it?

What was <u>women's role</u> anyway?

NB Their relationship to <u>men</u>: 'embodiments of their h's and f's status'.

                                'decorative'
They were expected to be fragile and innocent ∧ and to obey the rules of
'propriety' (correct behaviour) – e.g. only mix with equals ...

Figure 5.2   Sample of jottings related to the essay title.

Basically, what you are doing is trying to *trap* some of the ideas floating
about in your mind. As you study your course material, all kinds of thoughts
are set in motion. They are milling around in your mind in an unresolved
way. You now need to convert some of them into a more *fixed* form. You
also want them *outside* your head, where you can look at them and work on
them. You do this by *very quick, rough jotting.* Be prepared to flit from
point to point, so that you don't risk losing some thoughts while you are in
the process of writing others out. Once a few thoughts are out there on
paper you can move them around, draw arrows linking one with another,

cross bits out, tidy them up, think of better words here and there, and so on. But you need to get quite a lot of words on paper before you start too much 'organized thinking'. Trying to take a highly 'planned' and critical approach too early on may dry up the flow of your ideas.

Using a computer for word-processing

We saw in Chapter 3 how you can use a computer to communicate with other students and your tutor (section 2.5), and for a variety of other study activities (section 4.2). But by far the most common use of computers in arts and humanities education is for *word-processing*. Word-processing has transformed the age-old business of getting words and sentences onto paper. It enables us to make changes and corrections, and move whole sections of text around, without having to actually 'cut and paste' or start all over again. Instead of the laborious business of writing out a new draft each time you make major changes, you just alter the existing draft and it is done. This is a great liberation. Because you don't have to worry about the huge time-investment involved in re-drafting, you can be more relaxed and creative about the way you write.

You can start using your word-processor even at this early stage of getting some ideas down. Simply type in the questions and fragments you would otherwise have jotted on paper – starting a new line whenever a new thought occurs to you. You can print out at any point, have a good look at your jottings and perhaps alter them by hand before typing in changes. On the other hand, some people much prefer to begin by working on paper, and start word-processing only at the next (organizing) stage. Unless you are a fast typist, you probably *will* do a lot by hand at this stage just because you need to get your ideas down quickly, before you 'lose' them. You have to work out what suits you best – working almost entirely on screen, or switching back and forth between hand-writing and word-processing.

Incidentally, if you can't type well or at all, a computer program can teach you relatively quickly.

A very significant point about this jotting activity is that it helps you overcome the problem of the 'blank page' (or screen). It often happens that our minds seize up as we take the plunge and try to write the first sentence of an essay. That's why it is best *not* to begin by writing the first sentence – nor even to begin with sentences at all. When you are busy jotting down odd notes, with your thoughts in full flow, you will sometimes find that whole sentences come out fully formed. If so, you can set them aside to use later. But there's no need to force the pace.

Once you have a lot of words jotted down you have something to work on at the next stage, instead of sitting wondering where on earth to start. It is much easier to produce a basic supply of sound and interesting ideas in this informal way than to achieve inspiration on the run, while you are writing out a full draft. And it is worth generating *more* ideas than you will eventually need, so that you can throw some away and be left with just the best.

> **KEY POINTS**
> - The quality of the essay you eventually produce is closely linked to the richness and range of your initial, informal jottings.
> - If it is generally hard for you to find *enough* to write about in your essays, you should put more effort into this ideas-generating stage.

2.4 Organizing your material

When you have 'externalized' enough of your ideas (giving them an existence on paper, outside your mind), you need to start getting them into some sort of organized shape. Even a crude kind of dividing up will be useful to begin with. For example, you could begin by separating your jotted notes into points *for* and points *against* the proposition in the title. (In this case, points 'against' country life and points 'for' the town.) If it helps, cut up your notes into strips and sort them into piles. Then you can look at one of these groups and begin to work out the order in which to take the points within it, perhaps separating them into sub-groups. After that, you can sort through the points in the other group. Then you will be in a position to begin sketching out a plan of how the essay might be organized.

Simpler is generally *better* when it comes to essay plans. You will see that in my plan in Figure 5.3 I have opted for the classic structure for a short essay:

1   introduction
2   the countryside (points 'against')
3   the town (points 'for')
4   comparison between 2 and 3
5   conclusion.

In fact, I considered swapping the second and third stages around, thinking I might discuss the attractions of the town first since they seem so obvious. But when I tried to sketch out a plan, I found it difficult to know where to discuss the shift in these women's role from household manager to the more 'purely' decorative. According to Ellis, this shift is of underlying importance – before it took place women were (presumably) content to live in the countryside, and it was only as or after their role became more restricted that they migrated to the towns. So everything else hangs on that social change. Because what she discusses was, historically, a move *from* country *to* town I decided to stick with that as a structure for the essay.

> **KEY POINT**
> ● It is important to think in broad strategic terms in sketching your essay plan. You need to work out a *sequence* of points that enables you to arrive at the conclusion you would like to draw.

What I have sketched in Figure 5.3 is an *outline* of the *argument* for my essay. Later on I would add more words and short phrases indicating what illustrative examples I would use from Ellis's article, and the textual detail I would refer to at each stage.

Essay plan

Para. 1: Introduction   Why did women migrate?

Need to consider fact of migration (towns 'expanded dramatically') in context of women's changing role:

(a) women's conventional role	'embodiments... status' accomplishments/skills, fragile, innocent
(b) earlier, role more robust (incl. house/estate management)	but, incr. wealth → profs./servants → more leisure
(c) contemp. (satirists') explanation	escape male control, self-indulgence, but...
(d) Ellis's argument (in nutshell)	more leisure → frustration because less opportunity to use skills (irony)

Para. 2: In the countryside

(a) 'propriety' (i) mix w. socially = travel difficult	few living nearby, and... lack of transport, bad roads, bad weather
(ii) no country pursuits (unlike men) → sewing, reading etc.	
(b) few activities/pastimes	

Para. 3: Contrast with town life

(a) wider 'respectable' society (i.e. more opps. for company/display)	more people/smaller area easy to travel; lighting & safety
(b) more activities/amusements	theatre, concerts, shops, etc
(c) new, wider role	organizing events

Para. 4.: Comparison of country and town

To an extent, true that women were:

– escaping from country; restricted, and daily life boring

– attracted to towns: companions, and life more fun

Para 5: Conclusion

BUT (Ellis) the main cause of migration because in country could not fulfil conventional role (as status symbols) and in town could.

Figure 5.3   Sample essay plan.

When you have a longer essay to write and more texts to work from you may want a more elaborate structure than this. However, there is *no virtue in complexity* for its own sake. You will find your essay *easier to write* if it has a simple structure. Equally important, your reader will find it *easier to read*.

Working towards an essay plan

The stage when you are working towards a suitable plan for your essay is often quite unsettling. Because your thoughts are slowly resolving themselves, the 'shape' of your essay may take some time to emerge. When it does, it may be so simple as to make you wonder why it took so long. However, this simplicity is a sign that your thoughts *have* reached the stage of resolution.

When you are satisfied with your outline plan you can then go back through your essay notes labelling each point according to the section of the plan in which you think you will use it – or ruthlessly throwing it out because it doesn't fit. Remember that you also have to be *selective* in order to write *within the word limit* set for the essay.

From this point on, you can either work with your plan *plus* separate notes, or *incorporate* your notes into an extended, more fully worked out plan and work mainly from that. Although it may seem time-consuming to do a full plan before you start writing, it can save you a lot of time at that next stage. But it's up to you; it depends how thoroughly you like to be prepared before you get down to writing.

In any case, have your essay plan in front of you – so that you can keep in mind the *overall structure* of the essay as you start writing. Then you are less likely to get stuck, or waste time wondering what you are going to say next.

KEY POINTS

- The planning stage is of crucial importance, since it is at this point that your argument acquires its central coherence.

- If you tend to write *too much* in your essays, you need to make tough decisions at this stage. You *must* limit your essay plan to what can be managed in the space you have.

2.5   Writing a first draft

You have already decided *what* you are going to try to say. Now you have to concentrate on *how* to say it in a way that your reader will be able to understand.

It may seem that this ought to be a fairly straightforward stage, since it is simply the writing out of all you have planned in note form. However, it is more than that. In a way, writing is a very particular kind of *conversation*. You are 'speaking' to someone – your reader. You have to take the ideas set out in your notes and *explain* them in whole sentences. You have to give examples to *illustrate* to your reader what you are talking about, and provide *evidence* to support your points. And you have to take your reader carefully step by step *from* the question in the title *through* the points you want to make, *showing* how they follow one from another towards your conclusion.

> **KEY POINT**
>
> ● If you tend to write *too little* in your essays, you may not be giving enough attention to how much *explaining* you have to do to get your points across to someone else. You probably need to discuss more examples and show more carefully how your points link up with each other.

To write fluently and convincingly you have to be able to give all your attention to 'speaking' to your reader. That is why you need to have done so much preparatory work in the previous stages. If you are trying to 'think up' the *content* of the essay at the same time as you are *addressing* yourself to your reader, you will usually do one or other job badly. Either your points will be weak and disconnected, or your language will be insufficiently clear and expressive. Worst of all, you may run out of ideas and hit the dreaded 'writer's block' – when you can't think of anything worth saying at all.

> **KEY POINT**
>
> ● 'Speaking' in writing takes all your powers of concentration. Because of this you need to have the substance of the essay already worked out.

Finding your 'voice'

Writing is a very formal activity compared to talking. As I said in the last chapter, *you* have to make all the decisions about what the topic is, how it is going to be treated, what big issues are at stake and, especially, what kind of *relationship* you will have with your reader. In a conversation all these decisions are taken collectively. They 'emerge' as the discussion progresses. But in writing, you also have to take responsibility for making sure that the reader is continually kept in touch with what this one-sided conversation is all about.

Unfortunately, the strain of taking all that responsibility tends to cramp your style. You may find it difficult to get meanings over to your readers with the clarity and force you can achieve in conversation. You sense what you *want* to say but when the words come out on paper, and you read them over, you find you haven't managed to convey quite what you intended. The words are there to be read but they come across rather dull and leaden. There seems to be no 'voice' speaking them.

Most of us have had far more practice in establishing 'spoken' relationships than 'written' ones. So one approach to the problem is to *practise* occupying the role of writer: to do much more writing, on a regular basis. You might find it helpful to do just ten minutes writing *every day*, only for yourself, on any subject at all. Write quickly, without worrying about how 'good' it is, but write in sentences. Above all, just *keep going* for those minutes. When you have finished each day's writing, put it away. Then look it over some days later and try to find bits where you feel that your 'voice' breaks through – where your writing achieves some force: possibly a phrase, a sentence, or even a whole paragraph. In this way, over a period of time, a number of things should change:

- Sheer accumulation of practice in 'being a writer' takes some of the awkwardness and formality out of your writing style.

- The freedom to write 'anything' releases you from the constraints that normally crab your writing.

- The repeated hunting for your 'voice' sharpens your perceptions of when you are writing powerfully and when you are not.

- You become more aware of what kinds of orientation towards your writing help you to break through to an authentic writing voice.

You don't have to start your drafting with the introduction to the essay and then work steadily through to the end. You may find it easier to start somewhere else. For instance, it might be safer to get some of the main sections down on paper so you have a clearer sense of what it is you have to introduce – and how much space you have left for introducing and concluding the essay. (It is awfully easy to spend far too long beating about the bush in your introduction.) If you find a section going badly, it may be as well to break off and write another part, or else to start the section again, approaching it in a different way. But don't throw the old version away. You may end up preferring it, or being able to combine bits of both.

Once you have started writing, try to keep the momentum going; keep yourself writing. It is not helpful, for example, to spend ages going back over each sentence as you write it – changing this word and then that, and eventually changing them back again. It is better to press on to the end of the first draft, coming back to the whole thing afterwards to see how it reads. While you are writing you are too close to the words to make reliable judgements about them, and it is easy to waste time fiddling about with small changes. A fresh run at the piece might show a useful way of recasting a whole sentence or paragraph.

Experimenting with writing

Keep in mind that there is no right and 'perfect' way of making your points. Every piece you write has the potential to be written in many different ways. Yet when you start writing you may be able to see only one way ahead. It would be a good exercise to have to write every essay in three different versions – too idealistic of course, and exhausting. However, you *can* sketch several different outline plans; and you *can* write two or three different versions of a particular paragraph, or several ways of beginning and ending the essay. Working in this open, experimental way helps to make you feel less imprisoned within a particular approach to the essay and style of writing. It draws attention to a range of possibilities open to you, and to your powers of expression. Paradoxically, it also makes it easier to be content with what you do produce in the end, because you know it is only one of many versions you might have written, none of which would be the 'perfect' one.

It is easier to take an open, experimental approach to your writing if you use a word-processor to draft your essays. Because you know you can change anything at the click of a button, you can type away quite freely – it will not take long at all to come back later and add, delete or move things around ('cut and paste'). You can make several shots at composing the same sentence – starting a new line each time – and then quite easily move bits of each version around, combining them to form the sentence that satisfies you. If, as you type, an idea, phrase or sentence comes to you that might be useful in another part of the essay, you can put in a page break and 'dump' it clear of the part you are currently writing, ready for when you want it. This stops you worrying about 'losing' something you might just need and enables you to keep moving forward. Again, you may want to print off every now and then to see how things are coming along.

It is at this stage that it matters most whether you can type quite quickly or not. If not, you can't really take full advantage of the possibilities for writing spontaneously and flexibly that word-processing offers.

2.6   Reviewing your draft

When you have finished your first draft it is extremely important to force yourself into reading it over. This is an uncomfortable process but it is absolutely necessary. You are bound to have made mistakes and left things out. When you have your nose pressed right up against your sentences and paragraphs you cannot tell how they work, nor how the essay works overall. If you have the time, it is best to leave the reviewing to another day. Then you can view the essay from a greater distance – more as your reader will approach it.

If you are using a word-processor I suggest that you print out your draft essay and *review it on paper* rather than trying to read it through on screen. For some reason it is just easier to spot little mistakes on paper, in wording, grammar and spelling for instance.

As you read your draft through, check for those little mistakes as well as asking yourself the following questions:

- Do the sentences 'work'; that is, does the 'sense' keep moving along reasonably smoothly? A good check is to read the essay out loud. If you find you stumble, or have to pause to snatch at the meaning, then probably you have a sentence that is too long or has something important missing (such as a verb, or a link to the previous sentence).

- Do the divisions into paragraphs work? Do the breaks feel as though they come at the right places – when the focus of the discussion shifts?

- Have you given enough explanation and illustration for the intelligent 'person in the street' to be able to understand what the discussion is all about?

- Does the argument work? Does it make sense as you move from point to point? Have you signalled the main moves clearly to your reader?

- And perhaps the most important check of all, have you *answered the question in the essay title?*

To get a sense of whether your sentences and paragraphs flow and your argument works, it's best to read the essay through quite fluently. But in order to pick up small mistakes in wording, punctuation and spelling you will have to read slowly and deliberately, word by word. This means you cannot check everything at the *same* time. You need to read the essay through at least twice, looking out for *different* things each time. If you can, ask someone else to read it through as well – it is often quite difficult to spot your own mistakes.

Reading aloud

It is very helpful to hear what a written piece sounds like when read out loud. It gives you a new angle on how well the sense flows through the sentences. What is more, if you know someone who is prepared to listen (a fellow student, a friend, or a member of your family), reading to another person can help with the problem of establishing a *sense of audience* and a *voice*. It hardly matters whether or not the listener comments on what you have written, because in the process of speaking the words to someone you will *hear for yourself* which passages work best and which don't come across as you intended.

Most people feel rather shy about exposing their written work to other people, particularly when they are operating in unfamiliar territory. However, you are writing in order to be read by somebody, somewhere. If you can summon up the nerve to 'be there' as the message is received by someone, it gives you fresh insight into the process of communication you are engaged in.

As a result of the reviewing process, you may find there is some restructuring that can be achieved without too much disruption to the various parts of the essay. But it is more likely that you will be putting in extra words here and there, changing the punctuation and correcting spelling. You will rarely have time to consider any large-scale changes, and they are unlikely to be appropriate since you have other calls on your study time. That is not the point of reviewing. At this stage you have to 'go with it'. The review is essentially a tidying up process and usually a very necessary one.

2.7   Writing the final draft

At last you come to the stage when you write the words your tutor will see. In principle this is straightforward, since the final draft is simply a neat and tidy version of your corrected first draft. With all the other pressures off, you can now concentrate on keeping your handwriting legible and your page layout neat (assuming you are hand-writing rather than word-processing). You should write your name and essay title at the top of the first page, allow generous margins, and then set out to produce the polished end product of all your labour – remembering to number the pages afterwards.

Why bother doing more than one draft?

Since the last stage of 'copying out' a neat draft is rather mechanical, you might wonder whether it is really a sensible 'investment' of your study time. Could you not hand in a carefully corrected first draft? There are two reasons why I would say you shouldn't.

First, since you invest a lot of time in your writing, you might as well see the process through and produce something that *looks* as good as it is. It is important to the spirit in which you undertake the whole essay-writing venture that (like the craft worker) you are committed to taking some pride in what you produce. A well-presented essay is good for your own sense of satisfaction. What's more, your tutor is bound to be more kindly disposed if your essay is not peppered with illegibilities, inconsistencies and mistakes.

Second, and more fundamentally, the *intention* to write a final draft has a powerful impact on the process of producing the *first draft*. The fact that you know your first draft is *not* your final word takes a lot of the pressure off at that crucial stage, when you are trying to turn your plans and your notes into intelligible sentences and paragraphs. You will write much more fluently and creatively knowing that you can come back and change it later. Not only will you write better essays in the short term, you will also develop your writing style more effectively in the longer term because you will have more scope to experiment with your writing.

So although it *is* a slog writing out a neat final draft, it is far from being a fancy extra. If you are serious about becoming a better writer, you cannot really avoid writing more than one draft of your essays. And in the end I doubt whether it takes very much longer. Trying to write your finished version straight off builds up the pressure on you, stifles your creativity, and leads directly to problems of drying up. Mental blocks use up time far less productively than writing out a final draft.

Having said that, we all work differently. So don't let the thought of writing out a final draft put you off writing altogether. Think seriously about it, and then do what suits your purposes and your circumstances.

If you use a word-processor, preparing a final draft hardly seems like a separate stage at all. Once you have entered all the changes you decided to make as a result of reviewing your first draft, you have your completed second draft. But it is wise to print it off once more, and look through your essay for a last time just to make sure you are happy with it. You can check that you are satisfied with the lay-out of your work: your headings; the appearance of the type and any tables or diagrams you have included; the width of your margins, and so forth. These things are easy to change even at this late stage. You should use the *word count* facility to make sure that, having made lots of changes, your essay is still within the word limit. And you can call up the dictionary held in the computer in order to check your spelling automatically. In fact, this is the last check you should make; when you have made all the other changes you want to, tell the computer to do a final *spell check*. Then you are ready to hand in your work.

3 WHY TREAT ESSAY-WRITING AS A CRAFT?

As anyone who has tried knows, it is very easy to get stuck when you are writing essays – to sit wondering what you are trying to say and how you can get yourself moving again. It is enormously helpful to be able to break the job down into smaller, more manageable tasks, which you can take on one at a time. It helps to dispel some of the mystique that surrounds writing to think of it as a fairly ordinary activity of making a finished product through a series of practical processes; to think of yourself as a craft worker going through a series of closely-linked stages. It also gives you a chance to think *strategically* about your writing. You can *plan* a sequence of activities which makes sensible use of the time you have available. And since you have a set of identifiable tasks to work at, if you *do* become stuck it is perfectly possible to move on to a different task. If you find, for instance, that you have run dry as you are 'getting your ideas onto paper' then you can move on to thinking about your plan.

> **KEY POINT**
> - Awareness of the distinct stages of essay-writing greatly increases the options open to you and gives you more control over the writing process.

Now that we have been over the stages in detail, I'll summarize them.

The seven stages of essay-writing

Taking in the title	Underlining the key words in the essay title and thinking about it over a period of days.
Gathering material	Gathering together notes for the essay from various sources within the course.
Generating ideas	Getting ideas on to paper; quickly jotting down thoughts, sample sentences, etc.
Planning	Organizing your notes into a simple outline plan.
First draft	Writing a first draft; 'talking' your reader through your argument.
Reviewing	Reading over your work in the light of the essay title and correcting errors and omissions.
Final draft	Writing a final draft, paying attention to legibility, accuracy and general presentation.

Although it is very helpful to be able to think about these stages separately, it would be a mistake to treat them as completely separate and rigidly sequenced. In fact, they overlap considerably and are best tackled flexibly. As you plan, you may suddenly think of another source book you ought to have a quick look at, or some notes you made that you could use after all. When you are writing the first draft you may well realize that an aspect of your outline plan is not going to work out, and that there is a much better solution – leading you to go back and rework the plan. And when you are reviewing your first draft, you may suddenly think of a question you wrote down in your jotted notes which could be recast and used as a good introduction to the essay. All the stages of essay production are bound up with each other and you often need to move back and forth between them. Obviously there is a certain logical sequencing to them. You can't *start* your reading of the source texts *after* you have written the first draft. On the other hand, you might well go back to *check* something. So no single process is entirely complete until the whole is complete.

This might raise doubts as to whether it is really worth making distinctions between these stages. If you are moving back and forth between them all the time, can they really be regarded as separate stages? Is it even *possible* to distinguish between the 'first' and 'second' draft if you are using a word-processor? I think they *can* be regarded as separate stages, and *should* be even if you use a word-processor. That is because each stage makes a particular contribution to the end product. In other words, each stage has a different function in the production process. The *functions* of the seven stages are as follows.

Taking in the title	Formulating the overall purpose of the essay.
Gathering material	Working out what use you can make of the course material you have been studying.
Generating ideas	Capturing your own thoughts on paper.
Planning	Working out what shape to give to the argument of the essay.
First draft	'Speaking' your ideas to your reader, explaining your argument (translating your plan and notes from your own 'private' language into a shared, 'public' language).
Reviewing	Quality control.
Second draft	Presenting a polished end product.

These functions cannot be separated neatly from each other in terms of the practical operations you have to perform in writing the essay. However, *each* has to be fulfilled if you want to produce an essay of the quality you are capable of. So it is an advantage to be able to identify them and focus attention on each one.

Drawing on the image of a craft worker also reminds you that you would not expect to produce a perfect chair at your first attempt. It isn't done by a blinding flash of inspiration. Everybody makes a mess to begin with. You have to learn through experience how to blend a complex sequence of activities together, how much time to give to each, and where your own particular strengths lie. You should not be too despondent if your first efforts at essay-writing turn out less well than you hoped. Becoming skilled in a craft involves accepting that there will be a period when your output is not particularly impressive. As you practise you will get better. Seeing writing in these practical, workaday terms helps you to get stuck in and build up that practice – instead of sitting wondering whether you are an unacknowledged genius, or worrying about quite the opposite.

Finally, in case this list of very practical stages makes essay-writing sound a rather technical business, with much less scope for *originality* and *creativity* than you had imagined, I must stress that this is far from the case. It is a misleading notion of creativity that promotes the image of a free spirit wandering wheresoe'er inspiration takes it. Creative work is nearly always achieved within well defined *limits*. It is out of the struggle with constraints that creative solutions are born. If you *strive* to be original, you will often find that other people are unimpressed. By contrast, you may find you are praised for the originality of your ideas when you have done no more than say what seemed perfectly obvious to you. Originality is something you are likely to stumble across rather than achieve by deliberate effort. What you need is a framework within which you can see a way of taking the next step forward. Viewing your writing as a craft involving a series of stages will enable you to do that.

KEY POINTS

A 'craft' view of essay-writing implies that:

- You should treat essay-writing as a *practical* task, not as the search for some mysterious kind of 'inspiration'.
- Ideally, it is not a *one session* job, but should be spread out over several days.
- You do not simply sit down with a blank sheet of paper and start to write.
- In fact, you do the bulk of your work *before* you start writing 'proper'.
- You break the task into stages, so that you can tackle it *a bit at a time* rather than facing the whole thing at once.
- You think *strategically* about how to approach the writing assignment in all its stages.
- You work *flexibly*, moving back and forth between the stages as necessary.
- If you get stuck you move to a different stage.
- The quality of your essay-writing depends on a range of separate skills, not on a monolithic 'ability to write'.
- You can work at developing your strategies and skills within each separate stage.

4 MAKING YOUR ESSAY FLOW

During the discussion of students' essays in Chapter 4, we took a close look at the link words you can use in an essay to carry your meaning along and to 'signpost' the direction your argument is taking as it unfolds. This section reviews the issues raised there and looks at them in more depth.

4.1 Link words

In Hansa's and Philip's essays, we saw the way they sometimes link one paragraph to the next by referring *back*, in summary form, to what they have just said. Or, sometimes they use words that show the *relationship* between what they have just said and what they are about to say next. For example, they might indicate a *change* of direction in the argument by using words such as 'however', 'on the other hand' or 'but'. I also mentioned that Ellis's article is itself a good example of how you can make such links, so it is worth taking a quick look at how she, as a professional writer, achieves a 'flow' of argument.

ACTIVITY

Turn to the Ellis article again for a few minutes and look at the way she makes links between paragraphs 3–8. *Underline* the linking words or phrases, then work out how they help to achieve the transfer of meaning from one paragraph to the next.

(You may feel you have seen enough of the Ellis article by now. However, since you know it so well, it will be easier to look past the 'message' and concentrate on the way it is written. Also I shall be able to express points more succinctly, knowing that you already know what the article is about.)

How did you get on? I underlined the following words:

Paragraph 4:   '*This...*'
Paragraph 5:   '*With*', '*however*', '*these* tasks'
Paragraph 6:   No link word at the start; 'Women, *however...*' (beginning of second sentence).
Paragraph 7:   '*Even if...*'
Paragraph 8:   'Towns, *in contrast,...*'

Ellis begins paragraph 4 with the word 'This', which refers back directly to what she has just said at the end of the previous paragraph (that is, 'female behaviour was... dysfunctional in a rural setting'). She goes on to say 'This [dysfunction] was perhaps most obvious in the case of women from the higher ranks of society...'. So the meaning flows from paragraph 3 to 4 as Ellis takes up the 'story' of women's changing role, which in fact continues up to the end of paragraph 5. (Check this for yourself.) The connections between paragraphs 4 and 5, in the middle of this account, are more complicated. Paragraph 5 begins, 'With an increasing wealth and sophistication of society, however, many of these tasks were taken over by professionals…'. '*With…*' suggests a continuing story (or history, flowing on from paragraph 4), but the '*however*' that follows this opening phrase signals a significant *change* in these women's role. '*These*' tasks (another reference back to what was explained in paragraph 4) were now carried out by other people. This is a very artful and economical series of links I'd say, which imply processes of both continuity and change.

There is no link word or phrase between paragraphs 5 and 6 at all. However, Ellis doesn't need one because she simply repeats the last word of paragraph 5 at the start of the next. Notice that a change of topic is indicated part-way through, though, with 'Women, *however…*'. So in the space of some five lines Ellis has managed to change the subject from women to men and back again without ever leaving us confused.

'*Even if* a carriage was available…' at the start of the paragraph 7 suggests a *qualification* to the claim made at the end of the previous paragraph, about women's lack of mobility. And it also takes Ellis neatly on to another aspect of the same topic (the dangers involved in travel). She begins a new paragraph at that point precisely because it is a *different* aspect of the topic.

Finally, at the start of paragraph 8 'Towns, *in contrast…*' signals a complete change of subject.

In this way, Ellis manages to introduce and discuss different aspects of her subject while maintaining a thread of meaning throughout, which the reader is able to 'follow'. She links *analysis* in paragraph 3 with a developing (explanatory) *narrative* in paragraphs 4 and 5, to *further analysis* in paragraph 6 and *description* and *illustration* in paragraph 7 – and so on.

Breaking 'rules'

When I was at school we were told never to start a sentence with 'and' or 'but'. Is Ellis breaking the rules then, for example in the second sentence of paragraph 3? In fact, the rule *is* a useful one when you are not very confident about sentence structure. These two words can tempt you into leaving half-formed sentences lying around in the hope that an 'and' or a 'but' will connect them up to something.

In formal grammatical terms these words are 'conjunctions', which are placed between two equal items within a sentence to link them together. Strictly, they should not be used at the boundaries of a sentence. On the other hand, they are so useful as economical devices for carrying meaning over from one sentence to another that it is often worth breaking the formal rule, provided you know what you are doing. 'But' is particularly useful because it is such a quick way of saying 'I am now going to balance something against what I have just been saying'.

KEY POINT

- A writer carries a *thread of meaning* through a piece of writing by using linking phrases that take you on from one sentence to the next. These show you how to approach each new sentence, given what has been said in the last one.

4.2 Signposting

Some of the links we have just looked at serve a signposting function as well. For example, 'This' at the start of paragraph 4 both connects up with what Ellis has just been talking about (the reason for women's migration) and at the same time launches a different direction to the argument (an account of women's changing role). 'Towns, in contrast…' clearly signposts a new departure. At other times, Ellis uses a signposting phrase to draw things together: 'All the evidence indicates that…' in paragraph 1, for instance. And in the last two paragraphs of the article she signals a summary of what she has been saying with 'Although…, on the whole…'. This is followed by the suggestion of a final reckoning in the 'And yet…' of the concluding paragraph.

The need for sign-posts

When you are writing an essay you are 'talking' your reader through an argument. In order to follow your train of thought the reader has to know what questions and issues to hold in mind: what direction you are heading in and why. Readers have their *own* trains of thought which they are likely to follow in preference to yours unless you keep them in close touch with what you are doing. To maintain the thread of argument for the reader you have to pay attention to signalling what is going on. One of the main ways of doing that is to use *linking* phrases whose function is to pass the meaning across from one sentence to another, and *signposting* phrases which show your readers where they are in the development of the argument. Some phrases perform both these functions at the same time.

An important aspect of being skilled at the craft of writing is to have a good repertoire of handy words and phrases you can call on to do this job for you (see Chapter 4, section 2.3).

In an essay you may also need to indicate progress on a broader front, using phrases such as 'Before discussing X we must ask question Y', or 'having considered the arguments against, we should now…', or 'a final set of issues we must take into account is…'. But you don't have to place a dutiful 'sign-post' on everything you do. It can become boring and overdone. In the end, you have to make judgements about how much signposting your reader will find helpful. When in doubt, though, it is best to err on the generous side. It is seldom as obvious to your reader as it is to you where your arguments are leading.

> **KEY POINT**
>
> ● Signposting reminds your reader from time to time where you have reached in the argument and points the way you are going.

4.3   Sentences and paragraphing

Another way a writer signals the unfolding of an argument is through the organization of the words on the page: the way they are grouped together in *sentences* and the sentences grouped into *paragraphs*.

When we examined students' essays in Chapter 4, I pointed out the advantages of aiming at short sentences whenever possible. However, there are also advantages in *varying* the sentence *lengths* in order to shift the rhythm of the essay in places and maintain the reader's interest. Ellis, for example, writes fairly long sentences on the whole, so the occasional short ones in between have a somewhat 'dramatic' effect. Look for instance at: 'What women sought in the towns, the satirists argued, was freedom from male control.' (paragraph 3); or 'Unfortunately, well-born women were much less mobile than men.' (paragraph 6). Short, punchy sentences such as these can be used particularly effectively in the introductory and concluding sections of your essay. But you will probably need to use longer sentences when you are explaining and developing your argument.

Similarly, you can vary the *number* of sentences in your paragraphs to alter the texture of the writing. If you look at paragraphs 5 and 6 of the Ellis article, you'll see that they are quite a bit shorter than the surrounding ones. It is significant that they contain the two underlying planks of Ellis's argument about the 'dysfunctional' role of women in the countryside: respectively, the way their role became reduced, and the demands that 'propriety' made on them. Just as with the short sentences, they stand out from their surroundings and pack more 'punch'.

Paragraphs are clusters of sentences in which you normally discuss *a single* aspect of the topic, or one main theme. In other words, paragraphs mark the natural breaks in your argument, when the focus of your attention shifts. Each one should have its own job of work to do for your essay. And you should avoid making them *very* long. Because paragraphing is also a means of signposting the direction your argument is taking, readers will get lost if the signs are too far apart or are confused by a mixture of themes.

Playing with sentences and paragraphs

The way sentences and paragraphs are put together can do a lot to lead readers through an argument and bring out its force. Each paragraph does a specific job within the argument of the essay and each sentence makes a specific contribution to the paragraph, but as a writer you have a great deal of scope as to *how* you make them achieve those functions. For instance, you can make sentences and paragraphs long, *or* you can make them short, *or* you can vary them deliberately. Developing an effective writing style is partly to do with playing around with the effects that can be achieved and learning how to keep the focus of your reader's attention where you want it.

What we have been looking at is how you guide your readers through your essay; how in your introduction you pick up your readers 'from where they are', by getting hold of their attention and starting off a train of thought. Then in the main body of the essay you divide up what you want to say into paragraphs and lead your readers through from section to section. Finally you draw together the ideas you have been developing and try to show the reader what has been accomplished.

KEY POINTS

Guiding your reader through your essay involves:

- using link words to show the relationship between one point and the next
- signposting the stage your argument has reached and what direction it will take next
- grouping sentences together into paragraphs, in which you discuss different aspects of the topic
- varying the effect of your writing, by varying the lengths of sentences and paragraphs.

Having looked closely at Ellis's writing in these chapters, I hope you will now be in a position to make further explorations of your own. If you are interested in developing your writing style, the more time you spend working out how other people's styles work and the more attuned you become to the various effects that can be achieved, the greater will be your awareness of the range of options open to you and the greater the breadth of your verbal imagination.

5 MAKING A CONVINCING CASE

As you know, an essay should have an argument, but how do you persuade your reader to take your argument seriously? The fact that *you* hold a particular view means nothing to your reader unless you can show *why* you hold it. You have three basic weapons available to you in this cause. One is to show that you have drawn your ideas from an *authority* on the subject. The second is to offer *evidence* to support your case. And the third is to use *logic*. However, each requires a certain amount of know-how to be used effectively.

5.1   Using ideas drawn from other writers

Since one of the purposes of an essay is to show your grasp of the course you are studying, you are bound to draw heavily on other writers' ideas. In effect, the *point* of an essay is to provide a brief guided tour around established debates about the topic defined in the title. But as well as introducing a selection of relevant ideas from those debates, you have to give details of where they come from.

Listing references

Whenever you draw on another writer's ideas you should make a reference to the *particular* piece of writing you are working from. Then, if they want to, your readers can go and find it to check whether you have represented the author's views fairly and accurately – or just to read it themselves because it sounds interesting. The usual way to do this is to provide a list of references at the end of your essay, for example:

Ellis, J. (1995) 'On the town: women in Augustan England', *History Today*, vol. 45, no. 12 (December), pp.15–25.

There are different ways of presenting references and your tutor will tell you which 'convention' she wants you to follow. But, however you set references out, you must always include as *much* information as possible since the point is to help your reader find the article easily.

At the point *in the text* when you introduce the work, you simply refer to the author by last name and add the year of publication, in brackets: (Ellis, 1995). If you quote from an article, or refer to a very specific piece of information (a table of figures, for example), you must also include the page number of the quotation or reference: (Ellis, 1995, p.23). So, from your text, readers can turn to the list of references included at the end and find the information that enables them to locate the article; then, using the page number, they can find the table you refer to or the words you quote from it.

In most essays you are likely to be referring to quite a small number of texts over and over again. If so, you don't need to go through the full rigmarole every time you refer to them. After the first reference to Sharma (Sharma, 1994), you can say 'as Sharma argues' – assuming the same source as cited the first time, until you say differently. (However, if you are making a very specific point it would still be useful to put the page number in brackets.)

> **KEY POINT**
> - In an essay you have to work with *other people's* ideas. However, you are expected to *acknowledge* where the ideas come from – to say 'as Ellis argues' or 'according to Sharma's account', and provide the *reference*.

Quoting

At some points you may want to use an author's exact words, in order to convey the precise point he or she makes or to provide evidence that the author did indeed say such a thing. In most essays you shouldn't need to quote from secondary sources very often, since the essential point is to learn to write in your own words, not use other people's. However, when you do quote we have seen that you must provide a page reference in your text . In such cases it is also *essential* that you *use quotation marks*. For example, you might write:

> In Ellis's view it was 'vital that [these women] conformed to contemporary norms which had shifted...towards an ideal of delicate, innocent and essentially decorative womanhood'.

Notice that I have inserted the words 'these women' here, to allow the sense of the sentence to be read properly. To signal that this is *my* addition, I have put these words in square brackets. I have also left out a few words that I didn't need but, by using three dots (called an ellipsis), I have again signalled the change.

This exactness in the use of other people's words is extremely important. You may *think* you have done a pretty good job of capturing the essence of the author's ideas. But, when you attribute words to somebody, it is vital that you reproduce those words *completely accurately* or give a clear signal when you have made any changes. In some cases, getting just one word wrong can completely change the meaning of a quotation. So when you do quote you *must* be accurate.

In Chapter 6 you will find more detailed information about quoting from and making references to a range of sources.

> **KEY POINT**
> - Everything between quotation marks, including punctuation, should be *exactly* as in the original text. If you deliberately add or omit something, you should *signal* the changes with square brackets or with dots.

Avoiding plagiarism

While we are on the subject of working with other people's ideas, I must reaffirm an important point made in Chapter 4, section 3.3. The emphasis has to be on 'working with' other people's ideas, rather than 'reproducing' their words. If you rely on copying your material directly from a text, without using quotation marks and acknowledging your source, you will be accused by your tutor of *plagiarism*: that is, in effect, of 'stealing' other people's ideas. In the world of writing and ideas, plagiarism is a serious offence.

What's more, you might be guilty of plagiarism without even being aware of it. As you are reading an article you may jot down passages from it in note form and, later on, working through your notes for an essay, simply forget where you got these passages from and assume they are 'your' words. You can avoid such 'accidental plagiarism' by getting into the habit of including a reference to your source as a *heading* in your notes, and using quotation marks *whenever* you write down another person's words. But this also underlines the importance of the point made in Chapter 2, about 'translating' what you read into *your own words* as you make notes.

In any case, you have quite a fine line to tread between being 'accused', on the one hand, of not making *enough use* of the writers you have been reading in the course and, on the other, of having followed them *too slavishly*. One of your early tasks as a student is to get a feel for how to strike the right balance.

> **KEY POINT**
> - If you rely heavily on another writer's words and also fail to use quotation marks and references to acknowledge your borrowings, you will be accused of *plagiarizing*.

Avoiding idiosyncracy

If using other people's ideas is a delicate matter, so is using your own. (Again, I referred to this in Chapter 4, in section 2.2). You will find that the same tutor who criticizes you for staying too close to the course texts may also criticize you for being *idiosyncratic* – that is, going off into a discussion of your own pet themes. You may find you are both encouraged to bring your own thinking and ideas into your writing, and also criticized when

170

your tutor does not find them relevant. If you take off on a line of your own without showing how your thoughts are linked to the main debates in the course, you will be told your ideas are idiosyncratic. Until you get into the swing of this kind of writing it is safest to go for large doses of the ideas in the course and small doses of your own. In fact, your own ideas often emerge most clearly and convincingly when you are discussing the ideas of others.

KEY POINT

- You cannot assume that your ideas hold any interest for your reader unless you can show clearly how they connect with other debates in the subject.

5.2 Using evidence

What about supporting your arguments with evidence? What exactly *counts* as evidence? Simply 'telling stories' drawn from your own or a friend's experience does *not* count as convincing evidence. *You* are not a reliable witness as far as your reader is concerned. Your account will be seen as a 'subjective' one (because it is slanted in line with your personal opinions and beliefs). Your experience or views cannot be used to 'prove' a case. You need to draw your evidence from elsewhere.

Essentially this means drawing on research that other people (such as Ellis) have done. Ellis herself does this in her article, when she draws on the findings of demographic research. She has also researched primary sources such as contemporary diaries, letters and plays. In principle, we could check these sources for ourselves. (Providing 'evidence' in support of your judgements about these kinds of texts is discussed in Chapter 6.)

So, you are often drawing your evidence from information contained in the *same* course text from which you draw your basic arguments and ideas – as is the case with Ellis's article. Nevertheless, you need to get into the habit of referring to the *specific* evidence on which you are basing the points you make (Etherege's play, Sophie von La Roche's observations), even though it has already been done in the course text. It is important that *you* show how to draw appropriate conclusions from the evidence. The fact that the text author has already drawn conclusions is not going to convince the reader that *you* understand how the evidence works. You have to *show* that you do.

KEY POINT

- When you make a claim about the way things are or were, you must offer the reader *evidence* for that claim – as well as say where it comes from.

Illustrating

'Illustrating' your points is sometimes confused with giving 'evidence' in support of them. When you present an argument, you are often using words and ideas that are open to a range of interpretations. *Illustrating* a point is giving an *example* that makes your meaning clear and helps to fix what you are saying more precisely in your reader's mind. So, when Ellis says that men actively enjoyed their life in the countryside she illustrates this claim by giving specific examples of the pleasures they enjoyed: riding, hunting, fishing and shooting. This helps us imagine how they spent their time and so appreciate the point she makes.

And when she describes Lady Jane Coke's fate, stranded in her house for four months during the winter of 1748–9, Ellis is illustrating her point about the tedium of women's lives in the countryside in a particularly vivid way that sticks in our minds. However, at the same time as illustrating this point, the example *also* offers 'evidence' in support of the claim that these women's lives were tedious: the quotation ('continual rains') suggests that the information is drawn from an account given by someone who was actually there – possibly from Lady Coke herself, in a diary or letter. So it is 'first-hand' evidence.

Perhaps the fact that some examples can be used to illustrate a point *and* provide evidence to support it accounts for the confusion I mentioned just now. Of course, if you *can* find effective examples that do both jobs at once, they are very economical to use (taking up fewer of the words available to you). So Lady Coke's experience would be a good example to use in this essay.

5.3   Arguing logically

The third way of convincing your reader is by logical argument; in other words, by showing how the case you want the reader to accept follows *by force of reason* from things we assume the reader already accepts. In everyday speech people can be quite careless about saying that something follows from something else. Often they simply mean that most people accept that it does. However, when you *write down* an argument it becomes much easier to spot sloppy thinking or weak links in the argument. Your reader is quite likely to stop and think, 'Hang on a minute – that doesn't follow'. So you have to give more attention to what you claim follows from what.

We cannot go into the technical details of logical argument here (though, if your subject is philosophy, you may study logic in its own right). However, I can *illustrate* the form of a sound argument by taking an example from the opening of this chapter. On page 143, I said:

The fact that you are working your way through this book suggests that you are interested in the realm of ideas. So I would guess that the rewards of writing ideas down are likely to appeal to you.

How well does this work as an argument?

1   I have taken it as a premise that you *are* working your way through the book. (A premise is a starting point in a sequence of logic – a proposition that is assumed to be true (that is, which the argument will take for granted).)

2   I have concluded from it that you are interested in ideas.

3   Then I have gone on to draw a second conclusion from the first – to the effect that (since you are interested in ideas) you will find writing satisfying.

This gives a linked sequence of ideas: A leads to B; B leads to C. I am arguing that, if you accept A, you should also accept that B and C follow.

However, you might point out that the premise does not hold in your case, because you are *not* working your way through the book – only 'dipping in'. Or, even if you conceded this premise, you might challenge my *first* conclusion, saying, 'No, I'm not very interested in ideas at all. I'm just looking for a few tips for my essay'. Or you might object to the *second* conclusion, saying that it is perfectly possible to be interested in reading and thinking about ideas without wanting to write them down. So what I have argued may be weak on several fronts.

Even so, by setting the argument out as a sequence of linked points I have made it easier for you, the reader, to work out whether or not you agree. What is more, you can identify exactly the point, or points, at which you disagree. That is the reason for setting out arguments clearly; not necessarily because you think they are perfectly watertight, but so that they provide a worthwhile basis for discussion and debate.

Also, since you are aiming to be precise in analytical writing, you have to be careful not to claim *more* than you are entitled to. Because *very little* can be said with absolute certainty, you have to develop a style in which you say things in a cautious way (notice I said I would 'guess' that writing appeals to you). We see this when Ellis uses the phrase 'It is much more plausible to argue...' in paragraph 3 of her article. This *limits* the range of what she is about to claim: she is *not* saying that her position is absolutely true and the only one that could possibly be held.

It can actually *strengthen* your argument to put it cautiously. If you claim a great deal (for example, that 'All schoolchildren are lazy. Therefore they need perpetual goading'), then your opponent only has to find one instance to disprove you (one example of a hardworking schoolchild) and your whole argument falls down. By couching your argument more tentatively, with 'conditions' attached, it is harder for your opponent to knock it down. That is, it is a *better* argument. For example, '*Many* schoolchildren are lazy' (weaker claim); or 'Many schoolchildren are lazy *in subjects they don't like*' (a condition attached); or 'Many schoolchildren *feel* lazy *on Friday afternoons*' (weaker and with a condition attached). Initially, it may seem somewhat precious to be so careful. However, in the end, you can mount much more powerful arguments if you learn how to lay the groundwork carefully.

Having said that, there is no need to get too concerned about the formal rules of logic – especially if worrying about it cramps your style. What matters is that you try to sort out your points so that they follow in a sequence that leads towards your conclusion. Give time to the jotting and planning stages, when you can try grouping your points in different ways and presenting them in different sequences until you have a nice tight line of argument.

KEY POINTS

- You should try to say exactly what you mean and then check that your points really do follow logically.
- Don't be dismayed if you find this difficult to begin with. It takes practice.

---

6 THE EXPERIENCE OF WRITING

Writing is not an activity most people feel blasé about. Writing a carefully composed piece is often an intense experience, though not one people talk freely about. Why should writing evoke strong feelings? And why do we tend to avoid discussing those feelings with others who also experience them?

6.1 Revealing yourself

As skills go, writing is a special case. Communicating with other people is absolutely fundamental to our lives – unlike, say, skills such as juggling or ice-dancing. What's more, the ability to communicate well tends to be associated with perceptions of how intelligent a person is. Revealing a lack of talent at juggling is not too much of a threat, whereas revealing a poor ability to express yourself in writing is a much more 'personal' thing. The question is, why do so many of us tend to think we *lack* writing ability?

6.2   By what standards do you judge yourself?

In modern life we are surrounded by the printed word. We get the impression that the world is full of people who find writing easy. It seems almost shameful to be inept at it, just as we feel dreadfully inadequate at our first driving lesson. All those other drivers speed confidently about, passing each other by a cat's whisker, parking on a postage stamp. And driving is such a 'public' performance – how shameful to be crunching through the gears in the middle of the road, with a queue of people behind waiting to overtake. We can scarcely imagine all those other people going through the same humiliation themselves once upon a time.

With writing the situation is worse, because what we see in print is 'public' writing. Most of what we read is written by *experienced* writers *selected* for their talent in writing. We never see the writing of all the ordinary folk who muddle along as best they can. Rather, we see the output of writers who are the equivalent of rally drivers. So when, as beginners, we look at our own written work, what are we comparing it with? Almost inevitably our writing looks weak in the light of the comparisons we are in a position to make. This must be at least one reason why we are often very shy about our writing and are so ready to believe that we are chronically poor writers. Having compared ourselves only with seasoned professionals, we live with this private 'problem'. Nobody knows the dreadful secret that we are inarticulate in writing.

6.3   The private–public ambiguity

Although many of us feel compelled to treat our writing as a very private activity, it is paradoxically also a public activity. It is private in that we do it by ourselves, locked in our own thoughts and according to our own habits and perceptions, with very little idea of how other people cope with the challenges it presents. But it is also public in that what we are producing is intended to be read by others, perhaps strangers. Indeed, writing can become a kind of 'public property' which is discussed by all and sundry, with very little reference back to the author. Critics feel able to pronounce on what the words 'really' mean without needing to ask the writer who spent hours struggling alone with them, saying things first this way and then that. In fact, there is a large gulf between the private world of writing and the public world of reading and discussing.

The thoughts that float in our minds are potentially sparkling insights, whose possibilities all lie ahead. The act of putting them on paper immediately 'fixes' a particular formation of those thoughts and destroys all the other possibilities. It is a fateful act. We immediately have the urge to take the words back and recreate all that 'potential' – the great work inside waiting to be written one far-off day. Can the real words on the page ever live up to those hopes? And what of the further barbarity of showing these written words to others, who care nothing for the great possibilities but only for what they can see? And yet we *do* want the words to be read. This is the great contradiction in our impulses. We *want* 'the world' to read what we write, because that is the purpose of writing, but at the same time we don't want *anyone* to read it *yet*, because it is so personal and may not be understood as we meant it.

Obviously you do not write an essay with the public at large in mind as your audience. Nevertheless, these contradictory impulses arise: a desire to 'speak' in writing, immediately followed by a desire to retract; a feeling of vulnerability, and yet an urge to go on. In this, as in other respects, writing is a process that gives rise to intensely ambivalent feelings – surges of enthusiasm and satisfaction, accompanied by waves of doubt and self-criticism.

6.4   Taking advantage of criticism

One particularly ambivalent moment is when you get your essay back with comments written on it by your tutor. From talking to people about this, I gather that it quite common to take a quick look at the *grade* and then put the essay aside to 'look at later'. Indeed, it seems that some students find it quite difficult *ever* to get round to a close reading of their tutor's remarks. The comments the tutor has patiently thought about and written out are set aside as too intense and penetrating to bear. This, all too rare, offering of 'feedback' is put off to some future day that may never arrive. Why?

It is easy to take the comments made on your writing very *personally*, as though you are being told that you are stupid, that your ideas are no good and that you are inarticulate. It is very difficult to 'stand back' and see essay-writing as a process of 'skill development', in which you benefit from doing quite tightly defined exercises and receiving very direct comments on your performance. Each piece you write *feels* like a personal statement on the issue in question rather than simply a process of going through your paces in front of a 'coach'. However, from the tutor's point of view, there are probably some very specific things he or she is looking for and you will be told quite directly how well you measure up.

This relationship between you and your tutor breaks the usual conventions of politeness between adults. But by taking off the constraints and allowing very direct comment, you are being given the chance to try out new ideas and new techniques and find out whether they work. Your tutor may 'sound' very critical in the frankness of her comments. That is just the convention adopted in this particular type of relationship. It allows the tutor to tell you 'straight' when the point you want to make just doesn't come across, where a sequence of ideas is confusing, where the logic is unconvincing, and so on. This gives you the opportunity to try to remedy the problems so that, eventually, when you write 'for real' – for readers who will see your errors without ever telling you – you can avoid making mistakes.

Having direct and detailed comments on your writing is, then, a rare opportunity, but not an easy one to respond to because of the very personal feelings we have about our writing and because of the unusually direct nature of the relationship you have with a tutor. It is important to be able to put this relationship into an appropriate perspective; to be able to 'ride out' the irritation of criticisms that seem to miss your point; to be glad of the detailed crossing out of your words and substitution of others; to be able to pay close attention to the subtle nuances of the alterations suggested. Most tutors do their best to be civilized and considerate in their remarks. But that will not prevent you feeling annoyed and misunderstood sometimes. These are feelings you have to come to terms with in a teaching–learning relationship. If it helps, think of yourself as having made a temporary 'contract' with this person, your tutor: that is, for the time being, you 'agree' to accept her as '*an* authority' – on the subject you are studying and your development as a student of it – simply because this person has 'been there' before you, knows more than you do and so is in a position to help you. But of course your tutor is not '*in* authority' over you because, in all other respects, you are equal, adult human beings. It should always be your aim to treat each other as such.

6.5   Routine hardships

One major reason why writing is an intense experience is not at all deep and 'psychological'. Many people just do find writing difficult.

Open-endedness

For one thing, writing is a task in which the 'product' you are aiming for is very *ill-defined*. When you paint a door you know pretty well what you are aiming at and what a well-painted door should look like. When you are writing an essay the only thing you can be certain of is that the end product will be quite different from what you had in mind at the start. This means you have to think very hard at the outset, as you set about establishing a 'frame of reference' within which to set your remarks. And you have to continue to think hard as you develop your line of argument within that frame. This *struggle* to forge the way ahead gives rise to a mixture of feelings, from frustration and exhaustion at one end of the scale to satisfaction and elation at the other. Consequently, your mood may swing quite sharply as you write.

At the same time, the quality of open-endedness in the task of writing creates a more general feeling of uncertainty, aimlessness and an absence of solid 'meanings' to hold on to. As creatures dependent on being able to make sense of our surroundings, we find it intensely uncomfortable to be faced with sustained uncertainty, so the experience of writing tends to have a restless quality about it. You want to keep getting up to do something else – something more solid and routine. In fact it *may* be helpful to switch back and forth between writing and various routine chores, to give yourself a break from the pressures of uncertainty.

An uncertain 'relationship'

Writing is also uncomfortable because of the uncertainty surrounding your relationship with your reader. On *your* side, this relationship is a very personal thing because it involves the way you project yourself. But the other side of the relationship is shrouded in mystery. Your 'audience' is a mythical entity, in that the tutor who *actually* reads your essay will take on the role of the 'intelligent person in the street' in order to read it. This hypothetical audience is one you can never meet, to check whether you are adopting the right tone of voice. You can only guess, from the remarks your tutor chooses to make, whether you are anywhere near the mark. So you can go through great self-doubt as you re-read what you have written. Thinking of your readers in *one* way, it may read like a nursery story; but then thinking of them in *another* way, it may read like over-condensed gobbledegook.

Being too close to see

When you are in the thick of wrestling with your line of argument and trying to construct intelligible sentences, your attention is so highly focused that it is almost impossible for you to judge what the words you write will mean to someone coming to them fresh and without any emotional involvement. All you can do is press on and hope for the best. It is probably only after a period of several weeks, even months, that you can come back and look at your work with a feel for what its impact on others might be. Again, this adds a layer of mystery and uncertainty to the writing process.

Keeping going

Finally, essay-writing is a rather long drawn-out process. With so many different stages to it, you have to develop a certain stamina to write regularly. It can be tedious at some times and disappointing at others. Consequently it draws on your inner resources of will power and determination, as well your courage in facing possible disappointment. It is a great feeling when it comes 'right' in the end, but that moment can be a long time coming.

7 CONCLUSION

Putting the whole picture together we see that writing essays is a very challenging task. In the course of it you may feel:

- frustration when you are stuck
- uncertainty when you can't see where you are heading
- boredom when it goes on and on
- despair when you are overwhelmed by the time it takes
- nausea when you read what you have written
- gloom when you see the limitations of your own abilities
- annoyance when you read your tutor's comments.

But don't let me put you off. I am simply working on the principle that these experiences and feelings *will* come to you at some time or other and that, since writing is so private, you need to know in advance that *you are not alone* in having such reactions. You need to be *prepared* for a struggle so that you do not, unconsciously, keep putting off your writing tasks until it is too late to do them properly, or give up altogether when the going gets tough. If you are ready to cope with the hardships, you will still be around for the good times.

So why, you may ask, do sane adults bother writing essays at all? For the same reason people choose to do many other difficult things: because it is also *intensely rewarding*. No other experience in your studies is likely to be more satisfying than having completed an essay and handed it in, nor more elating than finding that you have done better than you expected when your essay is returned.

KEY POINTS

Some basic principles

- Your ability to express yourself is a fundamental aspect of your existence within a human society. Developing that ability is one of the most profoundly worthwhile activities you can undertake.

- You cannot learn formal *rules* of writing. Essentially you are learning to *communicate* ideas to a reader. Your style will only develop through practice at explaining things to a reader in your own words.

- Think of writing as a craft in which you are an apprentice. You learn by practising a range of different skills, and you get this practice by regularly turning out one piece after another and getting comments from a skilled craftsperson.

Some useful thoughts

- Don't worry too much about writing beautifully straight away. Just pitch in. You have to be prepared to write badly in order to learn how to write well.

- Remember that most of what you read is written by 'professionals'. If you are a beginner then compare yourself with other beginners.

- You cannot be a good judge of your own writing until some time after the event.

- You have to learn to 'let go' and allow others to see your writing, however far it falls short of your ideals.

- Think of your tutor as a 'coach' who is working on your technique. You won't agree with everything he or she says, but you *will* make more *progress* with the coaching than without.

Practical hints and tips for essay-writing

- Work to the question in the title at all times.

- Use material drawn from the course.

- Work at 'constructing' an argument – that is, putting points together in groups, organized around a simple essay plan, with a beginning, a middle and an end.

- Write clearly and simply.

- Write for the intelligent 'person in the street'.

- Read your work out loud to yourself (or to someone else, if you can) so that you can 'listen' for passages that don't work.

- When you get an essay back from a tutor, read any suggested corrections out loud and then read your original to 'hear' the differences.

- Keep practising. Write short pieces regularly (get comments from a fellow student if you can't get them from a tutor). This will:

  – help you to establish a 'writing voice'

  – extend your repertoire of the phrases that make your writing flow

  – help you to shape your writing style to the conventions of detailed analysis and objectivity

  – increase your sensitivity to the processes of structuring essays and signposting the direction your argument is taking.

CHAPTER SIX

1 INTRODUCTION

This chapter is different from the others in the book. So far we have been thinking about ways of approaching a range of different study tasks: reading and making sense of secondary source material in text books, articles and teaching texts; getting the most out of other ways of studying, from lectures, tutorial meetings and TV for example; and learning by 'doing' – making presentations and visits, using a computer and, especially, writing essays. In this chapter we turn to the *nature* of the arts and humanities themselves, and look at the main *processes* involved in studying them.

Broadly, when you study the arts and humanities you study aspects of *culture*. You explore people's ideas and beliefs, their cultural practices and the objects they have made. Human history is criss-crossed with the traces of people who did, said and made things and these people were to some extent aware of what they were doing. So all these things *mean* something. Your task is to look carefully at people's ideas, practices and products to try to *understand* what they mean. You achieve this understanding by:

- *analysing* the various 'objects' of your study (for example, plays, music, paintings, historical or legal documents, philosophical treatises, maps, buildings, religious ceremonies)
- *interpreting the meanings* of these objects
- *making judgements* of their value
- *communicating* your interpretations and judgements.

When you study a painting, for example, you take it apart to see how it 'works' as a painting. You *analyse* it 'as it is in itself', because this gives you many clues to what it might mean. But that analysis is complicated by the fact that the *way* we understand a painting *itself* changes over time. For instance, what a religious painting might have meant to the artist and his contemporaries in sixteenth-century Italy cannot be the same as it means to us now. We do not share their culture. And the painting does not 'appear' the same to us either. We study it close-up in a modern art gallery, or (much reduced in size) as an illustration in a book. Look at Raphael's painting, *The Madonna and Child* in Figure 6.1 (p.192). Imagine how different the painting would seem to its original audience – perhaps contemplating it during a religious service, high up on the wall of a church, lit by flickering candle-light. What might it have meant to them?

To make an *interpretation* of what the painting means, then, you not only have to study it 'as it is in itself' – you also need to learn as much as you can about the circumstances in which it was made and viewed (who painted it, what it was 'for' and, more generally, about the values, beliefs and way of life of those people at that time). This, too, presents certain challenges. Obviously, we cannot transport ourselves to sixteenth-century Italy. We live *here* and *now*. In the end, we interpret things in the context of our ideas and beliefs.

So it is as if the painting (or novel, vase, song, idea, document, event) has a kind of 'double life' – as it was to people in the past *and* as it is now, to us in the present. You have to try to understand why it means something now, and just what it means. Ultimately, you have to make *judgements* about its *value*.

These interlinked processes of *analysis–interpretation–evaluation* are what we will explore in this chapter. But it doesn't end there. You also have to *communicate* your interpretations and judgements to other people. To explain what *you* mean, you have to learn to speak and write in the appropriate 'language'. That way, you make your own contribution to an ongoing 'conversation' about our culture – a conversation that enables us to understand ourselves, and our purposes and values, as human beings who *continue* to live in society with each other.

KEY POINTS

- Studying the arts and humanities involves coming to *understand* aspects of human *culture*, past and present.
- You study the *meanings* of people's ideas, beliefs, cultural practices and products.
- And, by *communicating* your ideas, you make a *contribution* to our culture.

1.1   Different arts and humanities subjects

If studying the arts and humanities helps us understand our culture so that we can live together more meaningfully, then why do we study particular subjects or 'disciplines' in our universities? You may be studying a single discipline: a language (ancient or modern), history, art, music, literature, film, law, religion, philosophy – and so forth; or *some* subjects combined, in multi- or inter-disciplinary studies. Why not the arts and humanities in general?

It is partly because our cultural experience is very *broad*. If we want to *study* a culture, rather than just experience it, we have to make it *manageable*. We have to *analyse* it, or break it down into parts: making distinctions between the different *kinds* of experience we have – such as reading an account of the Roman Empire, watching a play, listening to the charts. By 'isolating' these things, and naming them (History, Literature, Music), we can see more clearly just what it is we are looking at and come to understand it better. We also make these distinctions because cultural experiences such as these are *different*. At bottom, if you can't tell the difference between a song, a painting and a poem then there is nothing much you can say about any of them. However, such discrimination depends on recognizing *similarities* as well as differences between things – for instance, recognizing that a great variety of visual images are all examples of what we call 'paintings'. But once you have learned the concept 'painting', and can distinguish between a painting and a song – which we all learn to do as children – then in a sense you 'know' what art and music are. (Incidentally, that means you already know a lot about arts and humanities subjects even if you have not studied them as subjects before. None of us is a true beginner in them.) This kind of analysis enables us to divide up our very wide experience of the world and organize it in our minds.

A main difference between the subjects that make up the arts and humanities, then, is that they have different *objects* of study – plays, poems and novels in Literature; documents, records and diaries in History; paintings, sculptures and buildings in Art History; and so on. Having identified such similarities and differences between the objects of our study, we can go on to to look at each of them more closely. And so, over time, we have been able to make even finer distinctions. Within poetry, for example, we come to recognize different *types* of poem (narrative, epic, lyric, satirical). That is the way we impose some *meaningful order* on our very broad cultural experience and 'discipline' our thinking about it.

'Living' disciplines

The subjects we study in the arts and humanities are not set in concrete. We make changes to them over time which reflect significant changes in our culture and the way we view it. For obvious reasons, *new* subjects such as Communications, Film and Media Studies have come into being quite recently. This has involved some shifting of boundaries in existing subjects such as Literature, Art History and Philosophy. And even within these older disciplines the focus of attention tends to *shift* over time. For instance, in recent decades feminist writers have drawn our attention to the roles of women as writers and artists, as characters in novels and as depicted in paintings, and as readers and viewers. Also, what was always called English Literature is now often referred to as Literatures in English. That extends the scope of our studies to include English language writing from Africa, the Americas, Australia, India and the West Indies.

These changes are sometimes dismissed as simply 'fashionable' or 'politically correct'. But that is a mistake. The rise of interest in Gender Studies since the 1960s is partly a result of an increase in the number of women working in universities – which itself reflects women's changing place in our society. And study of Literatures in English has arisen out of a deeper understanding of Britain's past role as an imperial power and the profound cultural effects this has had on its former colonies. As academics become aware that aspects of our cultural experience remain to be explored, their curiosity draws them towards those fresh pastures. For a while 'gender' or 'post-colonial' issues seem to be on everyone's lips. Eventually, they may become established as fields of inquiry and be drawn into the mainstream of a range of existing subjects – which are themselves *changed* in the process. Then other issues come to our attention, and so on. This process is what makes even 'traditional' academic disciplines *living* traditions of thought and practice.

It is by imposing order on our experience in this way that, together, we are able to examine the *substance* of our culture in great detail – not only the different ways in which we communicate with each other, but also the very 'stuff' of our ideas, history, literature, art, music, and religious and other practices.

KEY POINTS

- We distinguish between *different subjects*, or disciplines, in the arts and humanities.
- The distinctions we make impose *order* on our very wide cultural experience, enabling us to study it closely and understand it better.

1.2   Studying the arts and humanities

Having seen why and how distinctions are made between different arts and humanities subjects, does that mean we cannot think of these subjects 'as a whole'? The general label 'arts and humanities' suggests that there *is* something that unites them, at the same time distinguishing them from other subject groupings (such as 'the sciences' or 'social sciences'). What unites these subjects is that they focus on:

- cultural 'traditions'
- 'texts'.

Cultural traditions

Just now I said quite confidently that you already know a lot about the subjects that make up the arts and humanities even if you have not studied them before. But how can I be so sure? What makes me certain is that, like everyone else, you were born into a human culture. As you were growing up within that culture you were hearing and seeing all the things the people around you were busy saying, doing and making. And you were learning to think and understand, do, say and make similar kinds of thing. You were probably taught some things directly: by your parents; by other adults and children; at school; and through radio and TV. As soon as you could read you also learned from comics and books. But no doubt you just 'picked up' a lot of these customs along the way, as a member of the culture alongside other people.

In the process of growing up you learned to make sense of the world around you, to organize and represent it to yourself in your mind. You learned to recognize similarities and differences between things and formed the ideas or concepts that enable us to think. Among these concepts are the sort we are particularly interested in here – 'story', 'picture', 'song', 'the past'. Even before you could read, you were no doubt told stories and listened to them on the radio or on tape; you drew pictures and looked at them in books and on TV; you sang nursery rhymes and heard all kinds of music; and you learned to distinguish between 'yesterday' and 'today'. Even if you were not taught directly about these things you *experienced* them all, over and over again. And when you compare your experiences with those of your friends, you probably find that you sang similar songs, heard similar stories and (if you are around the same age) watched the same TV programmes. That is because you grew up in the same culture.

But we do not only have similar experiences. The very ways in which we think, the meanings we make, the ways we speak, our values and beliefs, and what we do, have all 'taken shape' *within* our cultures.

185

What is a 'culture'?

A *culture* is the collection of meanings, values, morals, ways of thinking, patterns of behaviour and speech, and ways of life, that a group of people *share*. And all modern cultures have histories – they are linked to the *past*. So, through our culture, what we have is shared experience and knowledge of certain customs or cultural *traditions*.

But this does not mean that we all end up like 'clones'. You are, of course, recognizably *yourself*. You experience things in your own *particular* ways too. And we know that not everyone brought up in the same culture believes *exactly* the same things or behaves in identical ways. You are probably also a member of a thriving 'sub-culture', which shares a certain kind of (perhaps, religious or moral) belief that is different from the mainstream. In any case, I hardly need to emphasize this point since the idea that we are all individuals, responsible for ourselves and in charge of our own destinies, is one of the fundamental beliefs in our culture. For us, it is more difficult to get our heads round the idea that, in a sense, we are none of us truly individual – because inevitably we live in, and through, our shared culture. Indeed, that is why we can communicate with each other. Perhaps we are more similar than we like to think.

What all arts and humanities subjects aim to explore, then, are aspects of human cultures, past and present. In fact, in the West, many of our values can be traced as far back as Ancient Greece (and beyond), so it is more accurate to say that we explore certain *cultural traditions*. It is because those traditions have been passed on through our culture, and are still alive today, that we can hope to make some sense of the past and of ideas and art of the past. If the culture in which we were reared and live had no 'links' to that past at all, the traces that have come down to us (ideas, values, written texts, pictures, buildings, artefacts) would be alien to us. It would be almost impossible to understand them.

But, equally, our culture is constantly changing – perhaps particularly fast in this age of electronic revolution. As we have seen, the way we 'slice it up' into subject areas, in order to make sense of it, changes too. What we study are *living* traditions.

Texts

We can think of all the 'objects' that we study in the arts and humanities as, broadly speaking, *texts*. They may be literary, historical, legal or philosophical *written* texts; *visual* texts such as paintings, buildings, artefacts, plays-in-performance and films; *aural* texts, as in the performance of music and in spoken languages; or *symbolic* texts, for example religious ceremonies, maps, architectural plans and music scores. These things are all

186

'texts' in the sense that they 'stand for' or represent the conditions of time and place in which they were created, and all the knowledge, ideas and activity that went into their making. We cannot re-create those conditions. And we can seldom study the actual knowledge, thoughts or intentions of their makers and doers, past or present. What we study are the results or *outcomes* of all these things – the written accounts, paintings, pieces of music, plays, maps, Acts of Parliament, buildings, and so on – that were and are being produced.

When we analyse and interpret these texts in appropriate ways, we can often get 'back' to some of the knowledge, ideas and activity that went into their making. But even when an author tells us how she wrote a particular novel and what she meant to say in it, or a painter records what was in his mind, those accounts are not the simple 'truth' of the matter. They are yet more *texts* which we have to scrutinize. *All* these texts are open to our interpretation of what they *mean*.

For instance, we know that the Battle of Waterloo was fought in June 1815. And if we know quite a lot about what happened then, that is because people made written, visual and symbolic records of it which have come down to us: official documents, records of speeches in Parliament, journals, diaries, letters, sketches, maps, and so on. These are what we study (not the battle itself, of course). If you were to compare different accounts of the battle – from the French or British side, or by men from different ranks of the armies – then you would probably find that, because they had different 'points of view', their versions of the event are different. They may even conflict. An historian has to study *all* these texts with a *critical* eye: weighing up the evidence for and against particular interpretations of what happened and why, before reaching conclusions. If Wellington himself had left an account of why he made certain decisions during the battle that would of course be very interesting. It would be important as 'evidence' which could not have come in a direct way from anyone else. But it would need to be seen as 'what Wellington *thought* he was doing', and be weighed in the balance along with the rest.

KEY POINTS

The different arts and humanities subjects are *living traditions* of thought and practice. When you study them, you learn:

- how to *analyse* a range of different *texts*; *interpret* their meanings and *evaluate* them
- to think *critically* and independently
- how to *communicate* your ideas to others in speech and writing.

The meanings and significance of human activities are never just 'in' the texts you study, ready to jump out at you. You have to question, or 'interrogate', those texts and interpret their meanings for yourself. How to do this is what we will explore in the next few sections of the chapter.

2   BECOMING FAMILIAR WITH THE TEXT

Before you begin your interrogation of a text, though, you have to get to know it in a general way. In a sense, you can 'see' *visual* texts (such as paintings, sculptures and buildings) all at once; there they are before you. You can move around them, looking at them from different angles. But with *written*, *aural* and *moving image* texts – in which words, sounds or images *follow on* from one another – you cannot become familiar with the whole thing until you have read, heard or seen it right through. If it is quite short there is no problem about this; before you begin your analysis you will do so several times probably. But what if it is a lengthy text, such as a novel or a symphony? How should you approach it?

2.1   Reading

There are many different *kinds* of written text, and you need to approach and read them *differently*.

On first reading a *novel*, it is best to read through the way you normally do – and enjoy yourself. Some people read very quickly. That's fine, because when you get down to analysing it you are anyway forced to re-read its various sections much more slowly and study some parts of it particularly carefully. Part of the process of analysing anything as long as a novel (a play, film, symphony) is finding a way of dividing it up into manageable 'episodes' – combining certain chapters, scenes or passages together to form groups. Then you can study each episode in detail, while keeping a grasp on the whole thing in your mind. So, as you read, you might just be thinking about some suitable way of doing that.

However, if you are reading a *philosophical* text you need to approach it in quite a different way. It is a mistake even to try reading it quickly because you will very soon lose the gist. If you keep going regardless, there's a danger that you will 'blame' yourself for failing to understand what you read, decide you are no good at philosophy and give up. In fact you are not even giving yourself a chance. *Nobody* can read a philosophical text at the speed they read a novel and *understand* what they read. You have to take it very slowly, trying to make some sense of it as you go along, a bit at a time. That is because these texts take the form of an *argument* about certain *ideas*. Unless you understand the first stage of the argument reasonably well you will not be able to make sense of the next stage, and so on. And, often, the argument is dense. Abstract ideas just *are* hard to understand, so every sentence may take a while to sort out.

Your reactions to the text

A few moments ago I said you might read through a novel and just *enjoy* it. But what if you are *not* enjoying it? What if you don't *like* a piece of music you will have to spend a lot of time thinking about? Or perhaps you feel thoroughly bewildered by a philosophical argument and at first you can't make head or tail of it.

Obviously, you cannot *force* yourself to find such a text enjoyable or interesting. But what you *can* do is give it a chance. At this stage you've hardly even been introduced. It may be that you are trying to read too quickly or expecting it to be something it is not. In any case, when you get down to studying it, looking more closely at this part and that, it will almost certainly make more sense to you. You may even come to enjoy it.

Having said that, you may not. We all have to study some things because they are important 'landmarks' in the subject, regardless of whether we enjoy the experience. So you need to be aware that, from time to time, you may have to just grit your teeth and press on.

However, it is always a good idea to talk things over with other people. See what fellow students make of the text. What they say may help you to 'come at' it from a different angle and see new possibilities in it.

Reading an *historical document* is different again. Much of it may be easy enough to follow, but there will probably be a number of terms that are 'of the period' or references to unfamiliar people and events that you need to look up. So reading it may be a stop–start process. In any case, you will be reading with certain questions in mind, such as:

- who wrote the document – what do we know about these people's background and particular interest in the matter?
- when was it written – how soon after the events it refers to?
- why was it written – who or what was it written 'for'?
- what was the author in a position to know; is it likely to provide sound information?

Then you can judge whether the document is a *reliable* source for your purposes, and just what it might mean.

So when you read philosophical texts and historical documents even for the first time, you will be beginning your interrogation. This is true of *symbolic* texts too, such as maps and music scores – you have to start 'deciphering' them straight away to make much sense of them.

2.2 Listening and viewing

If you are studying music, a foreign language, plays-in-performance, film or the media, you have to do a lot of listening and viewing. Again, you need to be aware that there are different *ways* of doing this.

For example, when you listen through some music for the first few times just to get a 'feel' for the piece as a whole, you don't have to do it in a studious way. You can listen in the car, or at home as you do some chores. But when you come to *study* the music, you have to listen carefully and in an 'active' way – *thinking* about the way the piece is put together or the contribution different instruments make. You need to get organized for this kind of listening.

1 *Try to make sure there are no other sounds or noises in the room.* Don't listen in the kitchen when there is a washing machine on, for instance.

2 *Find out where it's best to sit in relation to the source of sound and adjust the controls accordingly.*

3 *Concentrate on the silence before you start listening.* Sounds exist in what is otherwise silence. If you stop to appreciate that background, the textures and 'colours' of the music will be more vivid.

4 *Just listen and think – don't do anything else at the same time.* Get used to concentrating on what you hear. Shut your eyes if it helps.

5 *Try to listen without being interrupted.* If you are interrupted it is probably worth starting the piece again from the beginning.

Similar 'rules' apply if you are studying a language and perhaps listening to a tape of native speakers in conversation. You can listen through a few times in a less studious way, just to get the gist. But then, when you get down to work on it, you need to have quiet conditions in which to listen to the various parts of it carefully. And the same with poetry or a novel on tape, and a play on video.

When you are trying to become familiar with texts it helps a lot if you can *surround* yourself with them. You can pin the maps you are studying on your walls, and also illustrations of paintings, buildings and artefacts. And you can get into the habit of tuning in to a music or foreign language radio station, perhaps having it on in the background as you get up each morning.

KEY POINTS

- The *texts* you study in the arts and humanities are of *different kinds* (written, visual, aural, symbolic).
- There is also a *range* of texts within each of these categories.
- It is important to recognize the *differences* between texts, so that you *approach* them with the right *expectations*.
- You need to read, look or listen to the text in the way that is *appropriate* to it, and also suits your study *purposes*.

3 APPROACHING ANALYSIS

3.1 Why analyse?

Whatever kind of text you study, one of your main tasks is to try to understand it 'as it is in itself'. That means *analysing* it. You have to examine it *in detail* so that you can see what it is made up of and how it 'works'.

Just as you read, view or listen to different kinds of text in different ways, so you approach your analysis of them differently. In each case, you ask particular *types of question* using a specialized analytical *language*. We have just seen the sort of questions you will have in mind when approaching an historical document. Let's take another example.

Look at Raphael's *Madonna and Child* (Figure 6.1, over the page).[1] To understand how it is 'put together' you need to ask the following kinds of question about it, using some of the terms that appear in italics here.

- How much of the *picture space* is taken up by the three *figures* and how much by the *background* to them?
- Where are the figures *positioned* on the canvas and what are their *poses*?
- What is 'in' the background and how is this related to the figures in the *foreground*?
- Which parts of the painting are in *light* and which in *shade*, and where is the *source of light* – where is the light supposed to be coming from?
- What is the painting's *tonal range*; are there any striking uses of *colour* in it?
- How is the *two-dimensional* (flat) painted surface made to look as if it has a third dimension, of *depth*, so that the figures appear life-like?
- What is the relationship of the figures to you, the *viewer* – at your *eye-level*, 'looking' down, away, or what?

In the process of analysing the painting you study as many aspects of it as you can – not only the picture surface itself (the first four questions), but also your (the viewer's) relationship to it. All this gives you important clues to how the painting works. When you then combine the results of this analysis with what you have discovered about both the type of painting you are dealing with and the conditions in which it was painted and viewed, you are able to reach some informed and appropriate interpretation of its meanings and values, and to communicate your judgements to other people.

---

[1] We have only been able to reproduce the painting in black and white, so, among other things, you wouldn't be able to analyse the artist's use of colour. This is only one reason why you should always try to examine *original* paintings when you can. It is also difficult to get a sense of the scale and texture of a painting from a reproduction, however good it is. Of course, you will often have to use reproductions. When you do, you should always read the captions, which give you important information about a painting, including its size.

Figure 6.1 Raphael, *The Madonna and Child with the Infant Baptist (The Garvagh Madonna)*, probably 1509–10, oil on wood, 39 x 33 cm. (Reproduced by courtesy of the Trustees, The National Gallery, London)

KEY POINTS

When you analyse a text you *break it down* into parts and *examine* each part in detail, so that you can see how the text 'works' as a whole. According to the *type* of text you are analysing, you:

● ask particular *kinds* of question

● use the appropriate *language* of analysis.

Let's see how these processes of analysis–interpretation–evaluation and communication actually work in practice. To do this we will *separate* them out and *illustrate* each one, taking a short poem as a working example. As we discuss the poem, I hope you will be able to see how to *apply* what we are doing to *other kinds of text* you may be particularly interested in. From time to time I will draw out some of these implications.

3.2   Carrying out an analysis

Here, then, is the two-verse poem we will focus on in the next few sections of the chapter. As you see, I have left out the ends of the lines in the second verse. So it presents you with a kind of 'puzzle'. (But I have included the punctuation, and added line numbers for ease of reference.)

1   The grey sea and the long black land;

2   And the yellow half-moon large and low;

3   And the startled little waves that leap

4   In fiery ringlets from their sleep,

5   As I gain the cove with pushing prow,

6   And quench its speed i' the slushy sand.

1   Then a mile of warm sea-scented _____;

2   Three fields to cross till a farm _____;

3   A tap at the pane, the quick sharp _____

4   And blue spurt of a lighted _____,

5   And a voice less loud, thro' its joys and _____,

6   Than the two hearts beating each to _____!

ACTIVITY

Read the poem three or four times. Then turn poet and try to fill in the missing words in the second verse *before* you read on. (Don't cheat!)

A clue

Speak the first verse out loud, and notice which of the end-words in the lines have similar sounds (that is, which lines rhyme). Notice that lines 2 and 5 look as though they rhyme, but they don't strike the ear that way. However, in verse 2 the equivalent lines do rhyme.

A warning

Anxiety can Damage your Health – so do not get anxious about this. It's supposed to be *fun*. (But it will be even more fun if a group of you can get together to do it.)

I have no way of knowing what you wrote of course. But I should reveal that I have played this game before. And I am prepared to bet that, whether you got the right words or not, the ones you wrote were almost all words of one syllable. (Syllables are based on vowel *sounds*. So 'speed' ('ee') and 'loud' ('ow') are words of one syllable (even though they contain two vowels), and 'fiery' has two syllables because the 'fie' produces the sound 'i' and the 'y' is sounded 'ee' – 'fi/ree'.)

The poem is by Robert Browning and was published in the early 1840s; here it is in full.

1   The grey sea and the long black land;
2   And the yellow half-moon large and low;
3   And the startled little waves that leap
4   In fiery ringlets from their sleep,
5   As I gain the cove with pushing prow,
6   And quench its speed i' the slushy sand.

1   Then a mile of warm sea-scented beach;
2   Three fields to cross till a farm appears;
3   A tap at the pane, the quick sharp scratch
4   And blue spurt of a lighted match,
5   And a voice less loud, thro' its joys and fears,
6   Than the two hearts beating each to each!

(R. Browning (1940 edn) *Browning: Poetical Works*, London, Oxford University Press, p.215.)

ACTIVITY

Now read out the poem in full a few more times.

Note: It will help if you type or write the poem out accurately on a sheet of paper (including the punctuation). Then you can keep it in front of you alongside the book, as we look more closely.

The reason I am so confident that you wrote words of one syllable is that the majority of the words in the entire poem are of that kind, and all but one of the words that end the lines in the second verse ('appears'). (Just check that for yourself.) As you were reading through the poem several times your ear will have picked that up. So, if at first you wrote in two-syllable words, they would have 'sounded wrong' (unless, perhaps, English is not your first language or you happen to have very little experience of poetry). This is why I asked you to read the poem aloud. What your ear detects is a certain *pattern* of sounds – in this case a pretty simple pattern of mainly single sounds. And that is what a poem is, a particular pattern of words and sounds. That is why you should try to read poems out loud. Your *ear* tells you what you already 'know' about poetry, so you should always listen to it and put your faith in it, so to speak.

You may have noticed other *patterns of sound* that 'knit' these particular words together: each verse has six lines, and in each the end-words are paired in rhyming sounds as follows: lines 1 and 6; 2 and 5; 3 and 4. If you expected to find that kind of patterning, or picked up my 'clue', you probably worked out from the first verse which of the end-words in the second verse would need to rhyme. Another thing you may have 'heard' is how long and drawn-out most of the vowel sounds in these end-words are: 'low', 'leap', 'sleep', 'beach', 'appears', 'fears'. If you then look at the words *within* the lines you'll find many more that sound similar in this respect ('grey sea', 'half-moon', 'Three fields', 'hearts beating each to each'). Some of these long vowel sounds within the lines *also* 'echo' the vowel sounds in the end-words – for example, 'black land' in line 1, and 'yellow...low' in line 2 – producing 'internal' rhyming patterns as well. And, generally, the consonants are soft-sounding. If you find it hard to hear these things, read the words out loud in an exaggerated way.

There is another type of pattern here too, in the *kinds of word* the poet uses. A lot of these words appeal to our *senses*: of sight (the setting of 'grey sea', 'black land' and 'yellow' moonlight across the water); of hearing (the 'tap' and 'scratch' of lines 3 and 4 in the second verse); of smell ('sea-scented'); touch ('warm') and sensation ('two hearts beating'). In particular, the poem is very visual – in our mind's eye, we can see what is 'happening' at every stage. It is a little drama that would translate very well to film.

Finding 'ways into' a text

The hardest part of analysing a text is *getting started*. Here, the game of writing end-words for the poem forced you to start by thinking about *sounds*. But there are many possible ways into any text. So if you feel a bit bewildered at first, don't despair.

Generally, it is best to begin by thinking about some aspect of the text that seems to *stand out*, striking you forcefully in some way. In a written text, you may be struck by a particular *image* (or comparison), and begin thinking about what it brings to mind. (In the poem for instance, consider the way the waves are compared to ringlets in lines 3 and 4 of the first verse. Why 'ringlets'? What do you associate with them?) Or it may be the way the words are *laid out* on the page that attracts your attention: a pattern in the dialogue of a play or novel (such as very long speeches regularly assigned to one character and short utterances to another); in poetry, an unusual arrangement of the verses with some lines much shorter than others. In a piece of music it might be a sudden change in *rhythm*, or in *dynamics* (from soft to very loud perhaps). Or you may hear a particularly pleasing *melody* (or tune) repeated in a slightly different way at different points in the piece. You may see a certain *shape* repeated in a painting (lots of curves for instance), or notice a splash of vivid *colour* on one part of the canvas.

Wherever you begin, as soon as you notice a particular feature of the text and start thinking about it – or start to see or hear some sort of pattern – you will find yourself moving on from one observation to another (as we are doing here with the poem).

Once you think you have detected *any* kind of pattern you should look to see whether it runs right through the text. (Remember, from section 1.1, that analysis involves recognizing similarities *and* differences.)

ACTIVITY

Read the poem out loud again. Do any lines sound *different* – breaking the pattern of long vowel sounds and soft consonants we noticed?

I'd say there is a different pattern of sound in lines 3 and 4 of the poem. These lines are similar in both verses and also different from the slower, languorous movement of the other lines – especially in the second verse. There, you have to pronounce the words clearly because of all the hard, dental consonants; 't', 'st' and 'tch'. And there are a number of short vowel sounds too ('tap', 'quick', 'scratch', 'match') which, because they are short, make you speed up as you read. The sounds of these words seem to mimic, or *evoke*, the actual (short, sharp) sounds of tapping and match-scratching. Combining this observation with what we noticed about the rhyming pattern earlier, you can see that the middle two lines in each verse are knitted particularly closely together by this change in sounds and movement *and* by the fact that these are the only lines with adjacent rhymes. They are also the *only* lines we read through without stopping – they are not divided by a comma or semi-colon. They seem to be little 'units of meaning' in themselves, within each verse of the poem. But why? What's the point of this?

Once you ask that kind of question you are thinking about what the poem is *about* – that is, you are moving towards some *interpretation* of its *meanings*. In fact you will have been asking yourself that kind of question all along. It is impossible to read and analyse something without trying to make some sense of it as you go. However, we began by putting these 'why?', 'what' does this mean?' questions to one side. The point of suspending them – while you look closely at patterns of sound, movement, and so on – is that *meaning* in a poem is closely bound up in the *way it is written*. Indeed, the poem *is* the way it is written – these particular words on the page, in this order. (So too the painting *is* the marks on the canvas, the music *is* the particular arrangement of 'sounds in time'.) Discovering *how* the poem works is precisely the point of analysing it in detail. If you jump to conclusions about what it means too quickly, you will tend to shut off some other possibilities that may be thrown up by a more *thorough* analysis of it.

KEY POINTS

- Analysing a text shows you how it *works* and gives you many clues to what it might *mean*.

- First, examine a feature of the text that is particularly *striking*, and look out for *patterns* in it.

- Then go on to analyse the text as *fully* as you can before trying to reach any conclusions about its meanings.

So, although in reality analysing a text and interpreting its meanings are not separate 'stages' we go through, but are overlapping processes, I will keep them separate for the time being so that you can see more clearly what each involves.

4 INTERPRETING MEANINGS

After you had read the poem a few times, you no doubt pieced together that the 'I' of line 5 in the first verse, the speaker, is rowing in a boat at night. We probably realize that with the word 'prow'. By the end of the first verse the boat is beached in a cove. The journey continues over the beach and fields to a farm (by foot, presumably, since we hear about no other means of transport). There the traveller meets someone. It appears that they exchange signals – the tap on the pane and lighted match. And all this, together with the whispering voice and beating hearts, suggests that it is some kind of secret meeting. I imagine we would not disagree about that pretty bald account. It seems to be a poem about a journey and a secret meeting. In fact the title of the poem is 'Meeting at Night'.

But as far as I can see, we can't be sure about anything else. Although the verse is very visual, we don't know *where* this place is. We know the action happens at night, because of the grey and black of the surroundings in moonlight (and the title), but otherwise we don't know *when* it happens either. And we don't know *who* the speaker is, whether male or female, or who he or she meets, or *why* they meet. So there seems to be plenty of scope for interpretation here.

4.1   Knowledge about context and author

Starting with the 'central character' (traveller–speaker), I would guess that most of us just *assumed* he is male. If someone is doing something as strenuous and potentially dangerous as rowing about and walking alone through the countryside at the dead of night, we tend to expect that person to be a man. More to the point, what is known about mid-Victorian culture – the *conditions* within which this poem was written and first read – suggests that Browning's original readers would almost certainly have made that assumption. Then (and later) woman's place was firmly in the home, not pulling on oars and traipsing across fields at night (in a hooped skirt?). Given those conditions, then, we are in all probability right to think of the traveller–speaker as a man; this is an *appropriate* interpretation to make. The woman, if a woman is involved, is more likely to be the one who 'waits' in the farm ready to respond to the tap at the window-pane. And, if this is a poem about a lovers' meeting, then it is also reasonable to assume that the lovers *are* male and female – if that was obviously not the case Browning probably wouldn't have found a publisher for the poem.

However, I am speculating here. Is it right to do that? The answer is 'yes' and 'no'.

Interpreting texts from other times and places

Yes. Like everyone else, artists rely on communicating with their contemporary 'audience' on the basis of the understandings they *share*, as members of the same culture. So when you are studying a text that has come down from the past, or from a culture that is different from your own, it is important to find out as much as you can about that time and place – including the way of life, values and beliefs of the people for whom the text was written. Some knowledge of the *conditions* in which the text was written and received will guide you towards making *appropriate* interpretations of its meanings.

However, you need to be aware that acquiring that kind of knowledge is not a straightforward business. If your subject is Philosophy or History, you will be particularly interested in such questions as: what is 'true'?; in what sense can we 'know' what happened in the past?; how can we find out? In that connection, notice that what I have just said is carefully worded. I have said that our knowledge of this period 'suggests that...'; that we are 'probably' right to make certain assumptions about the poem on that basis; that it is 'reasonable' to draw a particular conclusion.

You have to be *cautious* in what you say about conditions in the past, and especially so when you are interpreting a text's meanings on the basis of your understanding of the past.

No. You have to be careful *not* to speculate on the basis of some kinds of knowledge though – such as what you know about the artist. For example, I know that Browning met a woman in 1844, Elizabeth Barrett (also a poet), and that they courted and married in secret. They fled to Italy immediately after their wedding in 1846. In view of this, I might be tempted to interpret the poem not just as the story of a lovers' meeting, but of the kind of clandestine meeting that may actually have taken place between these particular lovers. In this case I could simply be proved wrong: the poem was in fact published along with others in 1842, some two years before Browning met Elizabeth Barrett. But even if they had met earlier, I *still* couldn't be sure that Browning was writing about himself or about something he had actually experienced.

You should not make connections between what you know about artists' lives or times and their 'works of art' in a direct, *unqualified* way. We cannot get inside other people's minds, so we can never know for sure what artists feel or know or *intend* to do in their work. (And we can't just take what they themselves say at face value either because, like all of us, they may not be fully aware of what they feel or do.) Also, works of art are only ever *partly* 'true to life'. They always contain imaginary elements – even when they are portraits of real people or of actual landscapes. Artists create their work; what they are concerned with is its *composition*. A landscape painter, for example, may 'move' a tree in order to make a more pleasing pattern on the canvas, or add a figure to the landscape for the sake of visual interest. And these imaginary elements may so transform what was 'there' that it is pretty well impossible to disentangle the one from the other. So, even when there seems to be an obvious connection between 'real life' and 'work', you need to *argue your case* for that relationship rather than just assume it.

For all these reasons, you cannot just assume that the 'speaker' of the poem we are looking at *is* Browning. You cannot make assumptions about what the poet *feels* or *intends*, or what he *means* by the poem. You can only talk in terms of what 'the speaker' says and does; what Browning 'seems' to be doing in the poem; and what *the poem* might mean. The same applies when you are talking about the 'meanings' of a painting or a piece of music.

KEY POINTS

When you are interpreting the meanings of a text you should:

- try to *find out* as much as you can about the *conditions* in which the text was created and received (read, viewed or heard); but

- try *not to make assumptions* about relationships between 'real life' and 'the work', or about the artist's beliefs, feelings and *intentions*.

Figure 6.2 Nicolas Poussin, *Landscape with a Man Killed by a Snake*, 1648, oil on canvas, 119 x 199 cm. (Reproduced by courtesy of the Trustees, The National Gallery, London)

4.2 Meaning and 'form'

The question remains, what is this poem 'about'? Or, rather, we should ask, 'what *kind* of poem is it?' Poems (paintings, ideas, music, buildings, historical documents) are not all 'one kind of thing'. As we become familiar with poetry we learn to distinguish between different *kinds* of poem, or between different *poetic forms*.

Epic poems, for example, are extremely long stories about the doings of a noble warrior, voyager, or similar 'hero'. Other characters are involved too. They are always described in detail when they are introduced into the story and usually make a dignified 'set' speech which reveals their 'character'. Great battles take place, involving descriptions of the hero's appearance and weapons as well as the action. The style of writing is high-flown and elaborate, in keeping with the epic's lofty themes. These are the literary devices – or, *conventions* – traditionally associated with epic poetry. We interpret the meanings of an epic poem within that framework of understanding. So when a character makes a set speech we do not *expect* it to sound like 'real' speech. And it would be *inappropriate* to criticize the poem for not being 'true to life'. An epic is not supposed to be true to life; it is supposed to be far grander than that.

To say that the meaning of a poem is closely bound up in the way it is written, then, is to say that 'its *meaning* is bound up in its *form*'. When you analyse a poem you come to understand the elements of its 'formal' patterning. This gives you clues to the meanings it is *appropriate* to make.

'Conventions'

When you sit among rows of people to watch a play, first the curtain goes up – to reveal, say, a living room. We 'accept' this as an artificial device that indicates the start of the play (because of course curtains do not go up to reveal living rooms in real life). Then what you see is a 'room' with three walls. You simply ignore the fact that the fourth wall is missing. (Indeed, it would be odd to complain about this because, otherwise, you wouldn't be able to see the play.) These 'walls' are in fact flat, painted canvases, but you ignore that too. The furniture in the room is all turned to face the audience and people weave around it, wearing costumes, speaking very loudly and making exaggerated gestures, generally also facing the audience. And they perhaps even speak to each other in verse. *None* of these things is natural or 'true to life' (even sitting in rows in the 'audience'). They are all *conventions*: artificial devices that are 'generally accepted' as necessary to the business of presenting and viewing a play. Indeed, they are bound up in what it *means* to stage a play. If you, watching, do not 'accept' these things, then you will misunderstand what you see in a big way. As with the play, so with the epic poem.

Certain conventional 'rules' also govern the way a landscape painting is composed. (Look at the landscape in Figure 6.2.) As here, the scene is usually constructed in horizontal 'layers' that seem to recede into the distance – rather as scenery is positioned at the sides of a stage, with one 'flat' behind another – giving the illusion of depth on the two-dimensional canvas. This is another reason why a painting of a real landscape is never a faithful representation of that scene. It is not only that the painter may have added imaginary details to what she actually saw. It is that the landscape *form* will make its own 'demands'. In order to give the *illusion* of depth (light, and so on), painters *represent* what they see according to the conventions governing the painting's composition and uses of line and colour. A painting is always an '*imagined* reality'.

Some painters (composers, poets, playwrights) play around with these conventions, and so with our *expectations* of the painting, music, poem or play. A play may be presented 'in the round', for example, with no curtain, stage, or scenery. But they can only do that, and we can only *understand* what they are doing, if we all know what the (normally accepted) conventions are. It is only when we know what the 'rules' *are* that we can break them, or tell when someone else is breaking them.

Browning's poem is a *lyric* (in fact he called it a 'dramatic lyric'). When you analyse the particular patterns of words and sounds that make it up you are exploring the various *elements* of its lyric *form*. By convention, this type of poem is very short and usually expresses the feelings of a single speaker. Originally, lyrics were poems written to be sung. They are rhythmic and rhyming, and they appeal to the reader's emotions and senses. (Indeed, we have already identified some of these features in the poem.) When you can place Browning's poem as 'a lyric' you approach it with these kinds of expectations. Unlike the grandeur of epic themes, you expect it to engage with some aspect of a world that we know, and to appeal to your feelings as an 'ordinary' human being. So, in recognizing its form you are also accepting some *limits* on the kind of interpretation you can make of it – or, on the range of its *appropriate* meanings.

For example, if at first you thought the poem was about a smuggler meeting up with his accomplice (which I have heard argued, quite stoutly), that interpretation would not sit at all comfortably with Browning's use of the lyric form. Even if you argued that smugglers might well be rowing about in the night in an excited state, and meeting secretly using pre-arranged signals, still it would not be a likely interpretation of this poem – let alone a convincing one. Why then the mainly soft sounds and languorous movement of the verse; the attention to visual detail of 'yellow half-moon large and low' and the sensuousness of 'warm sea-scented beach'? No smuggler worth his salt would be responding to all that as he went about his business, nor registering the feel and smell of the sand. And while the two accomplices might well whisper to each other, would that be out of their 'joys' as well as fears? Would their, no doubt, pounding hearts beat 'each to each'?

And why, in the context of smugglers, would the poet be inclined to compare the waves in moonlight – 'startled' from their 'sleep' by unexpected oars – to 'fiery ringlets'? Ringlets are what women had in their hair. It seems much more likely that this image of being 'startled' from sleep anticipates what happens in the second verse – putting the idea of 'woman' into our minds earlier on, so that we are in a sense prepared for the meeting. In short, in view of the poem's lyric form and what we have understood about the way it works, it seems all the more appropriate to interpret it as a poem about a secret meeting between lovers.

KEY POINTS

When you are interpreting the meanings of a text you should be *guided* by:

- your knowledge of the *type* of text it is (of its *form*)
- your understanding of the *conventions* that 'govern' the subject matter, purposes, and (formal) elements of the text.

This enables you to make some *appropriate* interpretation of its meanings.

4.3   Analysis and interpretation

We have got to the point of recognizing that this is a lyric poem, and of thinking that it is probably about a lovers' meeting. But you cannot reach firmer conclusions about a text's meanings until you have looked at as many aspects of it as you can. I think we need to go back again to the detail of the poem, because the analysis is not full enough yet.

For one thing, there is something odd about the poem's syntax. If you look at the verbs in the first verse you'll see that they are all in the present tense: 'leap', 'I gain' and 'quench'. This is what the waves *are doing* or the speaker *is doing*. We might expect that pattern to continue into the second verse. But it doesn't. The next verb, in line 2, is 'to cross'. This does not suggest that the traveller *is doing* the crossing, but that crossing the fields *has still to be done*. What does that mean?

ACTIVITY

Just stop for a moment to confirm the change in verb tense for yourself. What are the implications of it; what do you think it might 'mean'?

While you're at it, have a really close look at the last two lines in the first verse. What is being compared to what here? And what does this comparison suggest to you?

Well, I think the change in tense means that at the end of the first verse the traveller is beaching the boat *looking forward* to, or anticipating, the rest of the journey and the meeting. In other words, the things that 'happen' in the second verse, the journey over land and the meeting itself, are going on in the speaker's *mind*. What are the implications of that? Notice, he knows this journey pretty well – 'a mile' of beach, 'three' fields – and he knows exactly what signals will be exchanged when he gets to the farm. What this suggests, then, is that it is not the first time he has made the journey and met his lover secretly. This is a 'love affair' we have here, not a one-night stand. And perhaps what *all* this means is that, in a secret love affair, what goes on in our minds – or, *anticipation* – is a large part of the excitement and pleasure.

Making meaning: 'Anything goes'?

'Making meaning' is a process that goes on in our minds when we come up against something in the world, or ideas in a text, that we try to make sense of. But it is clear from talking to other people that we do not always make the same meanings, even of the same events and texts. We may respond to and interpret them differently. Indeed, on that basis, some people think you can just say what you like about a poem, painting or piece of music; there is no 'right' or 'wrong' about it because we all 'respond' to it differently, emotionally and in our imaginations. So it *means* different things to us. In the realm of interpretation, 'anything goes'. (Lovers' or smugglers' meeting? – it's all a matter of personal response.) But this is a big mistake.

In the first place, just because we sometimes interpret things differently does not mean that we always or even usually do. In fact, I'd say that very often we make similar meanings to others in our culture. That's why we can understand each other, often in subtle ways, and laugh at the same jokes. But in any case, we *cannot* say just what we like about a poem, painting or any of the other objects we study. If we think we can that is because we are only thinking about *ourselves*, about our feelings and fancies. We are forgetting about the other half of the equation – the *text* we are studying and trying to interpret the meaning of. That text imposes some *limits* on the interpretations we may make. We are limited by our understanding of the *kind* of text we are dealing with – by its conventional *form* – and by our knowledge of the *conditions* in which it was created, and read, seen or heard. In view of those limitations, what we should say is that there is a certain *range* of *appropriate meanings* we may make.

It is *within that range* that we may well disagree because of the differences there are between us. In some texts the range is wide, so there may be much to disagree about. But this is far from saying that 'anything' goes. Rather, it suggests that we *can* be 'more' or 'less' right in our interpretations.

Another pattern you may or may not have spotted is Browning's frequent use of *articles* ('the' and 'a'), especially the *definite article*, 'the', in the first three lines of the poem. We noted before that we don't know where these events take place. It could be anywhere on and near a coast. Or is it 'nowhere' – not a 'real' place at all? The lovers are pretty shadowy figures too: one the muscular 'I' of the first verse, the other 'a voice' and, together, 'the two hearts beating'. Why all this anonymity?

Is it that we are not *supposed* to be thinking of them as *particular* lovers, meeting at a specific place and time? Are they rather meant to represent or 'stand for' lovers *in general*? If so, this seems to be all of a piece with the implications of the change in verb tenses we discussed just now. That, too, led us to think in more abstract terms – about the *role* of anticipation in affairs *of this kind.*

So, taking these elements of the verse together, perhaps what we should be thinking about – and our feelings be engaged by – is the *state* of 'being in love'. Rather than describing a series of events that actually happened in a real place involving particular people, what the poet seems to be doing is *evoking* this *state* for us: calling up our memories and feelings about it through the sounds and movement of the verse, and the kind of words and images he uses. Through that evocation, it is as if the poem 'asks' us to recognize that when we are in love, we human beings are fuelled with energy – we will go to extraordinary lengths and run all sorts of risk. We are full of excited anticipation, with every sense alert and heightened; we invest our surroundings with beauty and romance. And it is as if our very hearts beat a tattoo in our breasts. Perhaps the poem also suggests that, in a *secret* love affair, what we have is this romantic state 'writ large' – in its extreme form.

But are we quite right to think of this state as an extreme of 'romantic' love? What about the image at the end of the first verse? The male speaker is being compared to the boat: '*I* gain the cove with pushing *prow*'. Then the speaker's/prow's speed is quenched 'i' the slushy sand'. What does this comparison bring to mind? Well, within an interpretation of this as a poem about lovers, isn't it a sexual image? As people who live after Freud it is perhaps hard for us to interpret things like 'prows' penetrating sand (trains going through tunnels, and so on) as anything other than 'phallic symbols'. Come to think of it, the image in lines 3 and 4 of the first verse is beginning to take on a whole new meaning now. Maybe the 'spurt' of the match is significant too…

But perhaps you are protesting at this point. Isn't that going much too far – reading things 'into' this poem from our present ways of thinking? Isn't that interpretation *inappropriate*, given the time and place in which the poem was written? Actually, I don't see why. Browning certainly didn't know about Freud (1856–1939) when he wrote the poem. But full-blown love affairs were sexual then as now. Also, the promise of such an encounter fits with the idea of being driven to extremes of exertion and of taking risks, fuelled by the excitement of sexual passion. Anyway, if Browning were writing about sex we would precisely *expect* to find it only 'suggested' in his verse rather than made plain. If he wanted his work to be published he could not have written about it explicitly at that time.

However, having said all that, this is an example of the kind of interpretation we might *not* agree about – *within* our understanding of the poem's 'range of meaning' as a meeting between lovers. We can at least agree that it is unlikely to have some other range of meaning altogether. (It's safe to leave the smugglers behind us, for instance.) That is because, in carrying out a fairly full analysis of the 'formal elements' of this 'lyric' poem, and taking account of the 'conditions' in which it was written and read, *everything* we have discovered chimes with the interpretation of it as a lovers' meeting and *nothing* about it seems to suggest otherwise.

KEY POINTS

When you are *interpreting* a text, you should try to reach an understanding of the 'range of meaning' you may make by combining:

- your knowledge of the text's *form* (the *conventions* that govern its composition); and
- your understanding of the *conditions* in which the text was created and received.

When you also take account of

- the outcomes of your analysis of its formal *elements*

you are able to make some *appropriate* interpretation of the text's meanings.

Now, we will try to make some judgements about the text.

5 EVALUATION

As we have seen, you are fully *immersed* in the text while you try to discover how it works and what it is about. But in order to make some *judgements* of it you have to shift your stance a bit. You have to 'stand back', as it were, and ask yourself: What do I think about these things I have discovered?

Basically, you need to ask two *kinds* of question about the text's 'value':

1   *What values* are represented in the text (emotional/social/ moral/intellectual…)?

    Are they *good* values (for us, here and now), or not?

2   Is the text *of value*; is this text a good one of its kind?

Returning to the poem, we'll look at each of these questions in turn.

5.1 The values represented by the text

The first question here is, *what values* does the poem stand for? If the poem is about the nature of the romantic–sexual relationship – the state of being in love – what is it 'saying' to us about that?

Stop and think about this question of what values the poem 'stands for'. Jot down a few of the thoughts that occur to you – and also make a note of what their opposites might be.

For instance, the first things that occurred to me were:

(for) *romance*	('against') everyday reality	
(for) *risk*	('against') safety	

How did you get on? Other things I wrote down are:

For	Against
action/energy	passivity
intensity of feeling	quiescence
sexual passion	inhibition
the stolen moment	settled domesticity

The point of thinking about the opposite of whatever the text seems to stand for is that, whenever we *affirm* one thing we also (by implication) *deny* its opposite. So looking at what the text seems to be 'denying' can help you get clear what values it *does* represent.

Take the first pair of terms I thought of, 'romance' versus 'everyday reality'. Thinking about what the *reality* of Browning's scenario might be, draws attention to the *ideal*-ness of what he evokes – its make-believe quality. So, the energetic traveller does *not* disembark in the cove soaked in sweat (have you ever done any hard rowing, even for a few minutes?). Nor does he twist his ankle while ploughing through ruts or mud slicks in the fields, and no farm-yard dog barks to give his presence away. We do *not* get the sense that he will have to undertake the whole journey in reverse and then set off for work the next day thoroughly knackered.[2]

---

[2] In fact there is a companion-piece to this poem, entitled 'Parting at Morning', which raises some intriguing possibilities of a different kind.

Seen from this perspective, the poem seems even more concerned with the *possibilities* of human passion than with the reality of it. Looking further down my list, it is not that the poem 'says' anything as crude as 'whatever you do, don't get "married" and settle down'. But we can see that in evoking and *beautifying* this state of intense sexual passion (even, perhaps, a forbidden love) – the vigour, risk-taking and heightening of the senses involved – the poem *celebrates* all these things. And, in doing so, it seems to 'recommend' these *as values* over their opposites.

Making assumptions

You might think that, having examined the text carefully and reached some interpretation of its meanings, there should be no difficulty about deciding what values it represents. But this is not always the case – they may not be *obvious* to you at all. That is because values are often *assumed by* the text (simply taken to be true), and so hidden from view. It is as if the text speaks to us 'out of' certain *underlying* beliefs. So, at this stage, you may have to dig around the text a bit more to be clear about them (as we are doing here). As readers, we all make certain assumptions too – we are not conscious of everything we 'take to be true'. And some of the things we know we believe, we possibly haven't given much thought to.

For instance, you may have assumed from the start that the lover who 'waits' is a woman. And we saw that it is reasonable to think so, given the time and place the poem was written and read (so it isn't a totally unexamined assumption). However, we are now interpreting this as a poem about the state of being in love, rather than about particular lovers. If it is about human sexual passion *in general*, shouldn't we think again about this assumption? But, then, what about the 'ringlets'...?

Texts of all kinds, especially philosophical texts, challenge us to *explore* our assumptions, and really *think* about what we believe and why.

So, having identified some of the values the poem seems to stand for, are they 'good' values – for us, here and now – or not? What do *you* think?

You might take one of a number of positions on this. For example, you could argue along something like the following lines:

1   The poem evokes, beautifies and celebrates an 'ideal' of the romantic, sexual relationship. In doing so, it draws our attention to the possibilities of intense human passion – the energy, our willingness to risk, the heightening of our senses involved. And so, it espouses values that are positively life enhancing.

At this point there are at least couple of different directions your argument might take:

(a)   At a time when we seem to be obsessed with *practical* concerns of various kinds (with technology, the economy, material comfort…), it suggests that what we *are*, and may be in relationship to one another, is at least as valuable as what we *achieve*. The poem makes us question our modern assumptions; to think again about what it means, as human beings, to be fully *alive*.

(b)   In its unashamed celebration of human passion and absence of moral judgement, the poem takes what seems a surprisingly modern stance. These are not what we normally think of as 'Victorian values'. Reading the poem makes us think about relationships between then and now – re-examining what we understand by both 'Victorian' and 'modern' values.

On the other hand, leaving the first two sentences of (1) above pretty much as they are, you might add:

2   …espouses values that at first sight seem life enhancing. However, the poem celebrates a *particular* view of what that means. The values it represents are, traditionally, *masculine* values – 'risk' and aggressive 'action' taken towards the satisfaction of sexual desire. As the poem idealizes *these* values, at the same time it spurns the more passive or 'nurturing' values thought to be natural in the female. These differences were no doubt widely believed to be true of men and women at the time the poem was written and first read…

Again, the argument could then take off in different directions:

(a)   …even so, the effect of the poem is to glorify the 'male' at the expense of the 'female'. This hardly seems 'life enhancing' in our modern-day understanding. Perhaps the poem's greatest value to us is as a measure of how differently we view things now.

(b)   …so that the superior value of the 'masculine' is simply assumed. Knowing that, we can look beyond this assumption to the poem's central, essentially life-enhancing, message – the joy *both* lovers feel as their hearts beat 'each to each'.

Or, you might not take such a positive view of things at all, possibly arguing something like this.

3   The romantic setting of this little 'story' and the sensuous beauty of the verse are seductive. What we have here is a slight poem that celebrates what may well be a betrayal of some kind. It is a sort of 'adolescent fantasy' – of macho derring-do? or just nonsense? As such, it bears no relationship to reality and tells us nothing of value.

The point to note here is that there is no reason why you should *accept* the values the text seems to represent. We have seen that you certainly need to try to understand *what* those values are, and *why* they might have been held at that time – otherwise you are not in a position to make informed and appropriate judgements at all. But that is not the same thing as 'accepting' them.

Sometimes, you may find a text a good example of its kind *technically*, yet judge its values abhorrent – a painting that seems to 'celebrate' a bloody massacre, for instance, through the way the brush strokes are lovingly executed. This is why it is helpful to keep your assessment of the values the text stands for *separate* in your mind from your critical assessment of that text, as a painting, poem, or whatever. However, notice that *all* the 'arguments' I have just set out about the values the poem stands for depend heavily on critical assessment of it – which we are about to look at. Even argument 3 refers to, and recognizes, the 'sensuous beauty' of the verse.

This is just another way of saying that the processes of analysing a text and interpreting its meanings are fundamental to making judgements about it. The more thoroughly you analyse a text the better you will understand it and the surer your judgements will be.

> ### KEY POINTS
>
> When you are *assessing* the *values* a text represents, you should:
>
> - *question* those values (whether they are assumed by the text or are more obvious)
> - try to *examine* your own values, and the assumptions *you* may be making
> - firm up your judgements only when you have analysed and interpreted the meanings of the text as *fully* as you can.

5.2   The value of the text

We now turn to a *critical assessment* of the poem *as a poem*; the question is, is it a 'good' poem? To that we should add 'of its kind'. As we saw, we must judge it as a *lyric* poem – it would be inappropriate to think of it in the same terms as, say, an epic, because the conventions that govern the epic's form (its subject matter, purposes and formal elements) are very different. It is always important to understand what *kind* of text you are dealing with not only because that knowledge guides you towards some appropriate interpretation of its meanings, but also because it places limits on the *judgements* you can make of it.

As we have seen, by convention the lyric poem:

- takes as its *subject matter* some aspect of a human world we recognize
- has the *purposes* of appealing to our senses and engaging our feelings
- is in lyric *form*: short and song-like (rhythmic, rhyming).

These, then, are the *criteria* against which we make our judgements. I think it is safe to say that we have seen all these things in the poem during the last few sections of the chapter. The question is, how *well* does it do them?

As regards the poem's subject matter, we might ask 'does it "talk" to us about some aspect of the world we recognize, *in a meaningful and illuminating way*?' Looking at the series of 'arguments' I sketched out a couple of pages back, clearly the world of the poem is recognizable to us, and it is possible to make several different kinds of connection between what the poem 'says' and some of our current social, moral and intellectual concerns. These are meaningful connections and, I would say, potentially illuminating (response number 3 notwithstanding). But what do *you* think?

Turning to the poem's 'purposes', *how well* does it engage our feelings and appeal to our senses? Again, we have discussed the way the poem *evokes* our memories and feelings of 'being in love'. It achieves this through: the romantic setting (of moonlight over water…); the generally languorous movement and sounds of the verse, interspersed with the excited agitation of lines 3 and 4; the sexual imagery; the syntax (changing verb tenses and also the sensuousness of the words). On page 195 we saw that the poem appeals *directly* to our senses of sight, hearing, smell, touch, and sensation.

Here we have also impinged on our last criterion, the poem's song-like *formal elements* (especially its movement and rhyming, but also syntax, imagery, and so on). In short, on pages 195–6 we saw how the whole is 'knitted' closely together by interwoven patterns of sound, movement and imagery – that not a word of it is carelessly placed. Indeed, the verse is rich beyond what seems possible at first sight.

What is striking is how a poem so short and apparently simple can carry such a weight of analysis, interpretation and evaluation. But we must remind ourselves that this is, after all, a short lyric poem. We should not expect it to bear *too* much weight. (Incidentally, what do you think that exclamation mark right at the end means?)

Personal response

Do you think I like this poem? Perhaps it is obvious that I do. If you have 'picked up' my enjoyment of it, it must be something about the way I have written because it is the *poem* we have been concentrating on *all the time*. In fact I know it off by heart (which is perhaps not too surprising by now). But, anyway, I am only telling you so in this box.

That's because, if I say to you 'I love this music; it reminds me of lambs in spring-time', what I am telling you is something about *myself*. If you find me a fascinating person you will no doubt be interested to know how I feel. But if it's the *music* you are interested in then you are no closer to understanding it at all. Emotional or imaginative responses to a text are *not the same thing* as judgement of its values and critical assessment of it – arrived at through processes of analysis and interpretation. And it is the *texts* we study that are our main focus, not ourselves.

But that doesn't mean your personal responses are unimportant. Far from it. If you are moved by a novel, a passage of music, a sculpture or an idea, it is not only interesting but also a pleasure to work out why: what it is about the text that affects you in that way. Very often the text becomes more interesting and affects you more deeply the more you think and learn about it. Your feelings and intuitions are also very helpful guides to your analysis of it – showing you 'ways in', what to look out for. In any case, the very powerful effects art and ideas can have is perhaps why you are keen to study the arts and humanities in the first place. Even so, sometimes what you study may seem dull and uninspiring. Or, in extreme cases, you may find certain ideas and representations totally unacceptable or even shocking. In every case, the point is to understand *why* – what it is about *the text* – whether it is something you love or loathe.

However, if it seems to you that analysing texts simply 'spoils' your enjoyment of them then perhaps you shouldn't be *studying* these subjects. Why not just continue to enjoy your experiences?

In making a critical assessment of this poem it helps to be familiar with a range of other lyric poems, so that you have something to compare it with. And this is true generally. You become surer in your judgements as you become more familiar with the *kind* of poem, painting, piece of music, argument, or historical document you are faced with.

We should note here that the criteria for evaluating historical documents and philosophical arguments are different, both from each other and from the kinds of criteria we have been looking at here. As we have seen, the analytical questions you ask about a document are to do with the type of source it is, who its author was, when and why it was written; and therefore *what* it is actually telling you and how *reliably*. These are the criteria against which you judge it. A 'good' document is a reliable source that is useful for your purposes.

Philosophical texts argue through 'problems': such as an ethical dilemma, the question of free will, of what exists, and so forth. In evaluating this kind of text, you are concerned with the *logic* and '*truth*' of that argument. A 'good' argument is logically sound and also illuminating.

5.3   A 'circle' of understanding

It may seem as if analysing, interpreting and evaluating a text are 'stages' we go through, one after the other. But it's nothing like as mechanical as that. You do not analyse a text into separate parts, then 'add up' those parts to produce some interpretation of the whole, and then evaluate it. Rather, analysis–interpretation–evaluation are *overlapping processes*. They are different *kinds* of activity, as we have seen by looking at them separately. But when you try to understand a text you are unfamiliar with, what you actually do is 'circle around' it in the following sort of way.

● As you read, listen to or look at the text for the first few times, you form some impressions of what kind of text it is and what it is 'about'. And of course you respond to it, emotionally, in your imagination and intellectually.

● These perceptions help you find 'ways into' the text, and you start to analyse parts of it carefully.

● Then you draw back and have a think about how the whole thing looks now.

● Guided by that, you go back into the detail of another part of the text – draw back again, and see how that further analysis affects your view of the text's meanings as a whole.

● Meanwhile, you are beginning to make judgements about the text, which you also revise as you go along.

And so on, back and forth between the *parts* of the text and your conception of it *as a whole*, shifting your attention and revising your interpretations and judgements as you go. What we did in section 4.3 ('Analysis *and* interpretation') comes closest to this process.

You do this circling around as you *engage actively* with the text and *make meaning* of it in your mind. 'Meaning' is not a thing; it is not just 'inside' the text, waiting to be 'uncovered' when you apply certain analytical techniques to it. Making meaning is a *process*. What you do is more like 'communicating' with the text – looking at and 'listening' to it, as it were, and 'talking back' to it. The *last* things you firm up are your judgements: of the values the text represents, and its value as the kind of text it is. After all that, you are ready to communicate your interpretations and judgements to other people.

6 COMMUNICATING YOUR IDEAS

If you were talking to a friend about a picture hanging on your living-room wall, you might say: 'I really like that portrait because the man looks so life-like'. That is, you'd make some kind of *judgement* about the painting. (I've never heard anyone say 'I really like that portrait because of that little white brush stroke in the top right-hand corner'.) So, in effect, you turn the process we have just been through on its head. When you are communicating your ideas to other people, you *start* with what were the *conclusions* of that process – and you go on to present an *argument* in support of your judgements that draws on the detail you discovered in the text. Having previously taken the roles of investigator and judge (or 'critic') of the text, you now have to take on the role of *advocate* for your interpretation of it. As an advocate, you try to *make a case* for your view of the text's meanings and values that will *convince* other people.

6.1 Making a convincing case

Let's suppose you wanted to argue in support of the 'stem' of the first argument on page 208. Here it is again, broken down into its component parts.

(a) The poem (i) evokes, (ii) beautifies and (iii) celebrates an 'ideal' of the romantic, sexual relationship.

(b) In doing so, it draws our attention to the possibilities of intense human passion – (i) the energy, (ii) our willingness to risk, (iii) the heightening of our senses involved.

(c) And so, it espouses values that are positively life enhancing.

This is an outline sketch of the *argument* for, say, an essay. There are three main points (a, b, c), the first two of which contain several different claims (i, ii, iii.). *All* these claims have to be *demonstrated* in order to make both main points in a convincing way. In the process you will have demonstrated point (c), your conclusion, so at that stage you would just need to sum up.

But how do you 'demonstrate' a claim *convincingly*? If you look back to what we did in section 3.2 you will see how. You have to *explain* what you mean, using examples from the text to *illustrate* your meaning; and you have to provide some *evidence* from the text that shows you are right to say what you do about it.

Let's take the first claim in point (a), that the poem 'evokes' the romantic, sexual relationship. Earlier (in section 5.2) we saw that this depends on the poem's success in engaging our feelings and appealing to our senses. So you could demonstrate the claim by referring to:

- the romantic setting, of sea and landscape bathed in moonlight – offering textual detail as *illustration*

- the languorous movement of the verse – quoting some of the words of the poem to *illustrate* long vowel sounds and soft-sounding consonants

- the syntax – quoting a word or phrase that appeals to each of our senses, as *illustration*; the significance of the shift in verb tenses between the verses – *explaining* and *illustrating* this

- the imagery ('ringlets' and 'prow') – offering textual detail as *illustration* and *explanation.*

In each case you are also providing *evidence* in support of this claim, by referring to *precise* details of the text and/or *quoting* relevant words and phrases directly from it (see section 6.2). As a result, your reader should both understand what you are saying and find your argument convincing.

As you actually write the essay, the main difficulty you face is keeping this argument *going forward* while *also* including as much detailed reference as you need to explain, illustrate and justify what you say at each stage. So, at the points when you 'interrupt' the onward flow of the argument in order to provide this textual detail, you need to *remind* your readers where they have got to and where they are headed next, before you set off again. That is because, when you present a case in writing, you can't 'check' with your readers to make sure they are following your meaning. You need to keep 'signposting' the direction your argument is taking (see Chapter 5).

Why communicate?

Studying arts and humanities subjects involves learning particular ways of expressing ideas, and of 'arguing a case' that is supported by appropriate kinds of 'evidence'. That is, we learn to think, speak and write in the *terms* and *ways* that are appropriate to the subject we are studying. Those are the terms and ways in which *everyone* who has studied the subject speaks, so that we can understand each other and learn from each other. In short, we learn how to *join in* that ongoing discourse.

Indeed, each subject in the arts and humanities is itself a different kind of discourse (a way of using language and other symbolic forms (such as pictures and music) communicatively, so as to *produce meaning* and *understanding*). Poetry is one way in which human beings communicate with each other and art is another, different, way; so is music; so is a legal document or an Act of Parliament; and so is a philosophical argument. When we are actively reading and thinking about these texts, then, we engage in a kind of 'communication' with them.

Similarly, when you discuss your interpretations and judgements of these texts or write an essay, you become a participant in the *academic* discourses that are *related* to them – that produce meaning and understanding *about* the different subjects we study. You are making your own enquiries and producing your own 'texts'. The essays you write are judged according to how close you come to 'speaking' appropriately, within the terms of the academic discourse concerned.

The upshot is that, in the arts and humanities, the *knowledge* we have is what we have made and continue making through our *discourse*, past and present. Whichever way you turn, communication is the name of the game.

So, as an advocate for your interpretations and judgements of the text, you have to present a clear and consistent line of argument, that is well explained and illustrated and also supported by appropriate kinds of evidence. And you have to try to write simply and directly to your readers in order to *engage* their minds.

KEY POINTS

When you are *communicating* your interpretations and judgements of a text you have to make a convincing *case* in support of them.

At each stage of a written argument, you should:

- *explain* yourself clearly and give *examples* of what you mean by what you say (illustrations drawn from the text)
- provide appropriate *evidence* from the text
- use the appropriate *language* of communication
- 'signpost' the *direction* your argument is taking.

But what exactly is 'appropriate' evidence? And how do you know what terms are the 'appropriate' ones to use?

6.2 Different kinds of 'evidence'

The *terms* you use and the *ways* in which you support your argument depend on the subject you are studying and what *kind of text* you are talking or writing about.

Quoting from written texts

We have seen that when you are discussing a poem, you talk about its 'rhythms' or movement, its patterns of sound such as 'rhyme', and its 'imagery' and 'syntax', *quoting* words, phrases and lines from the poem as evidence of the points you want to make about it. And this applies to play-texts and novels, too. As you discuss the 'characters' involved, you quote parts of their 'dialogue' or passages from the 'narrator's' descriptions of them. You also *quote* from relevant parts of historical documents when you discuss their 'purposes', their 'reliability' as 'sources' of information and the 'evidence' they provide. And from a philosophical text when you discuss the 'premises' and 'logic' of an argument. However, in philosophical writing, part of the process of showing that you understand the ideas you have been grappling with is being able to *invent* examples of your own to illustrate the points you make. What matters most is how carefully you handle the details of the argument and how clearly you *explain* yourself.

Presenting quotations

Some general points about quoting from secondary sources are discussed in Chapter 5 (using quotation marks and three dots to indicate that some words have been left out, for example). Those conventions apply when you quote from *any* prose passage such as an historical document, novel or philosophical argument. But when you quote more than a few words you should *indent* the quotation rather than trying to incorporate it in the flow of a sentence, as follows:

Ellis concludes that:

> The steady migration of women into the towns was the logical consequence of conventional perceptions of femininity and of correct female behaviour.

In this case, you do *not* use quotation marks because you are indicating that it is a quotation by indenting it.

However, when you quote from poetry you have to show where lines end.

If you quote only a few words you can incorporate them into a sentence, separating the lines with a slash (/):

> In 'the quick sharp scratch/And blue spurt...' the consonants are dental and the vowel sounds short, in keeping with the sound of the match-lighting that the words evoke.

If you want to quote more than one line of the poem in full, you should indent the quotation:

> Here, though, the consonants are dental and the vowel sounds short:
>
>> A tap at the pane, the quick sharp scratch
>> And blue spurt of a lighted match,...

Notice that all punctuation marks must be included in the quotation too. Indeed, *whenever* you use quotation you must quote *accurately*.

Representing visual and symbolic texts

We saw that when you discuss your judgements of a visual text such as the landscape painting or *The Madonna and Child*, you talk about its 'composition': the way the 'picture space' is organized; the relationships between 'foreground' and 'background', and between 'figures'. You discuss the way 'perspective' is used in the painting to show 'depth'; the painting's 'tonal range', and its uses of 'colour', 'shape', 'line'; 'light' and 'shade', and light 'source'. This kind of description is based on detailed observation of the painting. But here – and when you discuss a sculpture or building, and symbolic texts such as maps, plans and music scores – you may *also* want to include your own *sketches*, *diagrams* or *notation* to demonstrate these relationships, and show precisely which elements of the text you are drawing attention to.

Precise reference to 'linear' texts

You may find it more difficult to provide evidence from texts in which sounds, words or images follow on from one another over time (such as music and videos, plays and novels). Music is perhaps particularly hard to pin down. Sounds weave in and out of each other so that at first you may experience the music as seamless. But there are different 'movements' or 'passages' in music; moments at which a 'melody' is first introduced and later passages when it is repeated, for example. You can distinguish between these and other, different passages in the music by locating them within a description of the music's 'development', making precise reference to its *structure*. A certain 'chord' sounds just *after* the 'first repetition' of the melody, for instance; or just *before* the trumpet 'fanfare'. You can also identify and *describe* the patterning and effects of different elements of the music, such as its 'harmony', 'rhythm' and 'timbre' (the quality of sound associated with different instruments or voices).

Although novels, play-texts and film-scripts are written rather than aural texts, they are similar in the way that they unfold bit by bit, in a linear way. Here too you can identify particular developments or moments by locating them within the overall *structure* – in this case, of the 'plot' – and again by reference to *time* and *event* (after the scene at the ball, when the characters first meet, before the picnic, during the thunder storm). And, as with music, you can *describe* and discuss formal elements, such as 'character', 'tone of voice', 'dialogue', 'point of view'. However, in these cases, you can *also* quote relevant words, sentences and short 'speeches' from the text.

When you are discussing the performance of a play or moving images, you again think in terms of 'plot' and structure, identifying particular moments in the ways we have just seen. Here again, you can include your own sketches or diagrams to provide evidence of the visual relationships you are discussing.

Multiple texts

Very often you will be studying 'the art' or 'the literature' of a particular period and therefore a *number* of texts rather than just one. Or perhaps you will be using a range of *different* documents as the basis of your interpretation of an historical event. And what if your subject is inter-disciplinary (Religious or Classical Studies, say) and you study many different *kinds* of text (written, visual and symbolic), 'bringing together' your judgements of them to explain certain beliefs, practices or ways of living?

In all these cases, the processes of analysis, interpretation and judgement we have discussed still apply to *each* particular work of art, building, document, ceremony and so forth that you study. And the kinds of evidence you use to justify your judgements of these different texts are also just as we have seen. However, the *danger* here is that you may be tempted to analyse and interpret these many texts less carefully than you might when dealing with only one or two – moving too quickly towards your judgements, and then too quickly again towards their implications for the times, beliefs or ways of life you are discussing. This is known as 'reading off the text' (that is, off its surface), and you should try not to do it.

For example, if your subject is Religious Studies and you are discussing the beliefs of, say, Browning's contemporaries, there will be many different sources you might study – hymns, paintings, scientific theories, church buildings, accounts of religious ceremonies… In this situation, it is better to select a few representative texts and talk about them in some detail rather than opting for thin coverage of a large number of them. In the end, precise and detailed reference to fewer texts makes for a more convincing case.

Evidence 'from authority'

When you present evidence for your judgements in an essay, you don't *only* draw that evidence from the text. You also often call on the 'authority' of other writers on the subject (critics, academics), drawing on their judgements. You can see in Chapters 2 and 3 how to read and 'make sense' of other people's ideas in books, articles, TV programmes, and so on; and how to weigh up these ideas and use them to help you form your own. As regards your writing, you have to learn how to use this kind of 'evidence from authority' – how to work other people's ideas into your argument, and also how to acknowledge your sources (see section 8.3).

> ### KEY POINTS
>
> You should present *evidence* for your interpretations and judgements of a text in order to *justify* them (showing your reader why you are right to say what you do).
>
> According to the *type* of text you are discussing, you should:
>
> ● use appropriate *kinds* of evidence
> ● 'speak' in the appropriate *terms*.

7 BELIEFS AND THEORIES

'Authorities' – critics, historians, philosophers and so forth – of course argue from *their* interpretations of what a work of art, an event or an idea means. And their judgements are based on certain *beliefs* – about the nature of the objects they study and about what they themselves do as readers and interpreters of them. From our discussion of 'Meeting at Night' you have seen what my beliefs are: that people can reach some understanding of a text through the processes of analysing its formal elements and acquiring some knowledge of the conditions in which it was created and received. Because I was talking about these very processes I said all that explicitly. But, very often, what writers believe about these things is 'assumed by' rather than 'stated in' their argument. For example, look again at these judgements about 'Meeting at Night':

> The romantic setting of this little 'story' and the sensuous beauty of the verse are seductive. What we have here is a slight poem that celebrates what may well be a betrayal of some kind. It is a sort of 'adolescent fantasy' – of macho derring-do? or just nonsense? As such, it bears no relationship to reality and tells us nothing of value.

Stop for a few minutes and think about what *beliefs* lie 'underneath' these judgements.

It seems to me that beneath the judgements lies the belief that there is quite a strong relationship between a poem and the 'real world' and that if a poem has no relationship to 'reality' then it does not tell us anything worthwhile. And the moral judgement here – that it is improper to celebrate what might be a betrayal – also implies that a poem should say something of *moral* value to us.

Now that we have unearthed these beliefs we can take a good look at them. We can see more clearly what is involved in agreeing with the argument (again asking, what does it 'deny'?). Then we can decide whether we do agree or, if not, what exactly we disagree with. So, do you agree with these beliefs or not? For instance, do you think that there is quite a strong relationship between a poem and 'real life'?

Of course I don't know what you think about that. But you have seen that I think there is. The poem's form is conventional (agreed, as it were, *by people*). It was created and received within certain conditions, and it is received now within different sorts of condition. I believe it does communicate something to us about both those 'worlds'. However, as we saw in section 4.1, I do not think this relationship between 'art' and 'reality' is either a simple or a direct one. What I was trying to say there is that *none* of the texts you study simply *reflects* the world of human experience 'as it really is'. As created objects, they are *artificial*. ('Artificial' *means* 'made by art, not natural'. That is, *people* made them, with different purposes in mind.) They are not simply 'true to life' and they do not 'tell' us things in the direct way this speaker suggests. Remember the painting of the 'real' landscape, with its imaginary additions and conventional form? But think too about an historical document, such as an Act of Parliament. We have to interpret the meanings of all these texts.

In my understanding of 'reality', human invention and imagining is as much a part of our 'world' as anything else. So I would not agree that fantasy is necessarily worthless (adolescent or otherwise). And I think that works of art can communicate all kinds of thing, not just about our moral values. In saying all this I am disagreeing with what the speaker appears to understand by both 'art' and 'reality' – which in both cases seems far too narrow – and about the relationship between the two, which seems too direct.

However, not everyone would agree with my beliefs (perhaps you don't). For instance, some people believe that texts of all kinds have no relationship to the 'real world' because there is no such thing; what 'really' exists are the ideas and beliefs that we human beings have – what we *construct* in our minds and *represent* in our texts. So a text can only be related to the constructions – or, other 'texts' – that have come before it.

These are just a few of the ideas people have about what a work of art *is* and what *relationship* it has to the 'worlds' of its makers and receivers. When such ideas are connected together in a thorough-going way we say we have a *theory* about these things.

Theories

A theory is a 'system of ideas' through which we *explain* something. In the arts and humanities we try to explain such things as the role of the artist, the nature of the text, the way the text is received and interpreted, and the relationships between these things. However, people have not developed a single, 'universal' theory that attempts to explain *all* these things, at all times and in all places. Rather, a number of theories guide us towards looking closely at different aspects of this 'complex' of issues and relationships. Some theories draw attention to the artist's role; some focus on the text and its 'context'; and others explain readers' 'reception' of the text, in their contexts.

In the course of your studies you will no doubt come across many different theories (indeed, it may seem there is a bewildering array of them). You will be asked to *apply* them to the texts you study. That is because theories suggest *different ways* in which you can view the text. As you approach a text from this or that 'point of view', you come to understand and *value* it differently. And, in the process, you become clearer about your own ideas and beliefs.

Using theories prompts you to ask different *kinds* of *question* about the text, from a range of points of view. For instance, can you see what kinds of question this speaker was asking when making judgements about the poem?

> The values [the poem] represents are, traditionally, *masculine* values – 'risk' and aggressive 'action' taken towards the satisfaction of sexual desire. As the poem idealizes *these* values, at the same time it spurns the more passive or 'nurturing' values thought to be natural in the female. These differences were no doubt widely believed to be true of men and women at the time the poem was written and first read…

I think the questions have to do with *gender*. The speaker has approached the poem from the 'point of view' of the way the words in it relate to ideas about the sexes, male and female. (I'll call the speaker 'he'; did you assume it was a woman?) His approach draws on feminist theory, broadly speaking. As a result of adopting this stance, he 'comes at' the poem from a different angle from the other speakers, 'sees' different things in it and makes very different kinds of judgement from them.

But, although adopting this (or any other) theory means taking a *particular* point of view, it does not act as a 'straightjacket' on your thinking – *forcing* you towards a particular conclusion. We have already seen that this feminist line of thinking could lead in quite opposite directions:

(a)   …even so, the effect of the poem is to glorify the 'male' at the expense of the 'female'. This hardly seems 'life enhancing' in our modern-day understanding. Perhaps the poem's greatest value to us is as a measure of how differently we view things now.

(b)   …so that the superior value of the 'masculine' is simply assumed. Knowing that, we can look beyond this assumption to the poem's central, essentially life-enhancing, message – the joy *both* lovers feel as their hearts beat 'each to each'.

If you had not thought about the poem in such feminist terms yourself, you may have found these interpretations and judgements surprising and interesting. And does this prompt you to wonder *why* you hadn't?

Whether you are aware of it or not, your interpretations and judgements of the texts you study are based on certain beliefs: about the world, about the nature of those objects, and about your role as 'critic' of them. If you are *not* aware of it, then these 'beliefs' lie beneath what you say, as *assumptions*. We can't be aware of all the assumptions we make, all the time. But, as you study, you should be thinking about at least some of these things. Our beliefs change, and our thinking becomes richer, as we assess other people's ideas and try applying their theories.

KEY POINTS

Examining other people's beliefs, and applying their theories to the texts you study helps you:

- recognize the *assumptions* that academics and critics make in their writing
- look at texts from different *points of view*, asking different kinds of question about them
- and so, become clearer about your *own* assumptions and beliefs.

Finally, leaving the poem behind, we turn to one of the main ways in which you can become a *participant* in the subject(s) you study. It is when you do some research of your own that you understand more deeply how all the processes we have been looking at actually work in practice.

8 MAKING YOUR OWN ENQUIRIES

Many courses in the arts and humanities now include a substantial *project work* component, which involves research even if it is of a limited and guided kind. This is an opportunity for you study a topic of your own choice in depth, working independently and extending interests and ideas of your own. It involves:

- setting your own targets
- posing central questions to explore
- seeking out the primary and secondary source material you need
- analysing and interpreting your material, and assessing its value
- producing a substantial text of your own.

These activities remind you that knowledge doesn't just appear in books by magic, but results from someone recognizing the importance of a particular question and setting out to find some 'answers' to it. They give you an idea of how knowledge is *created* in your subject. When all goes well, this kind of independent work increases your enthusiasm for your subject, brings a great sense of achievement and produces a deep kind of understanding. But it is very demanding. It can be very interesting and satisfying, but it can also go badly wrong.

The biggest pitfall is that almost everyone is *too ambitious* to begin with. Things always turn out to be more complicated than they seem and every aspect of project work is more time-consuming than you anticipate. There are several stages involved, each of which takes time and effort. One of the keys to success is recognizing the importance of each stage and spreading your time and energies across all of them. These *stages* are:

1   Formulating a question to explore
2   Planning the enquiry
3   Carrying out the research
4   Writing a project report.

At first sight, the third stage looks like the bulk of the work. But deciding on the question to investigate, narrowing it down sufficiently, and designing and planning the project always take a lot of thought. You can easily let these early stages eat too far into the time you have for the project as a whole. Then that third stage almost always throws up plenty of unexpected problems – sometimes quite minor, but enough to slow your progress. However, the writing phase is the one that really catches people unawares. You have to present your research in the wider context of the subject it arises out of, and also work out how to structure the report so that your line of argument is clear and leads to your conclusions. And you have to keep the forward momentum of that argument going while also introducing what you have discovered – of which there is plenty. All this takes several draft stages and a lot of time.

8. 1 Formulating a question

When you make your own enquiries you draw on your existing knowledge of a discipline or subject area and decide on a *specific* question to explore; a question that is relevant to some aspect of the subject and which interests you. That means you must have some understanding of what the important questions and issues are in your subject area, and why they are important. In other words, you must have acquired appropriate 'frameworks for thinking' within it (see Chapter 3, section 2.1). That background ensures that your topic is a significant one, from the outset. And, later on, it enables you to show *why* your investigation matters and just *what* it contributes to an understanding of the wider subject.

It is very important to be clear about what you are setting out to do, and not to be too ambitious. If you start from an interest in a broad issue in, say, social history – such as 'how independent broadcasting has developed' – you need to narrow this down to a more precise enquiry that is manageable within the *time* and *word limits* set for the project. One way of doing that is to take a case-study approach: to focus your enquiry mainly on a *particular* independent broadcasting company – let's say London Weekend Television (LWT). So your topic then is 'The development of London Weekend Television company'.

But it is most helpful if you actually put the enquiry to yourself *as a question* rather than a 'topic heading': for example, 'What factors influenced the development of LWT?', rather than 'The development of LWT'. The *question* focuses and channels your enquiries by forcing you to seek out some 'answers' to it. You must analyse the factors involved and explain and justify your conclusions. Working from the topic heading, it is all too easy to meander around the issues in a rather aimless way and, ultimately, find yourself on the receiving end of the project marker's most common complaints: 'Failed to relate project work to the wider context. Didn't *use* the information: too descriptive, not enough analysis and explanation.'

Focusing your research

Whatever subject you are interested in – music, art, literature, a particular period/place (such as Classical Rome) – you must try to define a 'do-able' project for yourself. If you are comparing the work of two composers or novelists, for instance, you cannot hope to look at all their work. And you cannot explore every aspect of an historical period, or of its art or literature. You have to be *selective*. But how do you know what to select, what to focus on?

This is where your knowledge of the broad subject-area comes in. When you are fairly familiar with a subject you *know* what the important questions and debates are within it. These are what your enquiry should contribute to in some way.

> You don't do research just for the sake of it, or to find out everything it is possible to know about D.H. Lawrence or Buddy Holly. You enquire into something because your particular and detailed work will shed light on some issue of more *general* importance within the subject.

While you are reading around the subject, and the question you will explore is taking shape, you need to make *preliminary enquiries* into what *resources* are available to you. If you cannot easily get hold of the main primary sources you need then you will have to re-define the enquiry and make changes to your research question. In the case of LWT, it might be difficult to get hold of the kinds of internal reports, papers and memos that document the company's development and may be held in a private archive. You will certainly need permission to use the archive and you need to seek it as soon as possible. You will also need access to the government reports and back numbers of newspapers that provide information about the context of public policy and opinion within which the company's decisions were made. If you ask, you may find you can use the reference section of any university library (though not borrow its books). And a library may be able to get books for you through interlibrary loan schemes. But if this primary source material turns out to be too difficult or impossible to access then you will have to alter your plans. Making these kinds of enquiries *early on* enables you to change the direction of your work before you have invested too much time in the project.

8. 2 Planning your enquiry[3]

At this stage, you will be deciding what *methods* of enquiry to use and the *scale* of investigation to attempt. Will examining company papers, government reports and newpapers provide enough of the right kind of information? Or, since independent broadcasting companies have developed fairly recently, is it possible to seek first-hand information by interviewing past and present LWT policy-makers? If so, which post-holders and how many of them?

Whatever decisions you make about method and scope, you will certainly need to consult secondary source material too. You might make a start by looking in a library catalogue to see whether there is a specialist encyclopaedia (a general collection of facts and analysis) on the subject of television. There you will find:

Sendall, B. (1983) *History of Independent Television in Britain*; Volume 1, *Origin and Foundation 1946–1962*; Volume 2, *Expansion and Change 1958–1962*, London, Macmillan.

---

[3] I am grateful to Tony Coulson, Liaison Librarian (Arts) at The Open University, for his help with this section; also to Magnus John, Information Services Manager, International Centre for Distance Learning.

There are specialist encyclopaedias for most subjects in the arts and humanities. Because they provide a general overview of the field, and usually contain extensive bibliographies, they are a very good place to start.

Or, if you browse in the library under the label 'Performing Arts (film, television and radio)', you will soon come across relevant books such as:

Briggs, A. (1979) *The History of Broadcasting in the United Kingdom*, Volume IV, *Sound and Vision*, Oxford, Oxford University Press.

I even found:

Docherty, D. (1990) *Running the Show: 21 Years of London Weekend Television*, London, Boxtree.

The references included in these books will lead you to other relevant books and articles.

But you will also need to read up-to-date work. For that you have to refer to the academic *journals* that regularly publish scholarly articles and the results of recent research in your field. Again, there are specialist journals that cater for all arts and humanities subjects and any good library will have access to lists of them. In this case, you might look through the contents lists of the *Journal of the Royal Television Society* or the *Historical Journal of Film, Radio and Television*, picking out articles related to your topic. You may well find that other people have carried out fairly similar enquiries, and you will want to learn from the methods they used as well as refer to their discoveries in your work. Having identified the material you need, you have to order it up or acquire as much as you can before the start of the next stage of the project.

Using a computer for research

These days you can conduct a 'literature search' by computer. You can also access data-bases and multi-media packages on CD-ROM. These developments are highly convenient and, as long as you know what you are looking for, fairly trouble free (see Chapter 3, section 4.2).

You may also have access to the masses of information now available on the Internet. But this is not without its difficulties. First, there is a problem about the *status* of this material. Some of the information available is offered by institutions such as universities, so you can be reasonably confident that it is reliable. Much is not. You may not know where it comes from nor what status this 'knowledge' has. When you surf the Internet you need your wits about you and your critical faculties on full alert.

Second, there is *masses* of it. More and more is becoming available every day. You can waste countless hours reading through what turns out to be useless for your purposes. Even if you find relevant material that you judge to be reliable, what are you going to do with it all? Do you have the time to read and analyse it carefully, and absorb it? At the least, you will have to be very selective. On what basis will you make your selections? Making these kinds of decisions alone takes time.

In short, the so-called 'knowledge explosion' seems a mixed blessing.

At this stage you also have to decide what *deadlines* you need to meet at each stage of the project and draw up an appropriate timetable for your work, perhaps week by week. (Remember to allow for the time you will spend travelling about to libraries and so forth.) And you may well be asked to submit a *project outline* for discussion with your tutor. Your tutor's advice will undoubtedly save you time and effort later on, so do not miss this and any other opportunity for guidance and help.

8.3   Carrying out research

During this stage you get down to the business of analysing and interpreting the meanings of all your primary and secondary source material (documents, reports, newspaper accounts, books and articles), in the ways outlined in the previous sections of this chapter and in Chapters 2 and 3. As you do so you will be making notes towards your project report. In this connection, it is very important to write down full *references* for all the material you use *as you read each item.* Then you can easily find particular parts of it again when you need to. And if you do that, you will also be building up your bibliography *as you go along.* A bibliography is a list of all the sources you refer to in your work which you attach to the end of your report, compiled in alphabetical order of authors' surnames. It is much better to build this list up gradually rather than leaving yourself with a lot of fiddly work to do at the end.

Presenting references in a bibliography

When you make a reference to a *book* you note: author, date of publication, title, place of publication, publisher – and any other relevant information, such as the edition, the volume number, and page references for any quotations you make. It looks like this:

Potter, J. (1990) *Independent Television in Britain*; Volume 4, *Companies and Programmes, 1968–1980*, London, Macmillan.

A reference for a *chapter* in an edited book is made as follows:

Sparks, C. (1994) 'Independent production', in S. Hood (ed.) *Behind the Screens: The Structure of British Broadcasting in the 1990s*, London, Lawrence and Wishart, pp.133–54.

And you enter an *article* in a journal in this way:

Kandiah, M. D. (1995) 'Television enters British politics: the Conservative Party's Central Office and political broadcasting, 1945–55', *Historical Journal of Film, Radio and Television*, vol. 15, no. 2, June, pp.265–84.

There are variations in ways of referencing and you may be advised to follow a slightly different convention. But, however you do it, you should always provide as *much* information as you can.

Whatever style of referencing you use, what matters is that you always make the references in the *same* way throughout. You should also keep your references together in one place as you work (on cards, loose leaf or in a note-book) so that you don't lose anything. You have to keep your source material and notes well organized too, or you will waste a lot of precious time hunting around for things.

Towards the end of this research phase you should be starting to make an *outline plan* for your project report and even to draft sections of it as they begin to take shape in your mind. And, as the deadline for this stage approaches, you will simply have to call a halt to your investigations. Whatever your topic, there is always more material than you can handle in the time available. You must be ruthless about keeping to your schedule.

8.4 Writing a project report

Finally, you write up your project report. It is important to recognize that this will go through several *drafts*. You can't just sit down and write a report on this sort of scale quickly or easily. You will have gathered far too much material for that. And it may take you a little while really to get into the writing. Towards the end of the research phase, as you face up to writing proper, you may reach a kind of plateau where nothing much seems to be going on. The excitement of the planning and discovery stages are behind you. You may have become so familiar with your topic that it seems trivial, and your findings insignificant. But push on. Once you are fully engaged in writing you will rediscover your enthusiasm in the intensity of the experience. Talking about your work with other students and friends helps at every stage, and especially now when you are really having to sort things out in your mind.

Try to achieve *different* things at each draft stage. For the first full draft aim just to get everything down on paper, even if you are dissatisfied with parts of it as you write. Writing a project report involves a lot more than producing a description of your work. You have to:

- explain the *rationale* for what you have done, outlining the background from which your question arose so that your readers can see its significance

- explain your choice of research *methods*

- plot a coherent line of *argument* for your report that takes you towards your conclusions, explaining yourself clearly and justifying your judgements.

So it is quite enough just to get things down somehow at this first stage.

As you work towards the second draft you can go back over the unsatisfactory parts of the report. Concentrate on the *structure* of your *argument*, making sure that ideas are adequately linked and sections follow on one from the other towards your conclusions. Then reorganize and prune your writing until it is closer to the required length. As we saw, the difficulty with writing on this kind of scale is keeping the forward momentum of argument going while at each stage adequately explaining your ideas and introducing appropriate illustrative material and evidence. So, to enable the reader to follow you, you must keep 'signposting' the direction your argument is taking. Finally, for the third draft, you will need to check that the meaning of each sentence is clear and polish up the report. Your writing is the means through which your ideas exist, so care lavished on expression is not an optional extra.

If you are using a word-processor these draft stages may not be as distinct as my account suggests. But it is very important *not* to try to do everything at once. So it is still worth behaving as if you were producing several separate drafts: at particular points going through your work with these *different* aims in mind.

8.5 Research skills

This kind of work teaches some very valuable skills:

- how to set about an enquiry
- how and where to find source material and information
- how to make your own investigations
- strategic planning
- time management
- cutting corners and being pragmatic

- analysing and interpreting primary and secondary source material
- forming your own conclusions
- writing clearly and concisely when you have a lot of very varied material to present
- making a convincing case.

You need to approach a project with care and allow yourself time to develop these skills. And you will need all the help you can get, especially if you are studying as a distance student. So start your project work early, seek your tutor's advice at every stage and study carefully any 'project guidance' material that is offered. Above all, be *modest* in your aims and take very seriously all *deadlines* for different stages of your work, for project outlines and draft reports.

KEY POINTS

When you undertake your own enquiries:

- don't be too ambitious at the outset: define a narrowly focused *question* which you can investigate fully in the time available
- make a *timetable* for your work and stick to all deadlines; start early and allow plenty of time for each project stage (especially writing the report)
- in your report show why your investigation matters and what it contributes to your discipline or subject-area; include analysis and explanation as well as description of your work
- try to achieve different things at each draft stage
- if in doubt about source material, ask your tutor or a librarian
- if in despair, don't suffer in silence; get in touch with your tutor and other students, or with anyone who is prepared to listen.

When it is successful, this kind of work is a great opportunity to explore your own particular interests. In spite of the time it takes, it is all-absorbing and very rewarding. It helps you really get 'inside' the subject you are studying.

CHAPTER SEVEN

PREPARING FOR EXAMINATIONS

1 WHY EXAMS?

Exams are not most people's favourite pastime. In fact they can cause a lot of stress and disruption in students' lives. So why do we have them? Is it just mean-mindedness on the part of teachers? Come to that, why are you, presumably of your own free will, putting yourself through a course that has an exam?[1]

Well, you might say that you take exams simply out of necessity, because that is the only way you can acquire qualifications. And indeed exams *are* used for 'testing' purposes – to check whether people have learned enough to be regarded as knowledgeable or skilful. However, to see them simply as an unpleasant but necessary way of certifying people's competence is a far too narrow and negative view of things. After all, many people take some kinds of exam entirely for the sake of it, without any expectation of practical benefit: people with no professional ambitions take tests and exams in piano playing, ballet dancing and swimming, for example. They do it as a way of setting targets and notching up achievements. An examination sets up a framework within which you make great efforts to develop skills and knowledge which, otherwise, you would never take the trouble to acquire. So being examined is not a wholly negative process. It presents a challenge that puts you under pressure, and so produces some very *positive* outcomes.

In fact, *pressure* has interesting effects when it comes to complicated mental activities. We are often able to think very efficiently in a crisis. In daily life, our minds churn away doing the work that has to be done – thinking through various issues that crop up, weighing things up, organizing our actions and so forth. But when we hit a *crisis* our whole mode of operation shifts. Instantly, our attention narrows down to the matter in hand and we sort rapidly through the main options open to us, cutting corners and ignoring lots of little questions that might normally occur to us. We go straight for the 'bottom line', as they say, drawing conclusions we would never reach under normal circumstances. When we have time on our hands there is always another day for thinking through the *really* tricky issues, but when it's 'now-or-never' we launch ourselves into them and drive on through until we reach a conclusion, regardless of any doubts that may arise along the way.

---

[1] Early on in your studies you may not be required to take an end-of-course exam, and in some later courses you may be able to substitute an extended essay or project work. But at some stages in your undergraduate studies you undoubtedly *will* have to sit, and pass, exams.

Pulling the whole course together

In a way an exam is a device for creating a 'mini-crisis', which enables you to find the resources of willpower and energy to take matters in hand and finally pull the ideas of the course together into the best shape you can manage. Studying is challenging work at the best of times, so there is always the temptation just to get on with the next task and put off the bigger job of standing back and asking, 'What is this all about?' Essays, of course, also have this effect of creating mini-crises in your life. And they too help you pull the course together. But they usually operate at a local level, helping you to organize parts of the course into a more coherent shape in your mind. Exams have a larger job to do and they create a correspondingly larger disturbance to your equilibrium.

The way exams create this pressure is through introducing the element of *performance*. In writing an essay you have flexibility in choosing when to write and how to organize your time, and you submit your work to your own tutor. But in an exam, you have to perform at a specified time and place, to the satisfaction of an audience you don't know. You have to 'think on your feet', so to speak, and you have to get it right first time. This brings considerably more pressure to bear on you. But this pressure is potentially a very creative force. In effect, the exam is a 'ritual' which creates the conditions of a public performance, so that you can draw a peak performance out of yourself.

Preparing for a 'performance'

There are many people who regularly perform in public, such as actors, musicians, athletes and politicians. They too experience the intense pressures of preparing for their performances and of the build-up of tension in the period immediately beforehand. Indeed, some of the most famous of them have reported feeling tense to the point of nausea immediately before big occasions, and yet have gone on to give outstanding performances – way beyond the everyday run of human activity and beyond their own normal standards. It takes the big occasion to bring out that performance. To be successful, public performers have to know how to make creative use of stress:

- how to channel it into an obsessive *drive* during the *period of preparation*, so that the impending performance is put above everything else in life around them; and

- how to use it to *'wind-up'* for the *occasion itself*, so as to reach performance pitch at the right time.

Stress, then, is powerful fuel. However, like many fuels it is also dangerous to handle. It has adverse side effects that need to be controlled. If you don't have strategies for channelling tension and putting it to productive use, then the side effects begin to override the benefits. At worst, a performance can 'go to pieces' if the effects of stress get out of hand. The sign of the old trouper is being able to remain in control whatever happens – keeping the tension working positively so that the show goes on. The same applies to taking exams. There is much to be learned from thinking about what professional performers do to get a consistently high standard of performance out of themselves, under difficult circumstances. Like them, you are not aiming for total freedom from stress, but to develop techniques for *managing* it successfully and *using* it.

I have begun this discussion of exams with the issue of stress because I think it permeates all aspects of the examination process and it is not helpful to pretend otherwise; but also, and more importantly, because I want to establish from the outset that it is not an entirely regrettable and unhelpful phenomenon. Stress in connection with exams, as in other aspects of life, is powerful but double-edged. It helps you accomplish a lot if you can handle it properly. So you should regard exams and the stresses they create positively, as an *opportunity* to *achieve* a great deal. You have set out to study because you want to learn. Properly approached, exams are an enormous help in achieving an overall grasp of what you have been studying.

KEY POINTS

- The stress created by exams is a positive force which you can harness to help you pull the course together and consolidate your understanding of it.
- Your aim is to find ways of 'managing' exam stress and putting it to good use.

2 SOME MYTHS ABOUT EXAMS

One side-effect of the tensions associated with exams is that our *perceptions* of them become warped. We develop distorted images of the processes involved in being examined and so we are unrealistic in our strategies for tackling what lies ahead. Worse still, the *collective* effect of generations of students experiencing these warped perceptions is that a good many unhelpful myths have grown up around exams. So we'll begin by trying to dispose of some of them.

2.1 Failure would ruin your life

One of the most valuable aspects of the stress of 'performing' is that you become very concerned to do well. This is excellent in that it focuses your energies intensely on the task in hand. But the reverse of the coin is that you may begin to think of *failure* to do well as the worst thing that could possibly happen to you. The whole enterprise begins to get out of proportion and you start worrying about it quite inappropriately. Of course it *is* very disappointing when you do less well than you hoped, after putting a lot of time and energy into something. But exams are *not* a life-and-death matter. Most people don't do too badly, but even if you *were* to fail – so what? Taking a course of study is a splendid and challenging thing to do, and you are almost certain to gain a great deal from it whether you pass the exam or not. In many cases you can have a second try at it. Life will go on. Indeed, some people go on to great success in their studies in spite of such setbacks. So, while you obviously don't want to approach an exam expecting to do any less than your best, it is certainly not worth turning your life into a misery over it. And if you recognize from the start that you can survive the worst the exam might throw at you – namely failure – it will help you keep things in proportion.

> **KEY POINT**
> - Failing an exam is not the end of the world, so keep your anxieties in proportion.

2.2 The exam could expose you as a fraud

It is not at all uncommon to have the lurking anxiety that an exam will suddenly reveal you as an imposter: that the hoax you have perpetrated all through the course – of understanding as much as everyone else – will finally be exposed; that stern examiners will probe for signs of weakness and mercilessly cast aside those who show less than watertight and comprehensive knowledge. (Incidentally, quite commonly people have recurring dreams along these lines years after taking exams. This indicates the intensity of the hopes and fears they arouse.) But of course exams are not at all like that. Examiners are delighted to have students pass and they usually go out of their way to seek out what is good in the answers they read. Nobody will think you are stupid if you don't do well, or that you have been wasting their time. They will just be sorry and hope you do better next time.

> **KEY POINT**
> - Everyone wants you to pass exams, including the examiners.

2.3 You should have studied everything in the course before attempting the exam

Most people have to miss out some sections of any course, and especially part-time adult students. Even the best students tend to specialize in the areas that interest them. You have done well to get as far as the exam. At that stage it's no use worrying about what you have left out. It is far better to consolidate what you *have* done rather than attempt any desperate catching up on what you haven't. An exam is when you gather together the products of your months of study and make use of them in achieving a peak performance. It is too late for studying from first principles.

To put things in perspective, just think about the practical constraints that apply to exams. How much can you write in a three-hour exam? Not very much. So you are not aiming to know everything there is to know and get it all down on paper. If you have to answer four questions, you need to know enough to produce, say, three or four sides of discussion on each question you tackle. Equally significant, the person who marks your script isn't going to be checking it over in fine detail to see whether it is worth a Nobel prize. He will spend around ten minutes on each answer, going quickly through it to see whether the general gist seems right, whether a reasonable number of the key points are there, and whether the argument is fairly well illustrated and supported and flows tolerably well. That is what exams are like. Your essays during a course are your chance to put together detailed and carefully thought-out arguments for close reading by a tutor. The exam is a much more rough-and-ready exercise. So you *don't* have to worry about leaving things out, so long as you can pull together enough from what you *have* studied to write for around forty minutes on chosen topics.

> **KEY POINT**
> - Don't worry about what you haven't done during the course. Work out how to make the best use of what you *have* done.

2.4 If you haven't understood what you have studied, it isn't worth taking the exam

It is quite normal to feel unsure as you reach the later stages of a course. Many other students will be experiencing similar doubts. A course that is any good will have set all kinds of ideas going in your mind, some of which you may still be sorting out a year or two later. Indeed, it is hard to imagine what a 'complete' understanding of a topic of any significance would be like.

Having said that, in any course there will be certain texts, central ideas and skills you will be expected to have made progress with. If you have *tried* to make sense of what you have studied, you have probably developed more understanding and ability than you realize. But if the course is at all challenging you can hardly expect to arrive at a resolution of every question it raises by the time of the exam. In fact the exam may be just what you need to spur you on to sort out some of these central issues. The point is to use your preparation for the exam to pull things together, to make the *best sense you can* of your studies.

> **KEY POINT**
> ● No one understands 'everything'. There are bound to be areas where you feel underprepared or confused.

2.5   Examiners are out to 'trick' you

The first time you look at a past exam paper for your course you may get a bit of a fright. Exam questions often look broad and demanding, and the wording may seem somewhat oblique. But they are *not* designed to 'trick' you. Examiners want to direct your attention towards particular parts of the course, without answering the questions for you, and they usually want to give you some choice about which texts you will discuss in your answers (plays, paintings, documents, or whatever). In other words, they are trying to be helpful. You need to remember at all times that the exam is a test of your understanding of the course you have been studying, not your general knowledge. So somewhere within what you have been studying lies an answer to each question and some texts it is appropriate to focus on. Don't panic at the sight of the paper. There is no mystery. Instead, carefully match what you know of the *course* against what the *questions* seem to be asking.

> **KEY POINT**
> ● Don't panic when you read exam questions. Each question is linked quite directly with something you have covered in the course. You have to work out the link.

2.6   Exams are for people who have a good memory

Everyone's memory is good enough. It is mainly a matter of how you use it. However, your memory is not really the point. Most of the exams adults take are *not* intended as 'memory tests'. The point of studying arts and humanities subjects at higher levels is to develop the *skills* of textual analysis, interpretation and judgement and your *understanding* of ideas (see Chapter 6). The purpose of the exam is to provide you with the chance to show how well you have understood the texts and grasped the ideas in the course. You will be expected to *use* your knowledge and ideas to *argue* a case. If you revise constructively before the exam, the role of 'pure' memory will be relatively small. When you have an organized understanding of what is in the course, and if you can see the relationship between the course material and the exam questions, you will have the core of your answers. On the basis of your revision, you will find it fairly easy to remember as much textual detail as you need to illustrate and support your arguments. So don't even think about your memory. Concentrate on organizing your notes and your thoughts during the revision period (see section 4).

KEY POINT

- Exams tend to be about what you *understand* rather than what you can remember. Getting your course material organized during the revision period will take care of your memory.

2.7   The exam will reveal the gaps in your education

Some people are anxious in a vague, general way before an exam – feeling that their whole educational background is somehow inadequate to the task ahead, and that past failings and omissions will at last come home to roost. This is a misleading trick that anxiety plays on us. As we have just seen, an exam is *not* a test of general knowledge. It is a test of your grasp of the course and its texts. If you have studied the course effectively, you can perform well in the exam regardless of your previous education. In fact it is a grave mistake to try to answer a question on an exam paper 'off the top of your head'. The examiners' marking guide will indicate some quite specific points from the course for which marks can be given. So going off on your own tack is a very risky strategy, however well informed you may be. If general knowledge and educational background do come through, it is in the 'roundedness' of answers to questions and refinements of writing style, which might push a 'good' answer up to 'excellent'. They may help to put a finishing gloss on a performance, but that is all.

KEY POINT

- Don't worry about what you didn't learn *before* the course. Consolidate what you have learned *during* it.

2.8 Exams are for 'speed merchants'

Can you think quickly enough and write quickly enough to pass an exam? Probably! As far as the thinking is concerned, you need to make sure you have done most of that in advance of the exam itself, as we shall see in section 4. So sheer speed of thinking is not the issue. What *will* matter is how well you have *organized* your ideas and how well you have *planned* your exam strategy. If you are working to a good plan, you can be extremely efficient in your use of the time available during the exam.

As regards the speed at which you can write, this *may* have an effect if it seriously restricts the amount you can get down. If you can write, say, 500–700 words in 40 minutes that should be sufficient to get a high mark. However, there are no hard and fast rules about this. Some students write short pithy answers that are very good, while others write pages without saying much. The fact that you have a lot of adrenalin pumping in an exam will help you to write much more quickly than usual. But if you have doubts, then give yourself some practice in writing at speed beforehand – especially if you normally use a word-processor and are not in the habit of writing by hand. If you suffer from a physical disability which makes you a slow writer you should get advice about whether you can be given special support in the exam, or extra time. In general, though, it is far more important to focus on the *quality* of what you write than the speed at which you can produce it. In any case, your progress is likely to be as much affected by the rate at which you can work out the next point in your argument as by the purely technical business of putting the words on the page – and, as we shall see, this has a great deal to do with how you prepare yourself in advance of the exam.

> **KEY POINT**
> - Speed in an exam is to do with having a very clear plan as to how you intend to use your time.

2.9 You have to revise till you drop before an exam

The folklore of exams is full of accounts of amazing last-minute orgies of work, deep into the night. There may be some truth in these stories, in that we *are* capable of extraordinary feats when the pressure is on. But the telling of them is more to do with the feelings that frenetic preparation for exams produces, and the intensity of people's hopes and fears. In any case, it is *not* true that all preparation can be done effectively at the very last moment, particularly as you get older and if you are studying part-time and have to keep your life going at the same time.

Our minds function somewhat differently under pressure, and you need to understand the differences if you are to 'manage' yourself well during the build-up to the big performance. In the period just before an exam the tension mounts and you become highly charged. This means that you have plenty of nervous energy and can get lots done, but it is harder to keep yourself under control and channel your energy to best effect. Being highly charged makes you very good at focusing attention on *concrete* matters in hand, but it makes you less good at sorting out *broad, abstract* issues. The obvious answer is to do your broad planning well in advance so that, by the final stage of revision (and in the exam itself), you have clear-cut strategies already worked out – strategies for tackling revision, for allocating time in the exam, for analysing the exam questions, for structuring your answers, and so on. If you have a well-developed sense of purpose, and a framework within which to work, you may find you can think surprisingly clearly once the exam has started. But none of this is likely to happen if you leave all thoughts of exam preparation to the last couple of days and nights before the exam.

KEY POINT

- You probably *will* do a lot of work just before the exam. But you need to do it in a planned way, using your time efficiently and conserving your energies.

These then are some of the myths about exams: that they are gigantic obstacles which can be surmounted only by people of extraordinary capabilities; that they are devised and marked by sadists to expose the weaknesses of ordinary mortals; that they threaten us with life-shattering consequences – the stuff of nightmares. As we have seen, the reality is much more mundane. Exams are just another part of the education process, although admittedly a part which presents a greater challenge and in consequence creates greater stress. The secret of achieving the results you are capable of in exams, and also of experiencing the least pain and discomfort, is to take a *practical* approach to them. You need to be *realistic* about *yourself* and about what is *required of you* by the exam, so that you can prepare yourself sensibly and carefully to give a 'peak performance'. The last thing you want to do is waste your energies dithering about in a panic, or spend all your time on useless activities because you can't let yourself stop and think straight about what is actually involved.

3 WHAT EXAMINERS DO NOT LIKE

Having disposed of some of the myths, let's look in more detail at the reality. One way of getting a sharp focus on what is wanted in exams is to consider what boards of examiners have to say in their reports after marking them. Since you are not likely to be in a position to do that yourself, I will summarize the comments made in some Open University examiners' reports for Arts Faculty courses. Often these reports stress *how well* many students answer the questions. However, here I think it is useful for us to think about the *faults* examiners find.

3.1   Failing to answer the question

In answering exam questions, it isn't just *what* you know that counts but *how* you say it. A great deal of emphasis is placed on being able to *use* what you know to *argue a case* that relates directly to the *specific question* you are asked. If you don't do this, the script-marker will sigh and write, 'Doesn't answer the question' below your answer. According to the examiners' reports, there are several ways in which you can miss the mark.

- Failing to recognize what one of the *key terms* in the question means (for instance, answering a question on 'primitive' art thinking that this term means 'uncultured'). You have to think carefully about what each of the words might mean, and also pay attention to the dates provided for any period you are asked to discuss. If there is a term in the question you are not sure about, it is best to avoid that question. You will get very few marks if you guess and get it wrong.

- Failing to offer *critical analysis* and *argument* relating to the question. However the question is posed, you are normally expected to present arguments *for* and *against* a particular point of view implied in it. As you read a question closely, your first job is to identify the *point of view* it presents. Your next job is to remind yourself of some *other* point(s) of view from which you can criticize that position. Your answer can then be constructed as an *argument* between two or more positions.

- Failing to take an *objective* stance in relation to the question. You cannot get away with 'haranguing' the examiner with your personal opinions, however strongly you may feel. You have to observe the same principles of objectivity in an exam as in your essays (see Chapter 4, section 3.5). That means you must provide *evidence* from the texts you discuss to support the points you make in argument.

● Failing to end the answer with any *conclusions* about the question asked. Your answer will impress the examiner as much more purposeful and relevant if, at the end, you make a point of coming *back* quite specifically to the *question* – briefly showing how what you have said helps to answer it. You don't necessarily have to come down on one side of the argument or another, but at least you should point out what is at stake.

These are familiar enough points. We have come across them all in connection with essay-writing in Chapters 4 and 5. So there is nothing particularly new for you to think about here. You should simply note that exam answers, although shorter and more scrappy than essays, are judged along roughly the same lines (but to lower levels of expectation, in recognition of the different circumstances in which they have been written).

3.2 Failing to draw on the course and its texts

Examiners complain that it is hard to tell whether some students have actually studied the course. In other words, these students completely forget one of the basic principles of any end-of-course exam: namely that it is set up for you to *demonstrate* that you have worked on and thought about the content of the course. It is essential that you treat each question as an opportunity to discuss the *objects* and *ideas*, and use the *terms*, you have been studying. When you are arguing a case you must *illustrate* and *support* your points by *detailed reference* to some of the texts you have studied. You may also need to draw on other people's ideas and theories about those texts, that is, on the judgements made by some of the 'authorities' in your field. (See Chapter 6, section 6.)

This means that you cannot write an exam answer on the basis of your general knowledge and an argument you have worked out on the spot, from first principles. In order to make good use of the primary and secondary source material in the course, you have to prepare yourself well for the exam.

3.3 Failing to be selective

Having said that, you have to use the course material discriminatingly. You are *never* asked, 'Write all you know about…'. The exam marker is not interested in whether you can memorize a section of a book and repeat it back. She wants to know whether you can put the ideas and information to work: whether you can *select* material appropriately from all that you have studied in the course, *using* it to answer the *particular question* you are asked. That includes making selections from among the *texts* you might discuss in relation to the question – part of the test is being able to make *appropriate* choices. If you cram your answer full of facts, dates, names, references to texts and quotations without placing them in the context of an *argument*, and without selecting them for their *relevance* to that argument, the marker will suspect that you don't understand the subject and are hoping sheer memorization will do instead. It won't.

3.4   Using time badly

Let's assume you have to answer four questions in a three-hour exam. A particularly common failing is to produce a very long first answer, followed by a somewhat short second one, a very short third, and finally a fourth which is just a paragraph and some scrappy notes. This is unfortunate because the allocation of exam marks is usually very straightforward. Each question carries a certain number of marks and good work on one question cannot be carried over in a general way to your overall score. It is extremely difficult to push your mark up beyond 90% for your best answer. But let's say you did manage a 90% for that. If you followed it with 45%, 30% and 15% then your overall score would be 45%. On the other hand, if you spent less time pushing the first answer into the highest ranges and got 75% for it, but used the time gained to do the much easier job of pulling the other questions up from the lower ranges, you might end up with, say, 60%, 55% and 50% for them. This would give you an overall score of 60% which, as you can see, is a far better result. It is *much* easier to accumulate marks at the lower end of the scale than at the upper end, so it *always* makes sense to spend roughly the same length of time on each question – however weak you feel on one or two of them.

3.5   Poor presentation

Finally, examiners also complain about answers that are:

- unstructured (that is, lacking a beginning, a middle and an end)
- lacking any division into paragraphs
- written in note form rather than sentences
- in unreadable handwriting.

Again, these requirements are familiar enough from your essay-writing. It is clearly much harder for you to pay attention to presentation under exam conditions. But equally the exam marker's job is harder than your tutor's, since she has to work through a mountain of scripts. With the best will in the world, it is hard for a marker to make sound judgements about an argument that is almost impossible to read. And, unlike your tutor, the scriptmarker does not know you and can't so easily guess what you might be intending to say. So it is all the more important to produce exam answers that are fairly coherent and legible. You cannot help the relative scrappiness and untidiness of your exam answers. But neither can the exam marker help being somewhat influenced by the difficulty of working out what you are trying to say.

These then are the things examiners complain about in their reports, alongside the very pleasant and encouraging things they also say. In order to make sure they say nice things about *your* answers you need to apply yourself as calmly as you can to the following aspects of the exam process:

- revising the course
- getting yourself 'geared up' during the last day or two
- sitting the exam itself.

4 REVISING FOR EXAMS

4.1 What is the point of revision?

The main purpose of revision is to pull together all the work you have done in studying the course. Revision is *not* primarily a massive memorizing task, as people sometimes think. It is a much more *constructive* activity than that. As you study, your existing ideas are constantly challenged and thrown into disarray. Revision is the process of tidying up the mess and getting your ideas and knowledge into a more useable form. It serves the function of rounding off the course. Without this period of revision the course might just drift away from you. Revising offers you the opportunity to *reconstruct* the course for yourself, so that the ideas you have developed as you studied become more coherent and are put in 'working' order.

Consequently, you have to make your revision an *active* process, not just a mechanical scanning through of pages in the hope that something will 'stick'. You have to plan it in a *purposeful* way, designing activities that are *meaningful* – engaging and thought-provoking rather than repetitive, tedious and mind-numbing. Revision is a substantial and time-consuming part of the course you have chosen to study, so you should make sure you get some pleasure and value out of it. Don't do it just for the examiner's sake.

So what kinds of things are worth doing, given the strictly limited time you have available and the importance of making all your efforts count? We'll look at some of the main strategic questions and activities.

4.2   When should you start revising?

There is no 'correct' answer to this question. It is something you have to work out for yourself. Some students leave it to the last fortnight while others make a start two months before the exam. The right time for you depends on:

- your personal commitments in addition to studying, and the time you can spare for revision
- your personal style of studying – whether you are more capable of short intensive bursts of effort, or prefer longer sustained periods
- what you want to get out of the course.

It would be a shame if you panicked and spoiled the later part of the course by becoming obsessed with revision too soon. On the other hand, it is a grave mistake to avoid all thought about the exam until the very last moment and then just hope for the best. If you leave yourself with no time for revision you will get far less out of the course and you will suffer in the exam itself. So it is a good idea to begin having some thoughts about revision a couple of months before the exam, even if you don't actually start revising until later. You might start simply by jotting down a plan for the last weeks of the course, sketching out how to fit in some time for revision alongside normal course work. It doesn't matter if you have to scrap the plan and draw up a new one (or have to keep scrapping plans and drawing up new ones). Making a tentative start on the back of an envelope will set going the shift in orientation you need to make as you move towards the final stages of the course.

4.3   Looking at past exam papers

This is an excellent idea, although we saw that your first look at an exam paper may make you gulp. Until you have done some serious revision you may not be able to imagine how you will ever tackle the questions. Nevertheless, it is much better to get the fright over in time to be able to do something about it. You certainly don't want to have that experience for the first time in the exam itself.

It is sensible to treat exams warily, particularly if you haven't done one for some time, and find out as much as you can about them in advance. There may be a specimen exam paper with printed notes that tell you about the nature of the exam and what is expected of you. And your tutor, or more experienced fellow-students, will be able to give you clues and tips as to how the exam process works in practice. In order to focus your mind on the task ahead, there is no substitute for looking at past papers or the specimen paper. You will be able to see exactly how the questions are set out on the page; how many there are; whether there are separate sections from which you have to choose questions; what kinds of questions are set; how the questions 'map' on to the content of the course; what sort of language they employ, and so on. For example, a three-hour exam paper might be in two parts with ten to twelve questions from which you have to select four, one of which has to come from the second part of the paper.

> ### Note
>
> Exams vary in length and as regards the number of questions you have to answer. Many, though not all, exams in the arts and humanities allow one hour for each of three questions. However, in what follows, I shall talk in terms of a three-hour exam in which you answer four questions, each of which requires an essay-type answer and carries 25% of the marks, because that is more difficult to handle. When you have found out the details of *your* exam, you will have to make the necessary adjustments to the figures I give for time per question, length of answers, and so on.
>
> In some exams, you may be asked to analyse a short text, such as an historical document or a painting. This will create a different structure for the exam and you will need to adapt your strategy accordingly.
>
> If the course you are studying is in its first year, there will not be any past papers. However, you may be supplied with a specimen paper. If there are past papers, make a point of finding out how to get hold of copies. Ask your tutor or more experienced students, or write to the examining body.

Whether you have a past paper or a specimen paper, you should first check to see whether there is an obvious relationship between the structure of the paper and the structure of the course: for example, whether a question is set on each major section of the course. This information is crucial as a guide to your *revision strategy*, helping you decide which parts of the course you will revise most thoroughly. The time you can spend revising will be limited so you need to make sure you use it wisely.

By the time you sit down to take the real exam you need to know what the paper will look like, and also be pretty sure about what questions you are looking for in it. Of course there is no guarantee that you will get the *specific* questions you want, but you should have formed a reasonable idea of the *general areas* the questions are likely to cover. You cannot afford to waste time dithering in an exam, or changing your mind halfway through a question. One of your most important projects before the exam is to form a clear *plan of attack* on the paper. So, for both your general revision strategy and your detailed planning for the exam itself, you need to be very familiar with the way the exam paper will look.

4.4   Should you re-read the whole course?

This is the sort of fantasy that floats across our minds in moments of remorse at past failings and steely resolve to set things right. It is hopelessly idealistic. It would take far too long. More important, it would be mind-numbingly tedious. You would learn little except a distaste for the course and for revision. You need to take a much more *selective* and *active* approach as you return to your earlier weeks of study. First, you have to make a careful judgement about *how* selective you can afford to be, based on your study of past papers and on any advice you can get from your tutor. Then decide exactly which parts of the course you are going to focus your efforts on.

Many exam papers are deliberately designed to allow you to be selective in your preparation. Provided you have made a point of carefully checking out the logic of the choices open to you, you can be quite ruthless about setting aside whole sections of the course and ignoring them. It is not 'cheating' to do this. Often, the most successful students are those who have the confidence to take an extremely businesslike approach; they select just as much of the course as they need to revise – always taking account of the need to have something to fall back on if a question does not come up in quite the form expected. They then give their full attention to revising these chosen areas very thoroughly.

4.5   Drawing up a detailed timetable for revision

As we saw, exam folklore is full of legendary people who leave things to the last few days and then study round the clock. However, as an adult student, possibly studying part-time and with several years of exams ahead of you, a more temperate approach is likely to serve you far better. You have to keep some balance between the exam and the rest of your life. You need to make out a timetable for the last few weeks of the course and the revision period to see how many hours, in total, you can reasonably hope to set aside for revision. Then:

● allow a proportion of your time for studying the last part of the course
● allocate some time towards the end of the revision period for polishing up your act (for example, practising writing out exam answers to time)

- finally, divide up the remaining time equally between each area of the course you have decided to revise.

It may be tempting to allow more time for the sections of the course you see as your strengths, and try to squeeze in your revision of weaker areas towards the end, or do the reverse of this. However, since each question carries the same number of marks, allocating *equal* time to each area is a better strategy. It is all too easy to end up with too little time for the areas that most need sorting out or, conversely, to leave no time for brushing up the very topics you hope to do best in. So, draw up a timetable showing what you hope to spend your time on. Although you won't be able to stick to it exactly, having a plan will help you to focus on the nature and the size of the task ahead. You can then keep readjusting your sights to take account of reality.

4.6   Sorting out your course material

Having made a revision plan, the first thing you have to do is get your course material organized. Unless you have an extraordinarily efficient filing system, you will have accumulated mounds of paper, notes, handouts, essays, photocopies of articles and half-read books. Before you can get down to revising your chosen areas you have to sort out exactly what there is to revise *from*. So setting aside an evening to do nothing but put everything into new, tidier piles is more than just 'housekeeping'. Only when you have looked around you to see what material there is and where, and have gathered together what you need, can you get a clear run at some serious revision.

4.7   Should you try to memorize your course notes?

No. It would be a complete waste of time and effort. If you set out to do routine, boring things such as dutifully scanning over and over old notes until you can recite them, your mind will switch off in protest. In any case, you need to be able to *think* in the exam, not recite back your notes. You need *ideas* in your head rather than strings of words. So you should do something much more constructive as you read your course notes, such as picking out *key points* and trying to work out what *questions* you might be asked on the topic. Any memorizing of course material should be done in the last day or two and should be based on 'summary' notes (see section 4.9).

4.8 Identifying key questions

As we have seen, this is a very powerful strategy. Try to identify one or two central questions in each of the sections of the course you are revising, and then write some notes that answer those questions. Sometimes your tutor or an author will have identified key questions for you. At other times you will have to tease them out and pose them for yourself. Similarly, they will sometimes have made a point of drawing conclusions about the main issues, while at other times you will have to summarize and draw conclusions for yourself. The process of seeking out key questions and answers to them gets your mind working the way it needs to work in the exam. It will alert you to the kinds of questions that *could* be asked about the course content you have been studying (in effect, you are making up your own exam questions). And it will help you think in terms of the kinds of answers you could put together, based on the course material.

4.9 Is it worth writing new notes?

Emphatically, yes. It is an excellent idea to work with a pen in your hand, actually *creating* something as you work. This is a constructive way of revising and will engage your mind to very good effect for long spells. Having identified a key (exam-type) question for the part of the course you are revising, you might go on to do something like the following.

1 Plan an answer to it in note form, drawing on the various notes, essays, articles, and so on, that you have gathered together for your revision of that part of the course, *including* detailed references to the particular *texts* you would discuss in relation to the question (paintings, poems, music, documents, or whatever). In other words, plan the *argument* and also the *substance* of your answer (see section 4.10).

2 After you have done that, extract the main points from these notes to produce a single *summary sheet* of headings for that question plus the key points of the argument, with textual reference alongside in summary form.

The effort to 'boil down' your course material in this way is extremely valuable because it converts both the broad themes and ideas of the course, and your detailed analyses of texts, into a form that is much more manageable for the purposes of answering questions in exams. As you know, you do not have much time to think about a question in the exam, or to write at tremendous length, so you don't want to be wading through mountains of detail in your mind trying to sift out your answer.

These *condensed* versions of the main points you might make, along with appropriate textual detail, are much closer to what you will have time to think through and write about. You can scan mentally through the main items on your summary sheet and select whichever are relevant to the question. This then leads your mind back to the fuller notes that 'lie behind' it. In other words, in your revision of the course you have in effect constructed pathways *down* from your basic source materials through notes in answer to questions to summary sheets of those notes. In the exam, then, you can quickly trace back *up* those pathways, to locate exactly the material that is relevant to the question. Perhaps the practice is rarely quite as neat as that, but at least this 'note-condensing' approach gives you a systematic way of overviewing and finding ideas and information. It also gets you into the habit of thinking in terms of *questions* and *answers* to them right from the start of your revision for the exam.

Furthermore, this strategy gives you a well focused and absorbing task to be getting on with, rather than the kind of aimless scanning back over old material that dulls your spirits and sends you to sleep. And finally, condensed notes supply you with just the kind of 'pulled together' version of the course that will be invaluable in the future, when you want to remind yourself of what the course was about.

4.10 Should you try answering exam-type questions?

Yes, this is an extremely useful revision activity, whether you use questions from past exam papers or questions you have developed yourself. As we have just seen, you can sketch out answers to such questions in note form to help you revise the course material, right from the start of the revision process. As you tackle each one, go through the routine of asking yourself the following questions.

- What is the question getting at? (Underline *key words* in the same way as for essays, see Chapter 5, section 2.1.)
- Which themes, ideas and texts can I draw on from the course?
- What main points of argument will I make, and in what order?

In the process of answering these questions you will be going over and over your course material in a purposeful way, *seeking out* appropriate ideas, facts, dates, texts and textual detail. As we saw, you will end up with a 'complete' answer to each exam-type question in note form, which you can then reproduce as a single summary sheet. This *activity* of sketching out answers on paper, over and over again, also helps to lodge ideas, facts, dates and textual details in your mind. Eventually you will find you 'know' a lot of them without ever having sat down to memorize them (and you can check your knowledge simply by going over your summary sheets, deliberately memorizing anything that has stubbornly refused to 'go in'). Furthermore, you will know them *in relation to* certain kinds of question, not as single, discrete items of 'information'. This *connectedness* of your ideas and knowledge is the basis of the 'tracing back' or retrieval process I described just now, that you do in the exam itself.

So, the reason this activity is worth doing many times is that it helps you develop the intellectual agility to do what examiners so clearly want you to, which is to answer the question that has been asked and to draw on relevant parts of the course in doing so. It helps you organize your knowledge in the right sort of way for the job in hand. You get used to going very quickly through the processes of:

- *sifting* through what you know of the course material
- *selecting* the items that are most relevant to the question
- *arranging* them in a suitable order for a coherent answer to it.

Just before the exam, you can use your outline answers to these questions to practise writing out a few essays within the time allowed. But a quicker exercise, which you can do much more frequently, is to rehearse the vital first few minutes of working on a question: the minutes when you examine the question carefully and sketch out rough notes for an answer. Indeed, you should do this over and over again during the final stages of revision. Give yourself, say, ten minutes to produce an outline answer to a question you haven't looked at before.

You don't need practice at writing out full answers quite so urgently because, once you have an outline plan, the writing itself is pretty much the same as writing an essay – except that you have less time. In other words, you have already practised that area of skill in your essay-writing during the course. What you have *not* had practise at is 'thinking on your feet' and fixing very quickly on a line to take. Our normal modes of thinking about essay questions are too reflective and lumbering for an exam. You need to practise a much more nimble style to get yourself into shape for it. Should you run out of questions, you can exchange them with other students.

One of the greatest benefits of this exercise of sketching outline answers to questions is discovering that the ground you covered early in the course, which had seemed no more than vague shapes in a mist, soon begins to come into much sharper focus. You discover that you know a great deal more than you realized.

4.11 Should you set yourself a full-scale 'mock exam'?

If you haven't taken exams for a long time it is obviously helpful to get some practice at working in exam 'conditions', against the clock. On the other hand, it might be hard to make the time, or find the stamina, for a full-length practice. It depends on your own inclinations and abilities. It might be just as useful and more practical to set yourself the task of writing a single timed answer every now and then, towards the end of the revision period. After all, you will have the benefit of a lot more nervous energy to help you perform great feats in the exam itself. You might find the experience of a full-scale 'mock' a bit demoralizing, and end up underestimating what you can do on the day. A further word of warning: don't be discouraged if the answers you produce look unimpressive compared to your essays. Answers produced under exam conditions are always more flawed.

4.12 Have you the time to attend tutorials during the revision period?

Make time! It is easy to develop a distorted perspective on exams during revision. You begin to think your problems are much worse than they really are, or you bias your revision too much in one particular direction. The best way to keep a sense of proportion is to talk to other people about what you are doing. I don't want to suggest that if you are studying on your own your chances are poor. But if you *can* get to classes you will make your revision easier and a lot more pleasant. It is a mistake to think that time spent at a tutorial is simply time lost from revising at home. Group revision can be extremely efficient. It throws up all sorts of insight into problems and misperceptions which might otherwise remain hidden. It helps you sort out your ideas, and you may pick up many helpful clues and tips from your tutor and other students.

4.13 Should you team up with other students for your revision?

It can be very valuable, particularly if you are new to exams, to meet fairly regularly with other students, to compare your revision strategies and your progress, to set each other questions, to comment on and criticize each other's outline answers and, generally, to offer mutual support. Since exams have a tendency to make us very anxious, it is extremely helpful to be able to make contact with other people's idea of reality. This helps you keep your own perceptions and plans within reasonable bounds.

5 'GEARING UP' FOR THE EXAM

Is it a good idea to relax and get plenty of sleep and outdoor exercise in the day or two immediately before an exam? Perhaps you ought to get away for a short holiday? Sounds great, doesn't it – but is it realistic? Probably for part-time students it isn't even within the bounds of possibility, given all the other demands of daily life. In any case, it is not at all obvious that it would be good for your exam performance. The few days before the exam is when you should be building up to a peak of preparation. You are able to concentrate wonderfully when it is too late to worry about the extras. You can forget your plans for re-reading that book, or the thorough going-over you were going to give that text you never really understood. With all those possibilities left behind, you are in a position to concentrate all your energies on making the best job you can of marshalling what you do know. 'Relaxed' is the last thing you want to be when you enter the exam. Calm and unruffled possibly, if you can manage it, but you should be keyed-up ready to give your big performance of the year – transcending your normal limits by force of all your nervous energy and single-minded concentration.

5.1 Changes to your mental powers

The last few days before the exam are about lodging your plans and strategies for the exam in your mind, going over your summary note sheets, practising sketching out answers to questions very quickly, perhaps writing out a full answer or two to time and, in general, winding yourself up for action. Because the pressures build up in these final days, your mental powers will change. You will probably be less good at deep-thinking tasks, such as sorting out the underlying meaning of a difficult text. But you will be better at more routine activities: checking over your notes, memorizing some quotations, practising answering questions, or reminding yourself of your strategy for the exam. So don't leave basic revision to the last few days – you will only depress yourself and get into a panic. *Plan* to switch your mode of work. Use these days as a polishing-up period for the big performance. As with the actor at the dress rehearsal, it is too late now to decide on a different approach. You just have to 'go with it' the way it is, and keep running over your lines in your head to make sure everything is in place.

5.2 Anxiety

As the exam draws closer, you may find the tension beginning to get to you. Various kinds and levels of anxiety can develop. You may experience a general uneasiness that builds up gradually until, in the period before the exam, it (very usefully) spurs you into a really intensive burst of work. This is a normal precursor to any kind of performance. What you need to do is to make sure that you use the tension productively. Set yourself practical tasks in preparation for the exam so as to keep yourself busy. Remind yourself from time to time that this is *your* exam; you are doing it because you have chosen to. Tell yourself that the tension it creates is a very *productive* force that will help you do some difficult learning. In other words, the ideal situation is that you learn to live with the pressures and use them to achieve things for yourself.

However, your anxiety may develop into a pall of gloom that spoils the last part of the course. All your thoughts may become centred on the exam. In this case you will find it helpful to *keep talking* to other students, your tutor, family and friends. You should share your thoughts about the exam and about your plans for tackling it. Talking to others releases tension and will help you keep things in a more realistic perspective.

For a few students though, this is not enough. Their anxiety in the period immediately before the exam builds up to a point where sleep is difficult and their health begins to suffer, or where work or family and friends begin to be affected. If you find this happening to you, then go to your doctor for advice. Some people find breathing exercises helpful, or meditation, or some other way of reducing the physical manifestations of tension. If you feel bad, don't suffer in isolation. Look for help.

5.3   Checking the arrangements

Because you need to get so 'geared up' in the last day or two, you may become rather inattentive to the ordinary details of life. People sometimes make quite odd mistakes, like turning up for the exam on the wrong day or at the wrong place. So it is a good idea to get all the details of the exam sorted out well in advance. You don't want to be worrying about anything trivial on the day. Mark the time very clearly on your calendar. You might even consider making a practice journey to the exam centre and finding the room, so that you don't have any last minute panics about which bus to catch, or where you left the address of the exam centre, or where the entrance to the building is. Finally, get together any equipment you need.

5.4   The exam day

On the day itself, try to approach the exam calmly. Go about the normal business of getting up and starting the day in an unhurried way. Don't worry if you didn't sleep well because adrenalin will see you through. Take a short stroll perhaps, or do a few exercises to get yourself tuned up and functioning properly. It is not a good idea to attempt any last minute revision because it will only make you feel panicky. Get to the exam in good time, but don't let the other candidates disturb you. Some people chatter away out of nervousness and you may begin to feel that, by the sound of it, they know a lot more than you do. Remain aloof if you need to, or keep walking around if you have to wait to get into the room.

When you are in the exam room find your desk and settle yourself in. Set out whatever you have with you on the desk and check that you have everything you need. If not, ask the person running the exam for what you want. The exam room always seems a strange place, full of people you don't know, all locked obsessively in their own thoughts – but try not to let the strangeness distract you. Keep your mind 'ticking over' in neutral, ready to slip into gear when the lights change. If you have prepared yourself sensibly there is no point in worrying. In fact once the exam has started you may find it surprisingly exhilarating and challenging.

However, if you are seriously distracted by anything at all – persistent noises just behind you, a radiator belting out heat next to you, a dreadful headache or the need to go to the lavatory – then raise your hand, or go to the front of the room and speak quietly to the invigilator. Make it clear what you want; ask to be moved to a different seat in the room, to leave the room for a few minutes, or whatever. Don't let your performance be adversely affected by anything that might be changed.

6 A TACTICAL PLAN FOR THE EXAM

Finally, we need to consider in detail what you are setting out to achieve in the examination itself. You can't afford to leave anything to chance. You need to work out exactly what has to be done and exactly how you think you will tackle it. If you do, you will improve your performance enormously.

6.1 The nature of the task ahead of you

When you enter the exam you have to be ready to work at peak efficiency. You have three hours to make the best show you can of all the work you have done during the course and the revision stage. You cannot afford to waste time dithering, moping or staring at the ceiling. You must have a clear plan of attack. You may not be able to stick to it, and in the end that may not matter. What is important is that you are clear at all times as to what you intend to do next.

This means that you need to have done a lot of your thinking *prior* to the exam itself. As we have seen, you should have decided which parts of the course you are going to answer questions on and have the central issues in the forefront of your mind. You need to have practised setting up arguments between different points of view on them. And you must have decided exactly how you are going to use your time in the exam (see section 6.10). Then, in the exam:

- you pick your question
- you settle after a few minutes on a particular way of using what you know to answer it, and then
- you stick to it, for better or worse.

In other words, you have to get yourself into a very particular frame of mind for the exam – that is, a highly organized, efficient and pragmatic one.

In order to give a practical flavour to the discussion I shall assume, as I said earlier, a three-hour exam in which you are asked to answer four questions selected from, say, twelve; that the questions are similar in style to essay questions and carry equal marks. I will assume also that you can take them in any order you like, that you can write any notes and jottings in the exam answer booklet (so long as you cross them out afterwards), and that you are not allowed to take books into the exam. If your exam is different, you need to find out how it differs and make the necessary adjustments to what I suggest below.

'Open book' exams

In some exams you are allowed to refer to course books and even your notes. This is a doubtful privilege. Thumbing through books and notes during the exam is scarcely consistent with the time limit imposed and the high-speed style of work required of you. You really need ideas in your *head*, so you can *think* with them, not scattered around in books and notes. You may be tempted to spend far too long looking up things, especially if you are the nervous type, and checking to make sure that you have got them just right. Having said that, it is helpful to be able to look up quotations and detailed information from set texts rather than having to memorize them. But unless you know exactly where to find the passages you want, this can take up far too much time. Even in open book exams you have to know your course texts very well. And you have to remember that arguing a good case is your top priority, not reproducing details from books.

6.2   Reading the question paper

The signal that the exam has started is when the invigilator tells you to turn over the exam paper. The general appearance of the paper should not surprise you, assuming you have done your work on the specimen paper or past papers. However, you may find it difficult to take in the words at first because you are so keyed up. So, although it might seem sensible to read carefully through the whole paper, you may not be able to do that effectively to begin with. It may be better to do something more active to get you going.

Certainly it is no bad idea to scan quickly through the questions, putting ticks against possible ones and crosses against those you definitely won't attempt. This will give you a first impression of what is on offer. But don't ponder over every question in detail. Search out the questions you have prepared yourself for, aiming to start with one of them. It is a desperate gamble to allow yourself to be deflected from a prepared subject onto an unprepared one because of the wording of the questions. Your chosen topic may look more difficult to you simply because you know so much about it. Other questions may look easier because you are not clued up enough to understand their full implications. Don't attempt to 'flannel' your way through an unrevised area. Try instead to work out what the question-setter must have been thinking of. You are much more likely to produce a solid answer on one of your prepared topics, even if you feel unhappy with the actual question.

6.3   How soon to start writing

It may be a good idea to find a question you *know* you are going to attempt and pitch straight into it. If your mind tends to go 'blank' under pressure, then starting on a question can be a good way of getting yourself past the opening moments and into action. There is no need to worry about starting your first question before reading the rest of the paper if you are *sure* it is on one of your chosen topics. Many people prefer to scan through the whole paper first, but if it suits you better to get straight into the swim of things, do it. However, as we shall see, you *will* need to think a bit about the wording of the question and to jot down some notes before starting to write your answer.

6.4   The order in which to take the questions

You are allowed to tackle the questions in any order you like, so you may as well follow your own best interests. Some people recommend starting with your very best question, so as to build up your confidence. Others say you should take your best question second, when you are warmed up and not so likely to be tempted to run wildly over your time allowance for it. In any case, it is a good idea to take your best questions earlier rather than later, to make sure that you have enough time to score well on them, to give you confidence and allow you to get nicely into your stride.

6.5   Examining the question

As with essays, it is an excellent idea to begin by underlining the key words in the question you are tackling. It helps you take a positive approach from the outset and it focuses your attention on developing an answer to the precise question set. The words you underline are the ones you will have to think about carefully in order to decide what material to use in your answer and how to organize it (see Chapter 5, sections 2.1 and 2.2). If you rush headlong into the question and make mistakes about the issues it addresses, you will seriously damage your chances.

6.6   Drawing together material towards your answer

When you have underlined the key words in the question, very quickly jot down some material you think you might use in answering it. Don't worry at first about *how* to use it. Just write words down to reassure yourself that you have enough to work on. Thinking back to the summary sheets you made during revision, make a note of the relevant texts, arguments, ideas and theories, as they come into your mind. A single word is usually enough to trigger off your memory and enable you to retrieve a point. Work fast and uncritically, and don't hesitate to make a mess of your exam booklet. You can cross out all your jottings later.

When you have some notes jotted down (perhaps only 10–15 words), you can go on to sort out what you will use, in what order, and what you might leave out. Plan a structure for your answer, identifying the main points you will make in each section, with appropriate textual detail noted alongside.

6.7 Taking time to plan your answer

It may sound all very well to do this kind of planning for your exam answers, but will you have the time? Making time for it certainly takes some nerve. But, bearing in mind the comments examiners make about 'failing to answer the question', poor presentation, and so on, it will be time very well spent. If you don't sketch out a plan you run the risk of 'going blank' in the middle of an answer. Expressing your arguments in writing tends to absorb the whole of your attention. Then, when you get to the end of a paragraph and reach for the next point, it's gone. Your argument jerks to a halt and you are too panic stricken to recall your intentions quickly. At this point you will waste far more time than writing a plan would have taken, trying to find some sense of direction for the rest of your answer and scratching about for ways of fleshing it out.

Of course, you have to plan exam answers very speedily. How long you will spend on each one is something you must judge for yourself. But between five and ten minutes is a reasonable target.

6.8 Keeping to the question

In your enthusiasm to demonstrate your knowledge, don't forget the importance of sticking to the point. It irritates exam markers, who are searching for points which relate *directly* to the question, to have to wade through paragraphs of uncensored and unsorted material. You will *not* gain marks if you give the impression that you are uncritically casting stuff before the examiners' eyes in the hope of fooling them into thinking you know what you are talking about. You must make sure to draw in plenty of material from the course, but you should always do it with a clear purpose. You must not pad out your answers, nor waffle on hoping to conceal your ignorance. Everything you write should have a clear relevance to the question. Anything else is just a waste of your time.

6.9   When to plan your later questions

When the first two questions are under your belt it is a good idea to 'rough out' plans for the other two in turn, *before* writing out your third answer. The reason for this is that you need time on your side when you are planning. It is very hard to think straight in the final stages of the exam, as you become aware of the approaching deadline. All too often a last answer represents the desperate casting about of a mind that has passed beyond the stage of thinking clearly. You will probably be able to write at your *fastest* during the last hour of the exam *provided you know what you intend to say.* So do the thinking that requires calm analysis at the half-way point, when you have got over any initial tension and have settled into a steady mode of working. Then you will be able to take advantage of your 'manic' energy in the later stages to get lots of useful material down.

6.10   Drawing up a 'time plan'

With time at a premium, it is important to be realistic and clear sighted about how you intend to use it. It is a good idea to draw up a plan of how, ideally, you would hope to use your time in the exam. Figure 7.1 shows one possible version.

10:00	Turn over the paper and glance through it, marking the questions you think you might attempt. (5 mins)
10:05	Start planning your first answer. Underline key words in the question. Jot down relevant material. Return to the question and work out an essay plan. (10 mins)
10:15	Start writing out your first answer. (35 mins)
10:50	Finish the first answer and plan out the next one. (10 mins)
11:00	Write out the second answer. (35 mins)
11:35	Finish the second answer and plan the third and fourth. (15 mins)
11:50	Write out the third answer. (35 mins)
12:25	Write out the fourth answer. (35 mins)
13:00	Finish

Figure 7.1 *Sample time plan for a three-hour exam.*

Of course this is a very idealized plan. You wouldn't be able to stick to it exactly. And other people might suggest different allocations of time. For example, some say you should set aside the last 5–10 minutes for reading through your answers and making corrections to them. You will have to see whether you have time for that, and whether your high-energy state towards the end, as you race for the finishing line, allows you to read with suitably calm concentration. In any case, it is not important whether this is the 'best' possible plan. What *is* important is to draw up a plan that suits *you*, so that you have a clear idea of how you intend to use your time. And, during the exam, you need to be prepared to modify the plan as you go along.

If you find you are falling behind schedule as you answer a question, draw the answer to a close as quickly as you can. Don't leave the question half finished in the hope that you will have time to come back to it. Since you are running late, most likely you won't. But, more important, by then you will have lost the train of thought. Make the best of a bad job and write out whatever conclusions you can manage to draw quickly, while the question is still alive in your mind.

6.11 What to do if you run out of time

If, in spite of all your plans, you do end up with too little time for the last question, write out some notes showing how your answer would have developed if you had had time. If you present an answer *entirely* in note form, you are unlikely to scrape a pass. However, if you have written out *part* of the answer and add some clearly written notes indicating where you had intended to go, you might convince the marker it is worth a reasonable mark. You will probably be given *some* credit for good notes, but it would scarcely be fair to the other candidates if the marker allowed you the benefit of the extra time you spent on the earlier questions *and* a generous benefit of the doubt on an uncompleted question. Basically, you need to write out an answer in full to be safely in the running for a good mark. So make sure you *don't* run out of time!

6.12 Presentation

Most people write less tidily and legibly than their best in an exam. But do *try* to make your work legible. Start each question on a new page and number the questions clearly. Draw a line across the page between your jotted plan and the essay itself, and remember to score through your jottings when you have completed the answer. It is too late now to worry about your handwriting or your command of written English. You can't do much to change these things at short notice. You can only work to improve them gradually, over your years of study. On the other hand, spare a thought for the reader as you write and avoid being so overwhelmed by the need for speed that your writing descends to a dreadful scrawl.

KEY POINTS

Practical tips for the exam itself

- Draw up a time plan for the exam in advance.
- Scan through the paper finding the questions you have prepared for.
- Start planning and writing your first answer straight away, if it helps to 'unfreeze' you.
- Take your best question either first or second.
- Spend some time planning your answer before you start writing.
- As you tackle a question:
  - examine the wording carefully
  - very quickly jot down some relevant ideas, arguments, texts and other material from the course
  - sketch an outline plan for your answer
  - remember that everything you plan to write should be relevant to the particular question asked.
- Consider planning the last two questions mid-way through the exam.
- Don't run wildly over your deadline for each question.
- Do your best to write legibly.

7 WILL YOU DO AS WELL AS YOU SHOULD IN THE EXAM?

Of course you should pass the exam, assuming you have been getting on all right with the course itself. In principle, the exam is just another way of confirming what your work during the course has already shown. But although this is more or less how things turn out for many people, it is not so in all cases.

1   A few people do *better* in exams than in their course work. Exams actually bring out the best in some of us. Perhaps you are one of them – or could be if you take the right approach to exams.

2   A number of people do just about *as well* in the exam as in their course work. This is fine and as it should be.

3   Many people tend to perform *less well* than their course work suggests they could. They pass, but at a lower level than they had reasonably hoped. If you are one of these people then this chapter is especially for you. Read it regularly every year as you start the revision period and remind yourself of all the very practical things you can do to get a better performance out of yourself.

4   A few people have a tendency to perform far below their potential in exams. If you are one of them, then I hope this chapter is helpful. But I would strongly recommend that you also try to *talk* to someone about exams and get direct support and advice. There is no point in struggling away on your own if you persistently ruin your good work when it comes to the exam.

However, whichever of these categories you think you fall into, you have nothing to lose by thinking positively. *Of course* you should pass. You will leave things out in the exam, but so will everyone else. Your exam answers won't look as impressive as your essays, but that will also be true for the other candidates. Your answers are going to be compared only with other fairly scrappy efforts. Be realistic about the exam. Yes, it may be a chore. Yes, you will have to focus a lot of attention and energy on it. But you will also *learn a lot* in the process. You *can* make yourself into a very efficient exam 'performer', achieving feats beyond your everyday powers. Don't let exams intimidate you. You are *likely* to pass.

POSTSCRIPT

You have now reached the end of this book. But of course you have not reached the end of the process of becoming a better student. That process never ends. Indeed, there will be times when you seem to slip backwards. Just when you think you have sorted out your note-making technique into a smoothly functioning routine you will find that it has become too mechanical – that you are making too many notes, or not the right notes – or you will come across a book that defeats your routine. Just when you are beginning to think you have 'cracked it' with writing, you will be faced with an essay that somehow won't come right or a tutor who criticizes the very things you thought you were good at. At all these times when your studies take an unexpected turn and knock you back, you will find it useful to return to this book and to basic study principles. Also, as you become more experienced as a student, many of the things you took in at an earlier stage acquire a different significance. When you come back to this book afresh, you will find you make another range of meanings built upon those extra layers of experience. So don't set the book aside for ever. Keep it where you will be able to find it, when you need it again. Learning to study is a lifelong process.

JOYCE ELLIS,'ON THE TOWN': WOMEN IN AUGUSTAN ENGLAND

Extracts from Ellis, J. (1995) 'On the town: women in Augustan England', *History Today*, vol.45, no.12 (December), pp.15–25

para.1   Modern demographic research suggests that in what is known as the 'long eighteenth century' the female population of England's larger towns expanded dramatically, producing what one demographer has called 'a remarkable predominance of women' in contrast with the more balanced or emphatically male-dominated populations of smaller settlements. [...] All the evidence indicates that urban populations were unbalanced principally by a net inflow of female migrants.

para.2   Hours of rigorous, computer-aided academic research has, therefore, vindicated to some extent the standard cliché of Restoration and eighteenth-century literature about women's enthusiasm for urban life. Women were consistently portrayed in plays and poetry of the period as being ready to adopt any stratagem, however underhand, to escape from the boredom and restrictions of the countryside. The young heroine of Etherege's *The Man of Mode* (1676), for instance, was so much in love with London that she 'can scarce endure the country in landscapes and in hangings'. In contrast, contemporary satirists represented towns in this period as 'female territory', meccas of unbridled consumption and frivolity to which women were irresistibly drawn.

para.3   Of course it was not only women who expressed a preference for urban life: many men would have agreed with the north-eastern landowner who contemptuously refused his mother's pleas for his return from London in 1720 with the rhetorical question 'Surely you don't think me such a fool as to prefer the charms of a stupid, dull, country life to the pleasures of the Town?' But these pleasures were thought to be especially attractive to women, not simply because women were by nature self-indulgent and superficial, but because urban life allowed them to gain the upper hand in their age-old struggle to escape their natural subordination. What women sought in the towns, the satirists argued, was freedom from male control. Such claims, however, reflected long-standing literary conventions and equally long-standing male anxieties rather than contemporary reality. It is much more plausible to argue that urban life attracted a disproportionate number of women not because they were trying to escape from or to subvert accepted gender roles but because 'correct' female behaviour was all too often dysfunctional in a rural setting.

para.4   This was perhaps most obvious in the case of women from the higher ranks of society, the main targets of male satirists, whose lives in the country were increasingly circumscribed by conventional expectations of female fragility and propriety. Women from wealthy families were seen as the embodiments of their husbands' and fathers' status. It was, therefore, vital that they conformed to contemporary norms which had shifted decisively in the seventeenth century towards an ideal of delicate, innocent and essentially decorative womanhood. Women's physical and mental inferiority had, of course, long been an accepted fact, but at the same time the wives and daughters of wealthy farmers and landowners had been expected to play an active part in managing their households or even their husband's land: thus girls were trained in the many practical and supervisory skills they would need as adults.

para.5   With an increasing wealth and sophistication of society, however, many of these tasks were taken over by professionals, allowing well-born women much greater leisure, but in the process creating a vacuum which the expensive 'accomplishments' that such women acquired from smart boarding schools or private tutors could not readily fill in a rural setting. Most of these new feminine skills were essentially designed to be shown off in public, and yet the demands of status and propriety meant that women's sociability was far more strictly controlled than that of men.

para.6   Men could to some degree socialize with those both above and below them in the hierarchy without losing face: a great landowner, for example, could dine with his tenant farmers and local tradesmen as a gesture of neighbourliness and courtesy. Women, however, could only mix with their equals, so that a woman's opportunities for sociability outside her immediate family were confined to those of her own social standing who lived within travelling distance. Unfortunately, well-born women were much less mobile than men. Relatively few women were able or willing to ride and were thus dependent on the availability of the family carriage unless, like Elizabeth Bennet in *Pride and Prejudice*, they were prepared to walk.

para.7   Even if a carriage was available, travel along unlit, unpaved country roads carried its own dangers: Elizabeth Montagu and her family were overturned so often on their way to visit friends that she 'began to think ... a bone-setter a necessary part of equipage for country visiting'. 'Fear', she declared in 1737, 'is never so powerful with me, as to make me stay at home' but floods, snow or mud sometimes made travel completely impossible. Lady Jane Coke, for example, was marooned in her house ten miles outside Derby for four months in the winter of 1748–49 by the 'continual rains' which made the roads impassable for a carriage. Of course, to some extent, her husband was marooned too, but men in this situation had many more resources to fall back on. The education given to men from the social elite was almost expressly designed for a rural setting. They were all, in effect, trained to be country gentlemen, able not only to manage their estates but also take an active pleasure from them through riding, hunting, shooting and fishing. Their womenfolk, meanwhile, had no outlet for most of their particular social skills: instead they had to make do with recreational needlework, writing letters and reading whatever books could be found in the house, with frequent walks in the grounds between downpours as their only exercise. [...]

para.8   Towns, in contrast, offered such women a variety of respectable occupations, amusements and companions, all of which they could enjoy in a degree of physical comfort. Young single women and widows were particularly prone to boredom in the countryside and had a greater incentive to settle permanently in town, but even married women felt the need for regular visits 'to brush off the rust a little'. The greater concentrations of both people and wealth found even in provincial centres meant that women could socialize on a much wider scale without sacrificing their status and respectability by mingling with those too far beneath them. The relatively compact built-up area of most towns was also an advantage, putting this wider circle of acceptable acquaintances within easy reach, especially as improvements in the urban environment, including better pavements and more efficient street lighting, and in public transport, such as sedan chairs and hackney carriages, meant that women were much more mobile in the town than in the country. [...]

para.9   The urban environment also offered so many more places to go. The delights of Bath or London were obviously exceptional but even in much more modest towns the social calendar was enlivened at least once a year by a regular season of balls, assemblies, race meetings, theatre performances and concerts. Women sometimes took a leading role in planning and running these events. [...]

para.10   The effects of maintaining these [social] distinctions meant that, in smaller towns, there were sometimes too few male partners for ladies anxious to dance, but at least they could (and did) dance with each other while their menfolk retreated to the card room. Moreover, whereas in earlier periods 'country ladies were stewed up in their father's old mansion houses and seldom saw company, but at an assize, a horse race or a fair', towns gradually developed a wide range of amenities such as landscaped walks, circulating libraries, and tea, confectionery or pastry shops where women could meet without the stigma attached to taverns or coffee houses.

para.11   Above all there were the shops, which in the course of this period were transformed into 'perfect gilded theatres' providing 'as agreeable an amusement as any lady can pass away three or four hours in'. Sophie von La Roche, a German visitor to England in the 1780s, was impressed by the shopping facilities even in provincial towns, noting in particular the wide pavements which allowed well-dressed women 'to pursue their way safe from the carriages, horses and dirt', and the combined effects of street- and shop-lighting which meant that window shopping could continue well into the evening.

[*Owing to the length of the original article, a section on poorer women and the town has been omitted.*]

para.12   Although a few contemporaries seem to have been sympathetic to women's attraction to what one character in *The Country Wife* (1675) termed 'the innocent liberty of the town', on the whole the opinion-makers of Augustan England seem to have seen every woman as a potential 'naughty town-woman', attracted to the urban environment by expectations of a liberty that was likely to be very far from innocent.

para.13   And yet in holding up the image of healthy, wholesome and rosy-cheeked countrywomen as the epitome of innocence and domestic virtue, such critics were ignoring the reality of rural life. The steady migration of women into the towns was the logical consequence of conventional perceptions of femininity and of correct female behaviour, perceptions which inflicted on country gentlewomen nothing worse than boredom but which made the lives of poor women a constant struggle for survival against the odds. In the towns, in contrast, these odds were tilted slightly in women's favour.

DICTIONARIES/COMPANIONS TO ARTS STUDY

Unless you are advised otherwise, always consult the most recent edition of these books. The dates/editions given here are as at the time of printing.

Art History

HAGGAR, R.G. (ed.) (1962) *A Dictionary of Art Terms*, London, Oldbourne.

HALL, J. (ed.) (1979) *Hall's Dictionary of Subjects and Symbols in Art*, London, John Murray.

Classical Studies

HORNBLOWER, S. and SPAWFORTH, A. (eds) (1997, 3rd edn) *The Oxford Classical Dictionary*, Oxford, Oxford University Press.

HOWATSON, M.C. and CHILVERS, I. (eds) (1993) *The Concise Oxford Companion to Classical Literature*, Oxford, Oxford University Press.

Film Studies

BAWDEN, L.-A. (ed.) (1976) *The Oxford Companion to Film*, Oxford, Oxford University Press.

History

There is no general dictionary or companion to the study of history as such. However, there are period and subject-specific companions and indexes, such as:

JONES, C. (1990) *The Longman Companion to the French Revolution*, London, Longman.

Consult those appropriate to your course.

English Language

MCARTHUR, T. (ed.) (1992) *The Oxford Companion to the English Language*, Oxford, Oxford University Press.

Languages and Law

Your course will recommend appropriate dictionaries, grammars and reference books.

Literature

DRABBLE, M. (ed.) (1995) *The Oxford Companion to English Literature*, Oxford, Oxford University Press.

Media Studies

WATSON, J. and HILL, A. (eds) (1984) *A Dictionary of Communication and Media Studies*, London, Arnold.

Music

BLOM, E., revised by CUMMINGS, D. (eds) (1991) *The New Everyman Dictionary of Music*, London, Dent.

ISAACS, A., and MARTIN, E. (eds) (1982) *Dictionary of Music*, London, Sphere.

Philosophy

FLEW, A. (ed.) (1979) *A Dictionary of Philosophy*, London, Pan Books.

BUNNIN, N., and TSUI-JAMES, E.P. (eds) (1996) *The Blackwell Companion to Philosophy*, Oxford, Blackwell.

Religious Studies

HINNELLS, J. R. (ed.) (1995) *A New Dictionary of Religions*, Oxford, Blackwell.

INDEX